Everyday Dining with Wine

Everyday Dining with Wine

ANDREA IMMER

BROADWAY BOOKS

New York

PRINTED IN THE UNITED STATES OF AMERICA

BROADWAY BOOKS and its logo, a letter B bisected on the diagonal, are trademarks of Random House, Inc.

Visit our website at www.broadwaybooks.com

First edition published 2004

Book design by Vertigo Design NYC

Library of Congress Cataloging-in-Publication Data

Immer, Andrea.
    Everyday dining with wine / Andrea Immer.
        p.   cm.
    1. Cookery.   2. Wine and wine making.   I. Title.
    TX714.I47 2004
    641.2'2—dc22   2004045854

ISBN 0-7679-1681-6

10   9   8   7   6   5   4   3   2

To John and Lucas, the loves of my life

CONTENTS

ACKNOWLEDGMENTS   ix

INTRODUCTION: EVERYDAY DINING WITH WINE   1

COURSE-BY-COURSE RECIPE LIST   23

chapter one
Riesling and the Aromatic Whites   28

chapter two
Sauvignon Blanc   54

chapter three
Chardonnay   72

chapter four
Champagne, Sparkling Wines, and Crisp Whites   98

chapter five
Pinot Noir   124

chapter six
Merlot and Cabernet Sauvignon   155

chapter seven
Shiraz, Rhône-Style Reds, and Zinfandel   180

chapter eight
Italian and Spanish Reds   208

chapter nine
Dessert Wines   237

chapter ten
Basic Recipes   263

appendices
WINE FAQS   273

GREAT MENUS WITH WINE   280

SOURCES AND RESOURCES   286

INDEX   288

ACKNOWLEDGMENTS

In my house, everyday dining with wine is always a collaboration; we take such pleasure in both the process and the results, which have included many delicious dinners, and now this book. I hope it will serve as a keepsake of fond food and wine memories for the people I love who've gathered to help chop, pop corks, taste, and pitch in with the dishes.

Loving thanks to John, who has made the kitchen one of the most romantic places in the world for me, who always served up the perfect antidote to my author's stress when I needed it most, and, between board meetings, helped create or refine so many of the recipes and pairings in this book. On top of all that, he helped shop and do mountains of dishes. And to Lucas, whose kitchen comedy routine makes preparing everyday dinner a delight for us. You're my champ—and not just for cheerfully chowing down on roast chicken, four nights in a row, and on all the other recipe experiments! You are gorgeous men, and I'm just crazy about you.

To my friend and colleague Cindy Renzi, thanks for your advice, incredible support, and friendship. You're the best!

To two great women: my editor Jennifer Josephy of Broadway Books for believing in this project, and for unleashing all your energy and talents at warp-speed to make it happen, and Lauren Chattman, whose culinary and literary wizardry made creating this book the pleasure it should be, for all of us. You all rock.

To Jee Levin, Ben Fink, Michele Michael, and Umi Kenyon, thanks for bringing to life on these pages the inherent beauty and simplicity of everyday dining with wine.

To founder Dorothy Hamilton and the deans, chef-instructors, and students at The French Culinary Institute in New York City, thanks for creating and sharing in a great environment, where we can all incubate new ideas about wine and food. Thanks to The FCI's Katie McManus for being such a gracious pro at everything, and to Rachel Soszynski for recipe testing.

To Fine Living Network and Follow Productions, thank you for your commitment to bringing the pleasure, beauty, and fun of wine and food via TV to their rightful place—millions of living rooms and kitchens across the country.

To my readers, website visitors, and *Simply Wine* TV show viewers, thanks for sharing with me your recipes pairing adventures and passion for wine and food.

And to my mom and dad, Sharon and David McKinster; Mildred and Garner Robinson; the Whittiers; the Taylors; the Steinmetz-Firras; and all the McMillan women—we are blessed to be able to gather with you over wine and food. Here's to all the priceless memories, and many more to come.

introduction

EVERYDAY DINING
WITH WINE

⊙

Wine with dinner.

What that means to you depends a lot on where and how you grew up. For most Americans, wine with dinner is strictly a special-occasions and fancy-restaurants deal. But to Europeans, wine with dinner is an everyday pleasure, a way of life, really.

It is for me, too. Although I didn't grow up in Europe or in a wine-industry family, I embraced the idea long before I became a sommelier. I remember the very instant as though it were yesterday: After a college abroad program in London, I took a train to Spain, and experienced the eating epiphany that so many American visitors to Europe do. In my case it was a meal of tapas and *tinto* (house red) that absolutely sang with flavor, yet cost only a song.

On the thread of my life, that eating experience was an exquisite pearl: simple, genuine, thrilling. Yet, unlike pearls, it was also cheap! It inspired me to think about wine with dinner very differently, and to embrace an equation that is the birthright of Europeans: Great flavor + affordability = Everyday dining with wine.

My Journey to *Everyday Dining with Wine*

SINCE THE AGE OF EIGHT, when I worked my way through *The Nancy Drew Cookbook,* I have been an ardent cook. By the time I was a teenager, a whole neighborhood of hungry high school athletes had become willing guinea pigs for my bread-baking, sausage-making, and tandoori experiments under a clay pot in my mother's oven. So when I first became interested in wine, it was a natural extension of my interest in food.

When I graduated from college I began a career as a New York City investment banker, but after hours I signed up for cleanup duty at cooking schools and wine schools so I could take classes for free. My parents, who had bought me that Nancy Drew cookbook so many years ago, weren't really surprised when I announced my decision to leave Wall Street for wine. Instead of going back to school for an M.B.A., I went for the M.S.—that is, I became a Master Sommelier. Obtaining this distinction wasn't an end in itself. Rather, it was a way for me gain the necessary knowledge so that I could help people discover, as I had in Spain, how the pleasure of food could be enhanced by wine, and how this pleasure could be experienced every day.

My first jobs were in restaurants, where I advised guests on food and wine pairings on their special nights out. I quickly concluded that many people were confused or intimidated by the arcane language of wine, not comfortable enough to make everyday choices on their own. What a shame, because when boiled down to the basics, choosing everyday wines is fun and easy. I put those basics in my first book, *Great Wine Made Simple,* an interactive wine course between two covers that shows you how to learn about wine the way I did, and the way I teach my waiters: by tasting it, grape by grape, region by region. I wanted to demystify the whole wine experience by explaining in simple language the differences among grapes, and how and why those grapes take on their unique flavor characteristics.

I went on to write *Great Tastes Made Simple,* a food-and-wine pairing book that's also interactive, because it teaches you the basics of matching food and wine so they taste better together than they do on their own. There are some recipes in this book, but it's really more about tasting than cooking—how does a tomato taste when paired with a glass of Chianti? What about popcorn and Chardonnay? This book put on paper the pairing principles that I and other sommeliers use every day in working with our guests.

At home in my kitchen, I make modest dinners and pour inexpensive bottles of wine, but I use the same sommelier pairing tricks and techniques to make the most of those everyday dinners with wine. Studying the shelves of wine books and cookbooks in our library at The French Culinary Institute (where I received my culinary education and now serve as a dean), it struck me that there was no book to guide people in the direction I had taken at home: using simple recipes and cooking techniques, combined with simple wine-pairing principles, to vastly improve everyday meals. So I decided to write *Everyday Dining with Wine.* In it, I have continued to perform my job as Master Sommelier: Not just to plug you in to the luxury wines and pairings (there's little value to you or challenge for me in that), but rather to enhance the everyday experience of dinner by providing you with recipes and wine matches that will cost you little in time and money but will pay off handsomely in pleasure.

Whether you sauce or sauté like a French chef or use an all-American method like grilling or slow-cooking in a crockpot, the result is the same. Good cooking showcases and intensifies the flavor of food. Wine, too, showcases and intensifies the flavor of food, so that a well-prepared dish tastes even better when served with wine. The French, and Europeans in general, have known this seemingly forever. But there's no reason that Americans can't improve their dinners by adding wine, too. This is where my journey has led me, and if you are interested in ending each day with a dinner that sustains the soul as well as nourishes the body, this is where yours can begin.

Your Journey Begins at Home

YOU WON'T NEED A PLANE TICKET to Madrid to experience the kind of pleasure I felt when eating my tapas and drinking my *tinto*. Begin in your own kitchen, where you can discover affordable, everyday wines that enhance great-tasting, easy-to-prepare meals. That's what this book is all about. Just as I began to savor every simple bite and sip after that meal in Spain, I hope that with the help of the recipes and wine recommendations in this book you will be able to slow down and savor everyday dinners, and to more fully enjoy all of the people with whom you share food and drink.

And I think the trip will be fun and easy, because to get there you won't have to jettison the things you hold dear, like kitchen speed and simplicity, ingredients available at your regular market, and foods and flavors that you already love. And one more thing: Just because "everyday" wine is inexpensive doesn't mean it can't be absolutely *great*.

The timing's never been better for great wine that really *is* affordable for everyday dining. In the last decade, Australia has realized the enormous potential of the $8-and-under (sometimes way under) bottle, finally forcing the rest of the wine world to focus on the value-priced category to remain competitive. Chile, Southern Italy, Washington State, California's Central Valley and Central Coast regions, and Spain are just some of the bright spots for value, which I define as lots of flavor and character for the money. Good thing dinner *is* a daily occurrence, because you've got lots of exploring to do!

A European Idea with an American Spin

AMERICANS JUST DISCOVERING the world of value-priced wines differ from Europeans who have always enjoyed inexpensive bottles with their dinners in this respect: For most Americans, the search for great bottles will take them all over the world (or at least to several continents). In contrast, most Europeans only have to travel as far as their backyards.

A FAMILY JOURNEY INTO WINE WITH DINNER

When I was growing up, my family didn't have a wine-with-dinner tradition, but we did have rich kitchen and dinner-table traditions that I treasure to this day. I remember my mom's fried chicken, and her hand-cut French fries and pickly tunafish salad—my favorite Saturday supper. During summers at my grandparents' Great Smoky Mountains farm, my mom and the aunts and cousins would can, freeze, and bake until even I was strawberry pied–out. From that point I was hooked on cooking, and by college had been on every cooking kick imaginable, from smoke-curing to bread-baking to stir-fries to Cajun—so much fun! Then I took a wine class at a little Dallas restaurant called the Grape (it's still there), and was captivated by the topic of wine. When the family came from Indiana to Dallas for my graduation dinner, I presented a wine tasting, parroting everything I'd learned at my last class at the Grape (it was a good thing no one asked questions, because my "expertise" went not a stitch further!). When my parents visited me in New York after I'd moved there to work on Wall Street, I took them for wine-tasting flights at a Soho wine bar, and within two years I'd left Wall Street for Windows on the World, where they enjoyed a wine class on another visit. Now wine with dinner is a fixture of my parents' table, and my dad's on a first-name basis with every wine retailer in town. My brother and sister-in-law's neighborhood gourmet group gathers for wine tastings. Via wine and the web we've reconnected with extended family we've not seen in decades—we set a record when twenty-seven of us met at the Epcot International Food and Wine Festival at Walt Disney World last year. For us, the combination of wine and food has delivered on what is, in my opinion, its true calling: It has both created and rekindled the people connections that make life worth living. It's the calling that brought me from Wall Street into a life of wine. In my work as a sommelier, it became my *job* to facilitate those kinds of connections for other families in a truly memorable setting. It is an honor and a privilege to continue that work in this book. I hope your family will enjoy its wine-with-dinner journey, too. I, and the McKinsters, Immers, Robinsons, Whittiers, McMillans, Taylors (and more), will see you on the wine trail!

Think about it: Part of what makes trattoria, tapas bar, and country auberge eating so magical is the immediacy and freshness of everything. The carafe wine, which costs pocket-change and tastes great, was most likely grown and vinified up the road, probably came straight from cask, and never touched a bottle or a cork. The tomatoes never saw a truck, the charcuterie was cured in the owner's lean-to, and the mushrooms probably arrived that morning wrapped in the neighbor's apron.

For most Americans, the food and wine landscape is quite different. The produce in our supermarkets comes from all corners of the earth. The spice, grain, and even canned goods sections speak in many tongues. You're likely to see Alaskan salmon and frozen fish sticks in the same sale circular. And of course the global world of wine, not the local, is our oyster. Such being the case, the recipes and pairings in this book, while often inspired by meals I've had in Europe, or techniques I've learned from European chefs and from French culinary training, often meld the diversity of ingredients, techniques, and wines that we have at our disposal.

In my culinary ecumenicalism, I'm all-American. I don't shy away from the bold ethnic flavors that Americans love—from the chili heat of Mexican mojo or the citrus tang of Caribbean ceviche—just because they have a reputation as being tough to pair with wine. I love the challenge! The reality is that these flavors are the perfect excuse to branch out and explore wines beyond the usual comfort zones of Chardonnay and Cabernet. How about a German Riesling with that Spicy Roasted Cauliflower and Okra? Or a Spanish sparkler with your Churrasco-Style Skirt Steak? By the same token, I love to take a beloved French classic wine like a Crozes-Hermitage red (made from the Syrah grape), and serve it with something completely foreign to France—Plank-Cooked Salmon with Indonesian Five-Spice Barbecue Sauce makes this old favorite taste brand-new. (Cracking the cover of this book has committed you to trying all kinds of new grapes, wine styles, and funky-on-the-face-of-it pairings—sorry if you didn't get the memo!)

Real-World Recipes for Exciting Eating

MY APPROACH TO SHOPPING, cooking, and pairing is an extension of the real-world approach I've always taken with wine, and seeks to balance its awesome pleasure potential with everyday pressures of time and budget. I relish the extremes of luxury dining and roadside diners pretty much equally. I love cooking and entertaining, but want shopping, prep, and cleanup to be as quick and painless as possible. And I'm not snobby about convenience products like store-bought sauces and takeout, when they make sense. I have a professional culinary degree, but like you, I don't have an army of prep cooks to tend to tedious procedures or a personal shopper to seek out specialty ingredients. A few of the recipes here feature expensive luxury items like foie gras and lobster, and wine pairings to match, because every once in a while I think we should all live it up. But for the most part, my recipes and pairings really are for every day. They're fast, affordable, and of course yummy. They're also loaded with variety—lots of different foods and, especially, wines—because constantly trying different wines is the easiest and most fun way to spice up everyday dinner, and you learn about wine in the process.

Everyday Wine and Good Health

I LOVE FOIE GRAS, bacon, and butter as much as the next cooking school graduate, but I fret about fat just like everyone else, especially since I was one of those kids who was teased on the playground for being chubby! As a mom, I want to enjoy food and wine without tipping the scales and risking my family's health. While *Everyday Dining with Wine* is no diet book, its recipes take a moderate approach, emphasizing fresh, zingy flavor over the heavy-handed use of fat. I believe that consuming a variety of healthy foods, deliciously prepared, is a prescription for long-term health, and this book is my personal recipe file for such a healthy diet.

And where does wine fit into the health equation? My wine students and website visitors ask me about this all the time. They also ask how, with my food-and wine-centric job, I stay in shape. The answer is simple. I'm neither a doctor nor an expert on wine's health effects, but like most reputable dieticians I believe that we should sip, chew, and swallow our nutrients, rather than pill-pop them. Just as important, I believe we should rigorously exercise both portion control and our bodies, rather than relying on a fad diet or diet pill, to maintain a healthy weight. That applies to wine, too, which of course has calories along with nutrients. The reported major benefit of *moderate* wine consumption, which is strongly supported by large-scale academic research studies, is a substantially reduced risk of heart disease, the number-one killer in this country. Researchers also cite the beneficial antioxidant properties of anthocyanins, which comprise the coloring pigments in the skins of red wine grapes, and of the circulation-enhancing qualities of resveratrol, also abundant in red wine.

My view, and that of many doctors with whom I've shared it, is that otherwise healthy people without contraindications for wine are highly likely to enhance their pleasure by enjoying wine in moderation with everyday dinner, and may strengthen their physical health in the process. For me, putting together dinner with wine is also a mental health boost. While cooking with a glass of wine, I get to turn down the loop-tape in my head, immerse myself in handwork and the smells and textures of things that recently came from the earth, and just enjoy the moment. It's also my most creative time, when I have my best ideas, or come up with the perfect solution to a nagging problem. Finally, sitting down to dinner with wine is that chance to make eye contact, talk about the stuff of the day or the stuff of dreams, and sustain for my son the dinner-table tradition that I so enjoyed growing up.

Another question I get a lot is, does my school-age son drink wine the way kids in Europe often do as they're growing up? His answer: "I'm underage, but I do smell it sometimes." (He's pretty good at describing those smells!) There you have it, and I didn't script it. Ironically, it seems that he's a product of our more conservative American drinking culture, a culture that assumes (wrongly I believe) that chronological age should be the determining factor in enjoying wine. If, or more likely when, he wants to start enjoying sips of wine with dinner as many of my friends' kids do, I'll be there to help him develop a healthy attitude about it, although living in our everyday-dining-with-wine household, I'm sure he's already begun to get the idea.

A Focus on Value

AS A WORKING MOM, I keenly understand that fresh food and everyday wine cost money. It's important to me that you get your money's worth when you make the commitment to serving wine with everyday dinner. I've tried my utmost to make the recipes and accompanying wines in this book pay off in affordability, ease, and flavor. A few recipes in each chapter are earmarked for weekends or special occasions—they're that impressive—but for the most part this is a solid repertoire of accessible, budget-conscious recipes for the home cook. Many of them come together in thirty minutes or less, because that's about all the time I've got on a weeknight to get dinner on the table and still wrap up homework, do laundry, and get ready for the next day. A lot of the recipes begin with good-value staples with which you probably already stock your pantry, refrigerator, and freezer: pasta, grains, eggs, and items that used to be expensive—boneless chicken breasts, salmon fillets, shrimp—but are now such a good deal when you buy them in bulk at a warehouse club and freeze them for later.

Similarly, my wine suggestions will correct the common misperception that wine has got to be expensive to be drinkable. I've included plenty of recommendations for cheap-but-good steals from unusual grapes or places that are hard to find unless you know what to look for. And where it's appropriate, I've also included some impressive (but not stupidly priced) bottles for special occasions, and for any dish that can really support a "big" wine.

How to Use This Book to Cook Up Delicious Everyday Dinners with Wine

THIS BOOK WILL SHOW YOU how easy it is to put together delicious everyday dinners with great wine pairings. There are several ways to enter the game. Choose your strategy depending on your interests and the way you like to shop and cook.

WHAT IF YOU CAN'T FIND THE WINE THAT I RECOMMEND FOR A DISH?

No sweat! You can take the book to the store with you and look for, or request from the merchant, a similar wine, one made from the same grape and/or from the same region. And as I hope I've already made clear, matching wine and food is a fairly free-form sport, so it's hard to go wrong if you veer off the particular pairing path I've set you on. In fact, if you do, chances are you'll find some interesting matches of your own. (I hope you'll share them with me in an e-mail!) For more specifics on shopping for wine in a variety of settings, from warehouse club to wine shop, see the Wine FAQs on page 273.

Learning a Little About Wine

If you are interested in getting the big picture before getting down to business in the kitchen, take some time to read through the chapter introductions. The chapters are organized by grape variety, because it is fun and easy to gain a lot of wine buying and pairing confidence by learning just a little bit about the major wine styles. Specifically, the intros will give you a basic understanding of the Big Six grapes, the three whites and three reds that comprise the bulk of the world's quality wines, as well as the key sparkling, Italian, Spanish, and dessert wine styles. Is the wine light or rich? Dry or off-dry? Reminiscent of apples and pears or tropical fruits? It's the flavor characteristics in both wine and food, not the color or protein type, that I use to create memorable and delicious pairings every day. So that's why you'll see combinations like beef and bubbly, or fish and Cabernet, that might seem unorthodox in the context of old pairing "rules."

Exploring These Combos Is the Next Step

Once you have gotten an idea of what a particular wine is all about and what kinds of food flavors generally pair well with it, take a look at the recipe titles in the chapter. These are my everyday (and some special-occasion) recipes for that particular wine type. Whether you start with a wine that interests you or a recipe that catches your eye, it makes no difference. At this point you will have all the information you need to start with either food or beverage and wind up with a delicious pairing.

But it's not necessary to read through and study this whole book to begin the process. (Happily, you've grown up and no longer have to do homework before sitting down to dinner!) There are several other ways to begin, and these may be more practical and convenient for tonight and every night:

You're in the Mood For . . .

If you've got a hankering for a particular food—salmon, chicken, steak—begin this way: Go to the Course-by-Course Recipe List starting on page 23 and see what's there. Browse through those recipes, pick the one that sounds the yummiest, then pick one of the wines I recommend for your particular recipe. Shop and cook. Simple.

Trying Something New

You've never tried a German Riesling, but somebody gave you a bottle that's been sitting around and you'd like to drink it tonight with dinner. Go straight to Chapter 1, read up on this grape, and choose a recipe that suits your taste, feeling confident that it will also showcase your bottle of Riesling.

Improvising with Basic Ingredients and Everyday Wine

You haven't had time to shop, but you have the basics in your refrigerator and pantry, and a few bottles of everyday wine on hand. Although I have hundreds of cookbooks and stacks of food magazines at my house, more often than not I improvise everyday dinner rather than follow a recipe. I look at what I have to cook, I glance at the wine rack to see what the choices are, and then I throw something together accordingly. In boxes scattered throughout this book, I've gathered together different ideas for improvised dinners—what to do with a pound of pasta, a package of chicken breasts, a half-dozen eggs—to transform these ingredients into wine-friendly dinners. Once you gain some confidence, you'll find there is an incredible feeling of freedom and creativity in cooking this way. When you come home from work and realize that all you have is a box of pasta, a hunk of Parmesan cheese, a handful of parsley, and a half-full bottle of Chianti, you can feel excited rather than desperate at the prospect of cooking and then sitting down to enjoy your dinner.

Planning a Menu with Wine

You've chosen a recipe from a particular chapter, but you need some ideas for rounding out the meal. Chapters 1 through 8 end with a meal-planning chart to help you take one recipe and add on to it to create a complete dinner. As you will see, some recipes are one-dish wonders, requiring only the addition of a loaf of bread or a salad and a glass of wine. Some go beautifully with other dishes from the same chapter or from another chapter in the book. Wine pairing suggestions are included, so all the information you need to make a simple menu will be right in front of you.

Stocking a Wine-Friendly Pantry

SOME OF MY MOST extraordinary food moments have included some of the most ordinary fare—eggs, rice, potatoes, chicken, even plain bread. What did it take to transform a slice of bread into manna from heaven? Nothing more than lush, fresh-tasting extra virgin olive oil and a sprinkling of crunchy sea salt. The oil and salt lent to the bread incredible sensory drama, as well as instant wine affinity. In fact, many of the best food moments I've ever had were just like this one, when I was surprised and delighted at the way one or two flavor-enhancing ingredients could elevate an everyday food to celestial heights. Before you pick out a recipe or choose a wine, take a good look at your pantry and refrigerator and stock up on some of these wine-friendly ingredients. You will be thrilled that you have purchased these items when you realize the endless array of exciting and quick dinner possibilities you can spin off from just a few of them.

The following list is comprised of purposefully chosen oils, vinegars, salts, nuts, and other intensely flavored add-ins. Most of these ingredients are easy to keep stocked in your pantry, so that even when you're cooking something simple, you can make it special with just a splash or a sprinkle. These are the ingredients I keep on hand to punch up the texture and/or wine-friendly flavor of my everyday cooking. Some of them are available at your local supermarket. Some are available only at specialty and gourmet stores and are somewhat pricey (see Sources and Resources, page 286), but in each of these cases the splurge is worth it, because just a very small quantity of one of these items will make a huge impact on your everyday dinner.

Great Olive Oil. A drizzle of top-quality extra virgin olive oil brings both bewitching perfume and texture to the table—it works on bread, baked potatoes, potato puree (a healthful alternative to buttery mashed potatoes), fish and shellfish, or just plain pasta. Try it in lieu of butter, brushed onto hot grilled corn on the cob, and follow with a sprinkling of great salt (see below). Big, rustic red wines are the best choices to spotlight the complexity of great olive oil. Look for French Rhône wines, Sangiovese-based Tuscan reds, and Spanish Rioja. Reserve the extra virgin for drizzling; its subtlety is lost in cooking. Use cheaper "pure" olive oil in any recipe where the olive oil is heated to a high temperature.

Great Salt. Coarse-grained specialty salts are a religion among chefs, and I'm a convert. Fleur de sel, a fine French sea salt, is probably the most talked-about gourmet salt, but there are all kinds of fun salts to try, including Peruvian pink salt, Hawaiian volcanic salt (black or reddish-pink), and even a smoked salt from Denmark that you can order from my friends at the Cooking School of Aspen in Colorado (see Sources and Resources, page 286). Coarse salts add both flavor and an exciting crunch to silky foods like scallops, fish fillets, and foie gras, and to tender meats such as filet mignon, duck, and veal. In my book, fleur de sel is a must for eggs, and I also use it on roasted vegetables. It is to-die-for on homegrown or farm-stand tomatoes. It is expensive, but a little goes a long way. Reserve expensive salts as "finishing" salts, for sprinkling on just before you serve the dish. For cooking, the savory recipes in this book call for kosher salt and the dessert recipes use table salt.

Great Vinegar. Almost always, my vinegars of choice for wine-friendly cooking are Spanish sherry vinegar and balsamic vinegar. The reason is that both are barrel-aged, a process that mellows and softens them, resulting in a richness and sweetness that mirror the sweet scent of oak aging in wines. My other favorite use: Sprinkle sherry vinegar onto roasted vegetables just before serving—the vinegar's tang actually kicks up the vegetables' caramelized sweetness. My favorite wine matches for sherry vinegar–dressed dishes are barrel-fermented Fumé and Sauvignon Blanc for salads, and barrel-fermented Chardonnay for roasted vegetables. Almost any sherry vinegar imported from Spain is a good bet. It costs more than domestic red wine vinegar that you buy at the supermarket, but it's a minimal investment that will pay off in the number of terrific, wine-friendly dishes you can dress with it.

Authentic balsamic vinegar is a different story. True balsamic vinegar is an artisanal product made in small batches in only two zones designated for its production: Modena and Reggio Emilia, both in Italy. It has a honeylike consistency and a complexity of flavor unmatched by any other vinegar. If a bottle is marked "Aceto Balsamico Tradizionale," it is the real thing—made by hand according to centuries'-old tradition and production and aging processes regulated by the Italian government. Aged in wood for years, it is very expensive. Tiny bottles of fifty-year-old balsamic vinegar can cost upwards of $100. So what are all of those bottles marked "balsamic vinegar" on the supermarket shelves and priced about the same as the cider vinegar in the same aisle? Most likely they are labeled "Aceto Balsamico di Modena," the designation for "industrial grade" balsamic that allows for the addition of artificial flavorings and colorings and not a bit of aging in wood. If you've got the money and the interest, by all means keep a bottle of Aceto Balsamico Tradizionale in the pantry. Use it as chefs do, a couple of drops at a time. Although there is no substitute for the real thing, industrial balsamic vinegar can be vastly improved simply by reducing it on top of the stove. For the everyday recipes in this book,

Balsamic Vinegar Reduction (page 264) adds some deep balsamic flavor without the high cost. My favorite wine matches include Spanish red Rioja, Italian Chianti, and any wines based on the Syrah and Zinfandel grapes.

Cured Meats and Vegetables. Curing intensifies the flavor, saltiness, and tanginess of a variety of meats and vegetables. Just a sprinkling of bacon, pancetta, prosciutto, or Serrano ham will add lovely flavor and saltiness to green vegetables (bitter greens and cabbage, broccoli, green beans, etc.). Capers, olives, sun-dried or oven-dried tomatoes, and anchovies do the same thing for salads, starchy beans, pastas, and bruschetta. The savory tang and earthiness of these ingredients call for a wine with acidity and earthiness to match. Italian Pinot Grigio and Vernaccia di San Gimignano are great choices for white. Dry rosé wines from southern France, Italy, or Spain are amazing with these flavors. And for red, try Italian Chianti Classico and Barbera d'Alba.

Dry-aged Cheeses. As cheeses age, some of the moisture content evaporates, concentrating the flavor (an added benefit of the lower moisture content is that they keep longer in the fridge). Grate dry-aged cheese onto eggs, pasta, risotto, grains (grits, polenta, barley, etc.), and soups. Shave or shred them onto salads. The style of the cheese determines my wine choice:

SHARP AND SALTY. Older Cheddars and pecorinos, Asiago. There are two ways to go. White wines such as Champagne and sparkling, and the aromatic whites like Riesling and Gewürztraminer, contrast the cheeses' sharpness and saltiness. Earthy-peppery Italian, Spanish, and southern French reds have enough bite and heft to stand up to it.

MELLOW AND MILDLY SALTY. Parmigiano-Reggiano, Spanish Manchego, aged Monterey Jack. These shine with any big red, from velvety California Cabernets to spicy Shiraz and Rhône wines, to exotic red Zinfandels.

Herbs. In my opinion, every wine lover should have her hand on this flavor lever. The ability of fresh and dried herbs to coax the complexity out of even everyday wines is uncanny. So I use them liberally, as you'll see in the recipes. I always keep dried thyme on hand. The following fresh herbs are relatively hardy and incredibly versatile with wine, so I buy them on every single shopping trip, and always have them in the refrigerator:

THYME: This herb never met a wine it didn't love—white, pink, or red— honest-to-God. I can't imagine life without it.

ROSEMARY, OREGANO, AND SAGE: These herbs shine with absolutely any red wine. As many of my recipes demonstrate, they make seafood and chicken, which you might consider to be white wine fare, delicious with reds.

Because they are less hardy in the fridge, I buy tarragon and cilantro for specific recipe and wine pairings. I like these herbs best with the white grapes: Riesling, Sauvignon Blanc, Chardonnay, and Pinot Gris/Grigio. And I buy basil and mint constantly in season. These herbs love, love, *love* Cabernet Sauvignon, Merlot, Shiraz, and red Zinfandel.

Nuts. I've always loved pine nuts in pesto, but my fiancé, John, has taught me some better tricks with them. Toasted until browned and fragrant, they add a toasty-butteriness to vegetables that's beautiful with rich oak-aged wines, especially California Chardonnay and French white Burgundy. Blanched, toasted almonds add a contrasting sweetness to earthy, cooked greens and tangy salads that amps up their wine affinity, especially with dry, aromatic whites like Riesling, Spanish Albariño, and Italian whites. The pleasant hint of bitterness in toasted walnuts added to greens or pasta creates great flavor tension with big, bold reds like Cabernet Sauvignon, Tuscan reds from Italy, and French Rhône reds.

Stocking a Wine "Pantry"

IT IS NOT NECESSARY (or even desirable) to become a wine collector or build a wine cellar to enjoy wine with dinner every night. But it does make sense to keep on hand a small selection of wines for everyday drinking, so that you have a few choices and aren't constantly running to the wine shop for fresh supplies. The same way that you shop every week for staples like milk and bread and vegetables, you might think about making a weekly or monthly stop at the wine shop or discount liquor store. As you taste more wines and discover new favorites, you will develop ideas about what you want on hand for everyday drinking. In the meantime, here are some suggestions for putting together a wine "pantry" for fun and convenience:

Sparkling. A must! Remember, it is *wine*, but with bubbles. One look at Chapter 4 and you'll see it goes with everything. Look for budget bottles labeled *brut* (meaning dry) from Spain and the United States.

Meat takes longer to cook, so I borrow a common chef's technique to add flavor to the outside while making sure that it is cooked adequately on the inside. After searing, I finish the cooking in the oven. Searing deepens any seasoning's flavor and bonds that flavor to the surface of meat. The classic French dish steak au poivre is a great example. The texture and taste of the cracked pepper coating after searing is much more intense and exciting than a grinding of black pepper onto an already cooked, plain steak. Whatever the seasonings, the caramelized crustiness and charred flavor of seared meat enhance the fruit and oak characteristics of wine. A final benefit of meat seared on top of the stove and then finished in the oven—there's only one pan to wash!

Roast Your Vegetables

Here's another method with several virtues. There's less prep time with roasting than with other cooking methods. Very often, you can skip peeling vegetables before putting them in the roasting pan. Think about how long it takes to peel potatoes before boiling them. With roasting, you just wash them, throw them in a baking dish, and put them in the oven. Roasting also has health benefits. While boiling leaches the nutrients from vegetables, roasting lets vegetables hold on to them. And those peels contain nutrients, too. Finally, the wine affinity of roasted vegetables just floors me. The oven's dry heat sucks out some of the vegetables' moisture, concentrating the flavors so they really stand up to and interact with the wine's flavors. In the oven, vegetables' natural starches are caramelized, lending them a sweetness and toastiness that's wonderfully suited to the deep fruit and toasty oakiness in many wines. Think about the taste of a boiled potato versus a roasted one and you'll see what I mean.

Produce: Seasonal-schmeasonal

In recent years, great chefs have become big boosters of buying and cooking what's seasonal. The quality and freshness of food grown on the local farm has inspired some of the best restaurant cooking ever. Seasonal produce, at peak freshness and simply but deliciously prepared, is also one of the attractions of the European countryside dining we dream about and experience on vacation. So if you live near a farmer's market or have an awesome garden, great. Go ahead and take advantage of the locally grown food that's available.

But, for everyday dinner most of us—me included—shop at the supermarket. And despite what purists would have you believe, it's not tragic. Far from it. Thanks to global shipping and staggered seasons in the different hemispheres, many of the most wine-loving vegetables really know no season. In my opinion, the season matters critically for just a few garden varieties such as peas, berries, tomatoes, corn, stone fruits (peaches, apricots, plums), melons, and summer squashes. Lucky for wine lovers, the veggies that aren't so season-centric happen to be some of the most wine-friendly of all. These include dark leafy greens, cruciferous vegetables like cauliflower and broccoli, the allium family (garlic, shallots, onions, etc.), mushrooms, starchy squashes like butternut and acorn, and root vegetables from potatoes to carrots to turnips to beets. Fresh herbs, so important in creating sparks between food and wine, are available year-round these days in most supermarkets. In any supermarket, on almost every day of the year, there will be a huge repertoire of wine-loving vegetables to enjoy. The recipes in this book focus not on precious produce like "heirloom" tomatoes, which are available for only a week or two of the year, but on supermarket workhorses like collards and potatoes. Would you be able to taste the difference between beets from the farmer's market and the supermarket? Probably yes. But that doesn't mean that the supermarket variety is not worth buying. Chosen and prepared with care, supermarket produce can be delicious, and wine-loving.

Make a Pan Sauce

This is a favorite technique of professional chefs and cookbook authors. Once you have seared your protein and removed it from the pan, you can use the flavorful browned bits stuck to the bottom of the pan to build an infinite variety of sauces to pour on top. To create the sauce, you pour liquid into the pan—usually wine, stock, or water. Boiling the liquid while scraping the bottom of the pan loosens the deliciously caramelized bits. Then you reduce the liquid to concentrate the flavors and thicken the sauce. From there you can season (always!) with salt and pepper, and add other aromatics, like herbs or mushrooms, and serve. Or you can add more body to the sauce: Southerners add flour or cornstarch, the French use heavy cream, but I usually just swirl in some butter or demi-glace (see Sources and Resources, page 286) or both, for the lightest and quickest result. I love pan sauces because they are quick, versatile, and appeal to my sense of frugality. Why would I waste the brown bits stuck to the bottom of the skillet if they could add so much taste to my dinner?

Brine Your Protein

Brining is another chef's secret—soaking uncooked meat, poultry, or seafood in a saltwater solution before cooking to plump it up and give it flavor. It is extremely easy, but requires some planning ahead. Small, delicate shrimp need only thirty minutes in the brine; larger cuts of meat or whole birds can be soaked overnight in the refrigerator. I've found that brining allows me to cook leaner or tougher cuts of meat such as chicken breasts or ribs quite a bit more quickly, without drying them out. I recently experimented with adding wine to my brine solutions to up the wine affinity of the dish, and it works great! Feel free to experiment with the various brines in this book, adjusting brining times depending on what you're cooking. The brine for Fast-Track Baby Back Ribs (page 50), for example, can also be used with chicken breasts, pork chops, or tenderloin, depending on your mood and what you have in your refrigerator. See page 196 for brining basics.

Make the Bed

This technique is perfect for both simple (grilled or baked chicken) and spectacular (prime steak) proteins. All you do is make a flavorful starch or vegetable bed to complement the wine, the protein, or both. For example, you can send plain chicken, which is pretty neutral wine-wise, in countless different wine directions: Spicy Fruited Couscous (page 193) for an Aussie Shiraz, creamy sweet corn polenta for a California Chardonnay, or Sweet Potato Puree with Garlic, Thyme, and Balsamic Vinegar (page 166) for a big Cab. If I've splurged on something really snazzy like a great steak or duck breast, I often want to serve it with a similarly special wine. A subtle bed such as a thickened, pureed version of Yukon Gold Potato and Cauliflower Soup with Truffle Oil (page 77) or Pearl Barley Risotto with Mushrooms and Carrots (page 138) is designed to complement both the wine and the protein, without stealing the spotlight.

Simple Salads

In the world of wine and food, salads generally get a bad rap of being tough to pair, but I don't buy it. It is true that very sweet dressings like raspberry vinaigrette, honey-Dijon, and commercially bottled "French dressing" are so sugary-tasting that they overpower the fruit in many wines, making the wine taste thin and tart. But otherwise, wine and salads match just fine, and they can match beautifully if you keep certain principles in mind. First, go for subtle dressings. Classic vinaigrette is easy to make and, according to the French, who should know, it is quite compatible with wine. Balsamic and sherry vinegars, which are mellowed by oak aging, will make a vinaigrette especially wine-friendly. Second, cheese dramatically ups the wine-friendliness of salads, so any of the classics that contain cheese—Cobb, chef's, Caesar, a wedge of iceberg lettuce with blue cheese dressing (a steakhouse classic), and goat cheese salad (I think it's achieved classic status)—are great ones for wine lovers to keep in mind. I also like to improvise wine-worthy salads by adding a bit of cheese to peak-of-the-season fresh vegetables such as lettuces, herbs, fresh peas, or tomatoes. Finally, roasting or grilling vegetables for a salad dramatically ups their wine affinity by reducing their moisture and caramelizing their starches, as I've described earlier. It takes a little extra time, but hardly any extra work, so quite a few of my salad recipes include this step.

If the Corporate Dude Can Do It, You Can, Too

DURING THE TIME that this book was coming together, I fell in love with a corporate type who learned to love wine while working overseas, and learned to cook largely, he's proud to say, by watching Emeril and Alton Brown on the Food Network. On our first his-place dinner date he commenced cooking with a quip: "I'm cooking for a chef and the wine dean at The French Culinary Institute . . . what am I thinking?" "I'm not picky," was my honest response (and having seen his cellar, I knew that at least one part of the meal would be a winner).

The meal was a keeper (the man, too), and in fact I've included John's salmon recipe from that evening (see page 150), because it was drop-dead delicious and wine-worthy, yet so easy—just a handful of ingredients that came together with warp-speed and not many dirty dishes. The technique—season, sear, and serve—was simple and gave a wonderful crisp-outside, succulent-inside texture to the fish. "I do 'guy cooking.' I sear protein," was John's description of *his* foundational recipe. But as the months served up more amazing creations—lobster tail fettuccine with vanilla bean, veal chop with a wine and herb sauce, cauliflower "popcorn" that even my son, Lucas, would eat—I realized there was more to it than that. John had a whole "guy cooking" playbook, shaped by his love of good food and wine and by the time constraints of his busy life as a corporate titan. What was incredible to me, though, was how similar his playbook was to my own—a set of cooking concepts and techniques developed and informed by my professional passion for wine and kept real by my working-mom budget.

When I realized how two very different individuals with such very different kitchen histories had come to such similar conclusions based on a love of good food and wine, I gained further conviction about the relevance of this book to a whole spectrum of people. No matter who you are, chances are good that you have your plate full (no pun intended) with work and family commitments. But if you have picked up this book, you are probably intrigued by the idea of a satisfying dinner and a good glass of wine at the end of each and every busy day. I know that my techniques and pairing principles will help you reach this end-of-the-day goal, whether cooking in your house is a passionate creative pursuit or simply a savory snippet in the day's work/family/friends agenda. My hope is that it will also renew the kitchen culture in your family. In my house, wine with dinner in the kitchen is where passion, pleasure, and the people I love all come together, every day. Here's to celebrating each other and life's simple pleasures each evening, with the help of lovingly prepared and paired food and wine.

Course-by-Course Recipe List

This isn't a conventional cookbook, and it's not organized according to recognized cookbook conventions. You won't find chapters here beginning with Appetizers, taking you through Main Courses, and ending with Desserts. (Okay—there is a dessert chapter, but that's just because there's a whole category of dessert wines paired with those recipes!) Instead, you'll find chapters on different types of wines, their general characteristics, rules of thumb when matching them with food, and recipes for dishes that pair well with the wines we are discussing.

But as wine-centric as I am, I do recognize that a lot of people ask themselves, "What should I cook for dinner?" before they ask themselves, "What kind of wine do I feel like drinking?" That may change as you read on. Maybe some of the information in this book will spark your interest in wine to the extent that at least some of the time you'll begin with wine and then move on to food. But in the meantime, if you are, say, in the mood for salmon, and not necessarily in the mood for Pinot Noir or any other particular wine, you can consult the following list of recipes, organized along conventional cookbook lines, to see if there's an interesting-sounding salmon dish that you'd like to try. *Then,* once you've made the decision about what to cook, you can start to think about what wine to drink with your dinner.

Soups and Salads

Apple, Sage, and Onion Soup with Cheddar-Bacon Croutons (page 36)

Yukon Gold Potato and Cauliflower Soup with Truffle Oil (page 77)

Roasted Tomato Soup with Leeks and Carrots (page 217)

Coconut Milk–Curry Shrimp Soup (page 64)

Summer Tomato Salad (page 58)

Shallot- and Thyme-Rubbed Roast Turkey (page 144)

Grilled Duck Breast with Red Wine Reduction (page 142)

Mushroom-Dusted Foie Gras (page 148)

Churrasco-Style Skirt Steak (page 112)

Sirloin Steak with "Beurre-Naise" Sauce (page 173)

"Red and Blue" Short Rib Ragù with Pappardelle (page 175)

Seared Filet Mignon with Merlot and Mushroom Jus (page 177)

Flank Steak Marinated in Spicy Herb Oil (page 226)

Fast-Track Baby Back Ribs (page 50)

Cuban-Style Asado Pork with Vino Mojo (page 94)

Seared Pork Tenderloin with Dried Fig and Mushroom Sauce (page 146)

Oloroso Sherry–Glazed Pork Chops with Mushrooms (page 228)

Cumin-Crusted Lamb (page 199)

Fish and Shellfish

Shrimps in a Blanket (page 114)

Shrimp Ceviche with Avocado, Cilantro, and Lime (page 113)

Seared Shrimp and Chorizo Bites (page 65)

Cheese Grits with Shrimp and Chorizo (page 225)

Tarragon- and Mustard-Crusted Scallops (page 66)

Lemon-Herb-Prosciutto Shrimp (page 201)

Roasted Oysters "Rockefeller Center" (page 116)

Pan-Crisped Oysters with Sesame Seeds (page 118)

Champagne-Steamed Mussels (page 119)

Mussel Salad with Seared Avocado Dressing (page 68)

Herbed Scallop and Potato "Napoleons" with Truffle Oil (page 92)

Crispy Artichokes and Squid (page 231)

Lobster with Smoked Mozzarella Sauce and Confetti Vegetables (page 89)

Wasabi Pea–Crusted Salmon (page 121)

Plank-Cooked Salmon (page 45)

John's First-Date Salmon Fillets (page 150)

Spice-Painted Salmon (page 202)

Mushroom-Dusted Tuna with Black Bean–Hoisin Sauce (page 151)

Seared Tuna with Preserved Lemon (page 233)

Whole Fish Baked in a Salt Crust (page 204)

Desserts

Honey- and Lavender-Glazed Fruit (page 244)

Tropical Fruits "On the Half-Shell" with Banana Crunch Topping (page 245)

Soft Chocolate Cookie Sandwiches with Mascarpone and Cherry Filling (page 246)

Gingered Cranberry-Pistachio Biscotti (page 248)

Ginger-Spumante Cupcakes with Apricot-Cranberry–Cream Cheese Centers (page 250)

Caramelized Banana "Pizza" (page 252)

Tarte Tatin with Bourbon and Vanilla (page 254)

Spiced Pear and Phyllo Dumplings (page 256)

Pumpkin-Pear Mini Soufflés (page 258)

Chocolate-Banana Sorbet (page 260)

Pear (or Pineapple) and Pinot Gris Granita (page 261)

Bittersweet Chocolate–Cassis Truffles (page 262)

chapter one

RIESLING AND THE AROMATIC WHITES

●

Riesling Rundown

HOME REGIONS
Germany and Alsace, France

OTHER GREAT RIESLING SOURCES
Austria, New Zealand, Australia, United States
(Washington State, California, New York)

STYLE
Light- to medium-bodied; elegant

FLAVOR
Tangy-crisp like apples to juicy-
mouthwatering like peaches and melons

What is Riesling?

As I've said to my culinary students, it's "the Riesling for living!" A fun pun, but in my book it's not a joke. I am passionate about this grape, for the simple reason that every time I pour one, it enchants me. The flavors and scents are so pure, so vibrant, and so thrilling that I'm drawn back to the glass again and again for more of that perfume. Sampled alone, Riesling's aromatic attributes certainly demand attention. But with food it is not a show-off. Like a perfect dance partner, it swirls and sashays lithely and elegantly across the table with virtually any dish. To put it plainly, I've never found a food that doesn't pair well with Riesling.

Yet, among average consumers, Riesling is the wallflower of wines, rarely getting a chance to show her charms. I think Liebfraumilch, the simple, sweet stuff we all discovered in the 1970s, is the reason. People see the traditional long, fluted bottle shape and think "sweet" and "not for me." Although Rieslings are bottled in the same distinctive container, the only other thing they share in common with Liebfraumilch is an original home base, Germany. To explore the wonderful world of Riesling, that's the place to start.

GERMAN WINE LABELS' "NEW LOOK"

You might say the wallflower has had a makeover. Many of the top German wine estates have radically simplified their labeling, with easier-to-read lettering and simpler designs. Some of the top wineries have begun to simply label their wines as "Estate," meaning grown in the winery's own vineyards. Leaving off the long vineyard names or shrinking them to a less prominent position helps the buyer get to the most important quality and style indicators—the producer and the ripeness level.

German Riesling Basics

SO YOU THOUGHT GERMANY WAS ONLY TOPS AT CARS AND BEER? German Rieslings are awesome. Admittedly, they can also be confusing, because the labels can sometimes seem engineered with as much technical detail and precision as a Porsche. But all that detail actually slows many wine lovers down. The hard-to-read script and multisyllabic names, while traditional, can make it hard for non–German speakers to figure out what style of Riesling is in the bottle.

That style is dependent on the ripeness of the grapes at harvest. The riper the grapes, the fuller the body, and the richer the wine. Now, the most important point. That richness can come in two forms: fruitiness or sweetness, or both. Here's the distinction: *Fruitiness* means the flavor and sweetness of fresh fruit, balanced by vibrant acidity; *sweetness* means the taste of fruit with sugar added. Think of the difference between a ripe apple (which is fruity-sweet) versus apple pie filling (which is sugary-sweet). The fruity wines are fabulous partners for savory food. The sweet ones are great with dessert, as dessert, or with cheeses and pâtés. Here are the different German ripeness levels from least to most ripe, and the fruitiness or sweetness associated with each:

Kabinett	Fruity	Light-bodied
Spätlese	Fruity	Light- to medium-bodied
Auslese	Slightly sweet	Light- to medium-bodied
Beerenauslese	Very sweet	Medium-bodied and luscious
Trockenbeerenauslese	Very sweet	Medium-bodied and syrupy

The Fruit Flavor of Riesling

OF COURSE, ANY EXPLORATION of the flavors in wine starts with fruit. Riesling is a virtual fruit-salad-in-a-glass, and the exact fruit flavors in any given bottling are a function of where the grapes were grown. The fruit flavors in any white wine range along a spectrum, from lean to lush. The "leaner," tangy fruit flavors are associated with cooler growing regions, while the "lush" riper fruits are associated with warmer, sunny climates, as follows:

LEAN   LUSH

apple pear lemon lime grapefruit kiwi peach apricot melon pineapple mango banana

Even in the same region, the fruit flavor can vary from one year to the next, with hotter growing seasons yielding lusher fruit flavors than cooler vintages. With this fruit flavor spectrum as a backdrop, here's a rundown of the other great Rieslings of the world, from leanest to lushest.

Austria. Try them! Although Austrian wines are labeled according to ripeness level like German wines, they are quite different because the growing regions get more sunshine. As such, Austrian wines are fuller-bodied, yet still have vibrant acidity and tangy fruit flavors of apple and citrus.

Alsace, France. Alsace was once a part of Germany, so it's no surprise that it, too, is a Riesling powerhouse. And while Alsace is a cool zone, it enjoys many more hours of sunshine during the growing season than does Germany, so the grapes get riper. They are fermented to a completely dry style (except for the late-harvest dessert versions; see Chapter 9, page 240, for details), and thus are fuller-bodied than German or Austrian Rieslings. Their fruit flavor ranges from Golden Delicious apple to lemon and peach, and the scent has a very distinctive "petroleum" quality that, while it may sound strange, is really great.

New Zealand. These wines offer great value and, not surprisingly, lip-smacking kiwi fruit flavor.

Australia. It always surprises my wine students that the land known for big brawny Shiraz reds also yields lively and elegant Rieslings. They are medium-bodied and dry, with zingy tangerine and peach fruit flavors.

United States. The desert growing conditions in Washington's Columbia Valley yield Riesling with vividly ripe, fragrant fruit, from mandarin orange to tropical. New York State also produces world-class Riesling, though in small quantities, and a few California wineries, including Fetzer, Wente, and Trefethen, produce juicy-tasting Riesling.

The Spice of Life: Chenin Blanc, Gewürztraminer, Pinot Gris, Muscat, Grüner-Veltliner, and Viognier

I INCLUDE THESE WHITE GRAPES, often referred to by wine pros as "aromatic varietals," in the Riesling chapter because they have a style similarity, and because similar food matching principles apply. All of them share a prominent "prettiness" and spiciness to their fruit flavors and fragrance, such

SUSHI, DIM SUM, TANDOORI, TACOS . . . BEER, HERE?

The flavor of everyday dinner sure has changed since I was a kid. In those days, Chinese food meant La Choy frozen eggrolls and canned chow mein, curry was a flavor of boil-in-bag rice, sushi was something completely bizarre my dad had tried on an exotic business trip, and "Mexican pie" at my school cafeteria was canned chili ladled over Fritos. Now supermarkets coast to coast carry bagged and ready-to-stir-fry fresh veggie mixes and preskewered kebabs ready to be curry-marinated and grilled, and have sushi chefs on-site. Mexican restaurants are more common than pizza parlors were when I was growing up. These new tastes are all welcome at my table, and perfectly compatible with wine.

With the exotic flavors and often sizzling spices of these foods, your natural instinct is perhaps to reach for a beer rather than a glass of Chard or Merlot. Fair enough: An ice-cold brew boasts the scrubbing bubbles and hoppy tanginess to cool and refresh your palate. In contrast, the full-bodied, oaky profile of many popular wine styles, coupled with bold food flavors, can be overwhelming. This doesn't mean you have to pass up wine with your favorite ethnic fare. Rather, it means you have a wonderful excuse to branch out from the "banker" wine grapes and regions, to Riesling and beyond! Pairing the aromatic grapes with Asian and Mexican food creates some truly great flavor fireworks.

Why do they work so well? There are several reasons. They all share a vibrant acidity that invigorates and refreshes your palate, just the thing to enjoy with food that has salty and/or fatty components. The acidity in these wines also puts a spotlight on the complex and exotic flavor layers in the food. If you think about it, the cuisines themselves echo this principle—from citrus or lemongrass to vinegar to yogurt to salsa, each is engineered with an acidic nerve center to fire the food's signature flavors. The wines also have distinctive scents and tastes, from herbal to fruity to spicy, that complement and that the scent is every bit as exciting as the flavor, and keeps you coming back to the glass to breathe the perfume. Also, they almost never possess oakiness because winemakers, conscious of those compelling scents, don't want to mask them. And without oakiness to overpower, the wines pair better with both exotic and delicate food flavors. Also like Riesling, they have the juicy acidity to tame intense flavors and kick up delicate ones. That said, they are all so unique you *must* explore each of them. Here's what you'll find.

even mimic those tastes in the food. No wonder they're the toast of the sommelier set. Some wine-savvy restaurants even spotlight separate sections of Food-Friendly Whites or Aromatic Varietals on the wine list, to draw your attention and encourage you to try them. It's hard to go wrong with any of them, but here are some fun recommendations for *your* exotic everyday dinners.

GERMAN RIESLING KABINETT OR SPÄTLESE

The touch of sweetness in this style acts as a coolant for your tongue with spicy dishes such as chips and salsa, Thai green curries, Indian vindaloo, and spicy Chinese stir-fries. This wine style also cuts through

and complements the rich meatiness of Peking duck and Chinese barbecued spareribs.

ALSACE OR WASHINGTON STATE DRY RIESLING, AND AUSTRIAN RIESLING AND GRÜNER-VELTLINER

The minerally citrus fruit and racy acidity of these wines make the sea-sweet flavors of sushi pop, and refresh against the kick of wasabi and the saltiness of soy. These wines also lift the earthiness of miso soup, tame the brininess of seaweed salad, and mirror the yogurt-tanginess of tandoori cooking. That cut of acidity also softens the lime in ceviches, allowing the fresh fish flavors to take center stage.

ALSACE, GERMAN, OR WASHINGTON STATE GEWÜRZTRAMINER, ALSACE MUSCAT, AND VIOGNIER

The floral-spiciness and tropical-apricot fruit of these grapes are luscious with Thai coconut milk or peanut-laced dishes like satay, pad thai, and Chinese kung pao chicken and cold sesame noodles. I also love them with the soy-sweet flavors of mu shu, teriyaki, and fermented black bean sauce. These grapes also pick up the earthy-sweet backnote of Latin starches such as plantains, yucca, and corn (in tortillas and empanadas), while kicking up the chili and pepper spices with which they're seasoned.

Chenin Blanc. This is the grape of the Vouvray and Savennières districts in France's Loire Valley, where its mouthwatering acidity and spiced apple and floral scents make for a wine that's at once exotic on the scent, lean and racy on the palate. While Savennieres is always dry, Vouvray may be sec (dry), demi-sec (off-dry), or moelleux (very sweet). Chenin Blanc is also widely planted in South Africa, where it is sometimes called Steen, and yields crisp, apple blossom–scented wines that are often value-priced.

Gewürztraminer. It's pronounced guh-VURTS-truh-mee-ner. *Gewürz* is German for "spice," and *traminer* means "grape." So there you have it—a delicious, spicy grape. The fragrance is a very complex blend of apricot, lychee nut, rose petals, and allspice. The palate oozes mouth-filling apricot-mandarin orange fruit and honey flavors. The best regions for Gewürz (the pro abbreviation) are Alsace, France, California, and Washington State. Although it is a German grape, not much Gewürztraminer wine is exported from there.

Pinot Gris. I include this here because the French Alsace version fits the aromatic and exotic flavor profile (while as the lighter-bodied and tangy Italian *Grigio,* it belongs with the crisp whites in Chapter 4). In Alsace, Pinot Gris yields succulent and exotic Asian pear and honey flavors, and a softer, "fatter" texture than Riesling. It achieves a similar style in California and in Oregon, where it's the signature white grape.

Muscat. Muscat has been a beloved grape since ancient times, I think due to the perfume and flavor: honeysuckle and orange-blossom, tangerines, cloves and honey. It is produced mainly in Alsace, France, and in California and Greece.

Grüner-Veltliner. In this grape, the most widely planted in Austria and, to my knowledge, produced exclusively there, the spice character is more savory than sweet: white pepper, mustard powder, and ginger. The flavor is tangy-grapefruit and lemon custard. It's really a treat!

Viognier. This beautiful grape is indigenous to France's Rhône Valley, where the main wine produced from it is the regionally named Condrieu. The fragrance is of lavender, lemongrass, and ginger; the flavor is like tropical fruit. Viognier is also grown successfully as a varietal wine in California.

Ready to start cooking with spice? Let the flavor fireworks begin!

OVEN-CRISPED RED POTATOES WITH THYME AND PUMPKINSEED OIL

SERVES FOUR AS A SIDE DISH • Creamy red potatoes are best for roasting, because they hold their shape during the long cooking time. Instead of cutting the potatoes into uniform pieces, I like to cut them all different sizes—from ½-inch bits that get really crispy to bigger 1-inch chunks that stay waxy-starchy. Thyme—fresh or dried—adds to the potatoes' earthy wine-friendliness, but the pumpkinseed oil—a specialty of Austria—clinches it. I first tasted this earthy-nutty oil, drizzled on some pâté, when I was in Vienna competing in the 1997 World Championship of Sommeliers. I love it so much I tend to drizzle it on anything starchy—bread, roasted vegetables, pasta, even lentils. Stir in the pumpkinseed oil and seasonings toward the end of cooking so that they perfume the potatoes but don't burn and become bitter. The garlic, herb, and pumpkinseed oil flavors are fabulous with the savory-herbal tang of Austrian Grüner-Veltliner and Riesling whites.

WINE RECOMMENDATIONS		
AUSTRIAN GRÜNER-VELTLINER Walter Glatzer, Nigl AUSTRIAN RIESLING Erich Salomon, Brundlmayer	1½ pounds red potatoes, scrubbed and cut into different-sized chunks, from ½ inch to 1 inch 2 tablespoons olive oil 2 tablespoons pumpkinseed oil	3 medium garlic cloves, finely chopped 1 tablespoon fresh thyme, or 1 teaspoon dried thyme 1 teaspoon kosher salt or sea salt

1. Preheat the oven to 425°F. Place the potatoes in a large bowl and toss with the olive oil to coat. Spread them in an even layer on a rimmed baking sheet and roast, turning once, until the small ones are very brown and the large ones light golden, 40 to 45 minutes.

2. While the potatoes are roasting, combine the pumpkinseed oil, garlic, thyme, and salt to taste in a small bowl.

3. Remove the baking sheet from the oven, drizzle the pumpkinseed oil mixture onto the potatoes, and turn the potatoes to coat them with the oil. Return the baking sheet to the oven and roast an additional 5 minutes to allow the potatoes to absorb the seasonings.

4. Spoon the potatoes into a serving bowl and serve immediately.

APPLE, SAGE, AND ONION SOUP WITH CHEDDAR-BACON CROUTONS

SERVES SIX • Here is my all-American version of onion soup, with Granny Smith apples providing some tart flavor, and Cheddar cheese taking the place of traditional Gruyère. While the flavors of the classic French version are tailor-made for Alsace white wines, I think this take trumps it for wine affinity—the sweet onions and apples mirror the fruit taste, while the savory bacon and cheese contrast it irresistibly—yum! Instead of homemade beef stock, which takes the better part of a day, I use canned chicken and beef broth with a dash of red wine. The wine instantly imparts a satisfying, beefy flavor to the soup without the hassle of starting from scratch.

WINE RECOMMENDATIONS

ALSACE WHITES

Pierre Sparr
Gewürztraminer, Josmeyer
Riesling, Zind-Humbrecht
Pinot Gris

2 tablespoons unsalted butter

3 medium onions, sliced thin

3 medium Granny Smith apples, peeled, cored, and cut into ¼-inch slices

Kosher salt

6 cups canned low-sodium chicken broth

1¾ cups canned low-sodium beef broth

¼ cup dry red wine

1 bay leaf

Freshly ground black pepper

6 ounces sharp Cheddar cheese, grated

6 slices bacon, cooked crisp, crumbled

1 tablespoon finely chopped fresh sage

1 French baguette, cut on the bias into twelve ¾-inch-thick slices

1. Heat the butter in a large stockpot or Dutch oven over medium-high heat. Add the onions, apples, and ½ teaspoon salt and stir thoroughly to coat the onions and apples in the butter. Cook, stirring frequently, until the onions and apples are deeply caramelized, and the bottom of the pot is coated with a dark brown crust, about 30 minutes.

2. Stir in the chicken broth, beef broth, wine, and bay leaf. Bring to a boil and scrape the bottom of the pot with a wooden spoon to loosen the brown crust. Simmer for 20 minutes to blend flavors. Discard the bay leaf and season with salt and pepper. (Soup may be covered and refrigerated for up to 2 days. Reheat to a simmer before proceeding with recipe.)

3. To serve: Adjust the oven rack to the upper-middle position and heat the broiler. Combine the cheese and bacon in a bowl and stir to distribute evenly. Place oven-proof soup crocks on a rimmed baking sheet. Stir the chopped sage into the simmering broth. Fill each crock almost to the top with soup. Top each crock with 2 baguette slices and sprinkle with some of the cheese-bacon mixture. Place the baking sheet in the oven and broil until the cheese is bubbling and well-browned, 2 to 4 minutes. Watch the soup carefully, because once the cheese is well-browned it will quickly burn. Serve immediately.

ROASTED SPAGHETTI SQUASH WITH NUTMEG AND BALSAMIC VINEGAR

SERVES TWO AS A MAIN COURSE OR FOUR AS A SIDE DISH • I could eat this rich, tender, yet toothsome squash all by itself for dinner, and I sometimes do, especially when I have a Riesling, Gewürztraminer, or Muscat to pair. The spicy-rich scent of the spaghetti squash is a gorgeous complement to the spicy aromatics of such fragrant grapes. And yet all the flavors dance on the thread of acidity from both the balsamic vinegar and the wine—the natural acidity of this category is its claim to food-friendly fame with the sommelier set. You can go either way with the wine choice. A totally dry version brings out the white pepper and balsamic grace notes, while a slightly sweet version makes the spaghetti squash taste richer and more buttery. A sprinkling of chopped smoked almonds over the top of the squash is a spectacular enhancement of both the dry and the sweet.

WINE RECOMMENDATIONS		
DRY RIESLING Paul Blanck (Alsace, France)	SLIGHTLY SWEET GEWÜRZTRAMINER Fetzer (California)	1 large spaghetti squash, cut in half lengthwise and seeded 1 tablespoon olive oil Kosher salt
SLIGHTLY SWEET RIESLING Hogue (Columbia Valley, Washington State)	DRY MUSCAT Trimbach (Alsace, France)	Freshly ground white pepper 2 teaspoons unsalted butter Pinch light brown sugar
DRY GEWÜRZTRAMINER Hugel (Alsace, France)	SLIGHTLY SWEET MUSCAT Famiglia di Robert Mondavi Moscato (California)	Pinch freshly grated nutmeg 1 to 2 teaspoons balsamic vinegar 1 tablespoon finely chopped smoked almonds, optional

1. Preheat the oven to 400°F. Brush the cut sides of the squash halves with the olive oil. Sprinkle with salt and pepper. Place the squash halves cut side down on a baking sheet and bake until tender, about 45 minutes.

2. Use a fork to scoop and shred the flesh of the squash, separating it into strands and then placing the strands in a bowl. Stir in the butter, brown sugar, nutmeg, and more salt and pepper to taste. Drizzle with the balsamic vinegar to taste, sprinkle with the almonds, if desired, and serve immediately.

CARROT SLAW WITH TOASTED PINE NUTS AND HERBS

SERVES SIX • The snappy sweetness of carrots and orange juice, the kick of pepper flakes, the fragrance and flavor jolt of fresh mint and cilantro—all signs point to "yum," especially with the Riesling and Grüner-Veltliner grapes. Their zesty fruit flavor mirrors the salad's crisp sweetness, and their savory spiciness and acidity cools the heat and launches the herbs' aromatics. I use this salad in summertime to transform a simple meal of grilled whatever's-on-sale-at-the-market into a keep-the-kitchen-cool wine-worthy dinner—only the toasting of the pine nuts requires brief indoor heating on the stove. Don't shy away from a match with red meats on the grill, because both grapes have enough flavor density to stand up to them. You can shred and refrigerate the carrots ahead of time, but mix together the salad at the last minute for the freshest flavor.

WINE RECOMMENDATIONS

DRY RIESLING

Wente (California)

Eroica (Washington State)

GRÜNER-VELTLINER

Freie Weingartner Wachau, Hirtzberger (Austria)

1 pound fresh carrots, ends trimmed

½ cup orange juice

2 tablespoons extra virgin olive oil

5 cloves Roasted Garlic (page 269), squeezed from their skins and finely chopped

½ teaspoon hot red pepper flakes

2 tablespoons pine nuts

½ cup finely chopped fresh cilantro

½ cup finely chopped fresh mint

1 teaspoon sea salt or other coarse salt

1. Use the grating disc of a food processor or a hand grater to shred the carrots. Place them in a medium bowl. Stir in the orange juice, olive oil, garlic, and pepper flakes.

2. Heat a small, dry skillet on medium and add the pine nuts. Cook, shaking the pan constantly, until they are fragrant and lightly browned, about 5 minutes. Add them to the carrots and toss. Add the herbs, toss, and season to taste with coarse salt. Serve immediately.

SPICY ROASTED CAULIFLOWER AND OKRA

SERVES SIX • This is an incredibly easy, drop-dead-delicious side dish. Roasted cauliflower's been a regular in my wine-worthy repertoire forever. The addition of bagged, frozen okra was a total gamble—I saw it in the freezer case and felt instantly nostalgic for what was a staple on the tables of my southern aunts. Would it be a slimy bust in my favorite cauliflower recipe, I wondered? Well, it's wonderful! The texture—at once tender, yet with crunchy little bits from the spices and caramelized edges of the vegetables—is a big wow. See page 286 for mail-order spice sources. You may not be able to find all of them at your local supermarket. (Don't worry if you don't have all of them on hand. Just use the ones you have and you will still end up with a very tasty dish.) A dry Gewürztraminer from Alsace or the United States, or an off-dry German Riesling from the Pfalz region, echoes the spice flavors beautifully.

WINE RECOMMENDATIONS	
AMERICAN GEWÜRZTRAMINER	1 teaspoon fenugreek seeds
	1 teaspoon mustard seeds
De Loach, Fetzer, or Sutter Home (California)	1 teaspoon coriander seeds
	1 teaspoon cumin seeds
Hogue, Chateau Ste. Michelle, or Columbia Crest (Washington State)	1 teaspoon fennel seeds
	½ teaspoon black peppercorns
	3 tablespoons olive oil, plus more for oiling the pan
ALSACE GEWÜRZTRAMINER	1 head cauliflower, cored and broken into florets
Paul Blanck, Pierre Sparr, Hugel	3 garlic cloves, finely chopped
	One 16-ounce bag frozen whole okra, unthawed
PFALZ RIESLING	1 teaspoon kosher salt
	1 teaspoon sugar
Lingenfelder Bird Label, Strub Niersteiner Paterberg	1½ teaspoons freshly squeezed lemon juice

1. Preheat the oven to 400°F. Combine the fenugreek, mustard, coriander, cumin, fennel, and black peppercorns in a heavy, dry skillet. Toast the spices over medium-high heat, shaking the pan frequently, until fragrant, about 2 minutes. Remove from heat to cool slightly, then transfer to a spice grinder or small coffee grinder and grind fine.

2. Oil a large, heavy casserole or lasagna pan. In a large bowl, combine the cauliflower, garlic, and okra. Sprinkle on the remaining 3 tablespoons of olive oil, 4 teaspoons of the ground spice mixture, salt, and sugar, and toss to mix the ingredients.

3. Roast, uncovered, for 25 minutes, stirring once after 15 minutes. Increase the heat to 450°F and continue roasting until the cauliflower has golden brown edges, about 10 minutes. Remove from the oven, sprinkle with the lemon juice, and stir to combine. Season with salt to taste. Serve hot.

BUTTERNUT SQUASH RISOTTO WITH BACON AND SAGE

SERVES FOUR • Risotto is not a difficult dish, but it does require frequent stirring, which releases the rice's starch and results in an incredibly creamy texture. I actually enjoy the work. It's fun and therapeutic to stand by the stove and tend my pot while sipping from my predinner glass of wine. The contrast of the sweet squash with the savory sage and bacon echoes the ripe fruit–smoky petroleum contrast of steely-dry Riesling, while the Riesling's zingy acidity cuts through the risotto's cheesy-richness.

DRY RIESLING

Pike's, Penfolds, Grosset (Australia)

Trefethen, Smith-Madrone (California)

6 cups chicken stock or canned low-sodium chicken broth

4 slices bacon

2 tablespoons unsalted butter

1 medium shallot, finely chopped

6 fresh sage leaves, finely chopped

½ small butternut squash (about 1 pound), peeled, seeded, and cut into ½-inch dice

½ cup white wine

1½ cups Arborio rice

½ cup grated Parmesan cheese

Kosher salt

Freshly ground black pepper

Oven-Crisped Sage Leaves (page 270), optional

1. Heat the chicken stock in a medium saucepan on medium until it reaches a simmer. Turn the heat to low to keep warm.

2. In a large, heavy saucepan, cook the bacon on medium until crisp. Transfer to a paper towel–lined plate to drain. Pour off all but 1 tablespoon of the bacon fat from the pan.

3. Add 1 tablespoon of the butter to the pan. Add the shallot and cook over medium heat until translucent, about 5 minutes. Stir in the chopped sage and the squash. Cook for 2 to 3 minutes, stirring to coat the squash.

4. Add the wine and 1 cup of the hot chicken stock and bring to a boil. Turn the heat to low, cover, and cook at a bare simmer until the squash is softened, 20 to 25 minutes.

5. Stir in the rice and 1 cup of the stock and bring to a lively simmer. Cook, stirring frequently, until the rice has absorbed the liquid. Continue to add stock, about ½ cup at a time, stirring frequently and allowing the rice to absorb the liquid, until the rice is al dente and creamy in texture, about 25 minutes. If you run out of chicken stock before the rice is cooked through, add warm water to the rice.

6. Remove the pot from the heat and stir in the remaining tablespoon butter, the Parmesan, and salt and pepper to taste. Divide the risotto among 4 warmed bowls. Crumble a slice of bacon over each bowl. Garnish with sage leaves, if desired. Serve immediately.

FENNEL AND APPLE HASH

SERVES SIX AS A SIDE DISH • When I was eleven years old, the quip about "pork chopsh and appleshaush" on a favorite *Brady Bunch* episode had me giggling all the way to the kitchen, eager to try the combination. But it was almost as much of a letdown as lamb with mint sauce (tell us how you *really* feel, Andrea!)—intriguing-sounding, but the two don't do much for each other. So I fixed it—at least to my taste and, I'll bet, to most wine lovers' taste. As the bed for simply grilled or pan-sautéed pork chops or chicken pieces (seasoned with salt and pepper before cooking), it really makes the match with an Alsace or Oregon Pinot Gris. Why? The licorice taste of the fennel brings out the licorice note in Pinot Gris, and the apple flavors mirror the wine's juicy fruit.

WINE RECOMMENDATIONS

ALSACE PINOT GRIS

Trimbach, Weinbach

OREGON PINOT GRIS

Willamette Valley Vineyard, King Estate, WillaKenzie

2 slices bacon, cut into ½-inch pieces	½ cup dry white wine, such as Alsace Riesling
1 fennel bulb, cut into ½-inch dice	3 tablespoons fresh sage, finely chopped
2 Granny Smith apples, peeled, cored, and cut into ½-inch dice	2 tablespoons unsalted butter
1 medium onion, cut into ½-inch dice	1 teaspoon kosher salt
3 garlic cloves, finely chopped	Freshly ground black pepper

1. In a medium sauté pan, cook the bacon pieces over medium heat until they begin to crisp.

2. Add the fennel, apples, onion, and garlic to the pan and cook, stirring frequently, until they begin to soften, about 10 minutes. Stir in the wine. Turn the heat down to medium-low, cover, and cook, stirring occasionally, until the vegetables are very soft and caramelized, about 20 minutes.

3. Add the sage and butter and stir until the butter is melted. Season with salt and pepper to taste. Serve immediately.

PLANK-COOKED SALMON

SERVES SIX • I serve this dish to my wine and food pairing students at The French Culinary Institute with Riesling, and the match is always a surprise hit. Students expect such big food flavors to clobber Riesling's delicacy. But Riesling's flavor concentration without heaviness, and its great acidity, enable it to share equal billing with the dish. And the way the tropical fruit and Asian aromatics in the wine (five spice, lemongrass, ginger) harmonize with the spicy-sweetness of the sauce creates a magic carpet of tastes, borne aloft by the smoky richness of the salmon.

Finally, the lightness of Riesling is so cooling and refreshing in summertime, when you're most likely to turn to this grilled main course. Grilling the fish atop a cedar plank gives it a marvelous flavor from the wood smoke. Soaking the plank in water before grilling makes the wood smolder (as opposed to going up in flames!) when it is placed on the hot grill. Cedar cooking planks are sold in some cookware shops, but I get mine (untreated with chemicals) at the hardware store.

WINE RECOMMENDATIONS	NEW WORLD RIESLING	OLD WORLD RIESLING	
	Jacob's Creek Reserve (Australia)	Robert Weil Riesling Spätlese Trocken (Germany)	1½ pounds center-cut salmon fillet, 1 inch thick
	Allan Scott (New Zealand)	Josmeyer Riesling, Trimbach Riesling (Alsace, France)	Extra virgin olive oil
	Eroica (Washington State)		Kosher salt
			Freshly ground black pepper
			1 recipe Indonesian Five-Spice Barbecue Sauce (page 267)
			Special equipment: cedar cooking plank

1. Soak the cedar plank in cold water to cover for 30 minutes. Preheat a gas grill to medium-high.

2. Brush the skin side of the salmon lightly with the olive oil. Put the fillet, skin side down, on the soaked cooking plank and season the flesh side with salt and pepper. Brush the barbecue sauce on the salmon generously to coat. Place the plank on the grill and, as soon as it begins to smolder, reduce the grill's heat to medium and close the cover. Cook the salmon, covered, until medium rare, about 10 minutes for a 1-inch fillet.

BRAISED COQ AU RIESLING WITH LEEKS

SERVES FOUR TO SIX • This dish was born of a craving: I wanted a melding of the wine-friendliness and comfort-food richness of coq au vin—a lusty chicken braise traditionally made with red wine—with the tongue-tingling zinginess of choucroute, because I love how its acidity actually makes the meat taste even meatier. My version uses a dry Riesling and leeks cooked until they're meltingly tender and sweet. The result is a texture like choucroute, with a tangy-sweet flavor that's much softer compared to the vinegary taste of choucroute, and thus wonderfully suited to wine—the one you cooked with, or really any crisp white. I like to finish the chicken in the oven, in an uncovered pan. This way the skin gets a little crisp (a covered braised chicken's skin is always a little soggy), but doesn't dry out thanks to the flavorful cooking liquid underneath it in the pan.

WINE RECOMMENDATIONS		
DRY RIESLING	ITALIAN PINOT GRIGIO	3 medium leeks
Wente, Kendall-Jackson (California)	Pighin, Maso Canali, Zemmer	4 whole chicken legs
		Kosher salt
		Freshly ground black pepper
Pikes, Jacob's Creek, Grosset (Australia)		1 tablespoon olive oil
		2 medium garlic cloves, finely chopped
Robert Weil Estate, J&H Selbach "TJ" (Germany)		1½ cups dry or off-dry Riesling
		½ cup chicken stock or canned low-sodium chicken broth

1. Preheat the oven to 400°F. Trim off the tough green leaves of the leeks, leaving about ½ inch of green. Halve the leeks lengthwise and rinse well under cold running water to remove all grit. Slice into ½-inch-thick pieces and set aside.

2. Season the chicken legs all over with salt and pepper. Heat the oil in a large oven-proof skillet over medium-high heat and brown the chicken pieces on both sides, turning once, 10 to 12 minutes. Remove chicken pieces from the pan and set aside.

3. Discard all but a thin film of fat from the pan. Lower the heat to medium and add the leeks and garlic. Cook, stirring frequently, until they begin to brown, about 7 minutes.

4. Add the Riesling and chicken stock and bring to a boil, scraping the bottom of the pan with a wooden spoon to loosen any browned bits.

5. Return the chicken legs to the pan and place the pan in the oven. Bake, uncovered, until chicken legs are cooked through, about 20 minutes. Serve immediately.

OATMEAL-CRUSTED CHICKEN WITH GEWÜRZTRAMINER PAN SAUCE

SERVES FOUR • I'm always looking for ways to pump up plain chicken breasts, and flavorful, crunchy "crusts" are one of my favorite ways to do that. The coating here is like a savory oatmeal cookie—spicy and nutty-tasting. The spices toast up and intensify during sautéing, creating a delicious savory-sweetness that pairs gorgeously with Gewürztraminer. Pounding the chicken with a meat mallet to a thickness of ½ inch allows the chicken to cook through quickly before the crust burns. A side note: Tim Schaefer (known as "The Beer Chef"), whose salmon recipe inspired this dish, serves his with Irish stout!

WINE RECOMMENDATIONS

GEWÜRZTRAMINER

Columbia Crest, Chateau Ste. Michelle (Washington State)

Martinelli, Sutter Home, De Loach (California)

1 cup old-fashioned rolled oats

½ teaspoon ground cinnamon

¼ teaspoon allspice

¼ teaspoon ground ginger

Pinch freshly grated nutmeg

1½ teaspoons kosher salt, plus more for seasoning

1½ teaspoons freshly ground black pepper, plus more for seasoning

1 large egg

1 tablespoon water

¼ cup all-purpose flour

4 skinless chicken breast halves (about 1½ pounds), rinsed and thoroughly dried

2½ tablespoons unsalted butter

1½ tablespoons olive oil

½ cup Gewürztraminer

1. Combine the oats, cinnamon, allspice, ginger, nutmeg, salt, and pepper in a blender or the workbowl of a food processor and grind. Place in a shallow bowl or pie plate.

2. Whisk the egg and water together in another shallow bowl. Place the flour in a shallow bowl or pie plate.

3. Trim any fat and remove the tendons from the breasts. One at a time, place them between two sheets of plastic wrap and place on a cutting board. Use a meat pounder or lay the side of a large chef's knife on the breast and pound with your fist to flatten the breasts to a ½-inch thickness.

4. Working with one half at a time, press each side of a chicken breast in the flour, shaking over the bowl to remove any excess. Then dip the breast in the egg and let any excess drip back into the bowl. Finally, press each side of the chicken breast half into the

oatmeal mixture to coat. Place the coated breast on a plate and press on the coating lightly with your fingertips to make sure that the crumbs adhere.

5. Heat 1½ tablespoons of the butter and the olive oil in a large, heavy skillet on medium-high. When the butter is foaming, place the cutlets in the skillet. Cook until brown and crisp on one side, about 4 minutes, checking the underside once or twice to make sure the coating isn't burning. If it is getting too dark, reduce the heat to medium. Turn the chicken and reduce the heat to medium. Cook until done, another 3 to 4 minutes. Transfer to a platter and cover loosely with foil to keep warm.

6. Add the wine to the pan and bring to a boil, scraping up the browned bits from the bottom of the pan with a wooden spoon. Cook until the wine is reduced to about 3 tablespoons, about 2 minutes. Remove from the heat and swirl in the remaining tablespoon of butter. Season with salt and pepper. Pour over the chicken and serve immediately.

HERE'S THE RUB

Most any meat that is suitable for grilling—steaks, pork tenderloin and chops, butterflied leg of lamb, lamb chops—will be more flavorful and wine-friendly with a spice rub. It'll also be easy because the ingredients—dried spices, salt, and sugar—are all nonperishable and probably sitting in your pantry. You can even stir up big batches of a favorite rub so you always have it on hand for grilling. The rub flavors the surface of the meat and helps give it a caramelized crispness. Choose your spices according to taste, what you have on hand, and/or what wine you feel like drinking.

To season a 1½-pound flank steak (or chops or other grillable meat), begin with 1 teaspoon salt and 1 tablespoon light brown sugar. Then add the following flavorings to complete your dish and your match:

SOUTHWESTERN: 1 tablespoon chili powder, 1 tablespoon cumin, 1 teaspoon dried oregano, pinch cayenne pepper. Serve with red Zinfandel

NORTH AFRICAN: 2 teaspoons ground ginger, 2 teaspoons ground coriander, 2 teaspoons ground cumin, 1 teaspoon ground black pepper, ½ teaspoon cardamom. Serve with Australian Shiraz

JAMAICAN JERK: 2 teaspoons ground ginger, 1 teaspoon allspice, 1 teaspoon dried thyme. Serve with Gewürztraminer

HERBES DE PROVENCE: 2 tablespoons herbes de Provence, *or* 1 teaspoon each dried rosemary, marjoram, oregano, thyme, and basil, and 3 crushed bay leaves. Serve with Côtes du Rhône

INDIAN: 2 tablespoons garam masala. Serve with Shiraz/Cabernet

FAST-TRACK BABY BACK RIBS

SERVES SIX • When I want barbecued ribs but I don't have a lot of time, I choose baby backs. The ribs are smaller, so they need less time on the grill to cook through, and are less tough, so they don't need hours of slow cooking to make them tender. To really put them on the fast track, I brine the ribs ahead of time with a wine-infused brine, which makes them cook even more quickly and plumps up the meat with extra juiciness and flavor. Most any aromatic white is wonderful with this dish. (The wine you choose for the brine need not be the wine you plan to pair with the meal.) There are two particularly great ways to go here: A slightly sweet Riesling or Chenin Blanc will temper the peppery heat of the rub; a completely dry Austrian Grüner-Veltliner has a white pepper/herbal character of its own that complements the rub's spicy-herbal elements. Each of these wine styles has great acidity to cut through the ribs' fatty richness, just as beer, with its hops flavor, cleanses the palate after every bite.

WINE RECOMMENDATIONS

SLIGHTLY SWEET RIESLING

Dr. Loosen Estate, Lingenfelder Bird Label (Germany)

Hogue Fruit Forward, Columbia Winery (Washington State)

SLIGHTLY SWEET CHENIN BLANC

Sutter Home (California)

Huet or Prince Poniatowsky Vouvray demi-sec (France)

AUSTRIAN GRÜNER-VELTLINER

Walter Glatzer, Erich Salomon, Prager, Pichler

FOR THE BRINE

½ cup kosher salt

½ cup packed brown sugar

2 teaspoons whole black pepper-corns

½ teaspoon hot red pepper flakes

2 bay leaves, broken

1 cup aromatic white wine such as Riesling, Chenin Blanc, or Grüner-Veltliner (leftover is fine)

FOR THE SEASONING RUB

1 teaspoon coriander seeds

1 teaspoon yellow mustard seeds

2 teaspoons whole black pepper-corns

1 tablespoon kosher salt

1½ teaspoons garlic powder

1 teaspoon dried thyme

1 teaspoon dried oregano

1 teaspoon granulated sugar

2 slabs of baby back ribs, about 3 pounds

1. Prepare the brine: Combine the salt, brown sugar, black peppercorns, hot red pepper flakes, bay leaves, and 2 cups hot water in a large bowl. Stir to dissolve the sugar and salt. Add the wine and 5 cups of ice water and stir to combine.

Place the ribs in a large nonreactive baking dish. Pour the brine over the ribs, cover with plastic wrap, and refrigerate for 4 to 6 hours. Remove the ribs from the brine, rinse well under cold running water, and pat dry with paper towels. (Brined ribs may be wrapped in plastic and refrigerated overnight.)

2. Prepare the spice rub: Heat a heavy, dry saucepan on medium-high. Add the coriander, mustard seeds, and whole peppercorns and toast, shaking the pan, until fragrant. Grind the toasted spices in a spice grinder or small coffee grinder. Transfer to a small bowl and stir in the salt, garlic powder, thyme, oregano, and granulated sugar.

3. Rub both sides of the rib slabs with the seasoning rub and let stand for 30 minutes at room temperature. Preheat a gas grill to medium-high and lightly oil the grill rack to prevent sticking.

4. Place the ribs on the grill, meat side down, and grill, covered, for 10 minutes, checking frequently and reducing the heat slightly to control excessive flame-ups (a little bit of charring will give the ribs nice flavor, but you don't want to blacken them completely). Turn the rib racks and grill, covered, until cooked through, about 10 minutes more. Serve immediately.

Everyday Dinners with
RIESLING AND THE AROMATIC WHITES

PASTAS AND OTHER ONE-PLATE DINNERS

WHAT TO COOK	WINE PAIRINGS
Apple, Sage, and Onion Soup with Cheddar-Bacon Croutons *(page 36)*, with spinach salad	ONCE-A-WEEK ($–$$): Pierre Sparr Gewürztraminer (Alsace, France) Josmeyer Riesling (Alsace, France) ONCE-A-MONTH ($$$ AND UP): Zind-Humbrecht Pinot Gris (Alsace, France)
Butternut Squash Risotto with Bacon and Sage *(page 42)*, crusty bread, green salad	ONCE-A-WEEK ($–$$): Trefethen Riesling (California) Smith-Madrone Riesling (California) ONCE-A-MONTH ($$$ AND UP): Pike's Riesling (Australia)

TRADITIONAL (MAIN-AND-SIDES) DINNERS

WHAT TO COOK	WINE PAIRINGS
MAIN COURSE: Seared Pork Tenderloin with Dried Fig and Mushroom Sauce *(page 146)* VEGGIE: Wine-Braised Leeks *(page 167)* STARCHES, ETC.: Roasted Spaghetti Squash with Nutmeg and Balsamic Vinegar *(page 38)*	ONCE-A-WEEK ($–$$): Fetzer Gewürztraminer (California) Hogue Riesling (Washington State) ONCE-A-MONTH ($$$ AND UP): Trimbach Muscat (Alsace, France)
MAIN COURSE: Fast-Track Baby Back Ribs *(page 50)* VEGGIES: Carrot Slaw with Toasted Pine Nuts and Herbs *(page 39)* STARCHES, ETC.: corn on the cob	ONCE-A-WEEK ($–$$): Freie Weingartner Wachau Grüner-Veltliner (Austria) Wente Riesling (California) ONCE-A-MONTH ($$$ AND UP): Eroica Riesling (Washington State)
MAIN COURSE: Cumin-Crusted Lamb *(page 199)* VEGGIES: Spicy Roasted Cauliflower and Okra *(page 40)* STARCHES, ETC.: couscous	ONCE-A-WEEK ($–$$): Lingenfelder Bird Label Riesling (Germany) Chateau Ste. Michelle Gewürztraminer (Washington State) ONCE-A-MONTH ($$$ AND UP): Paul Blanck Gewürztraminer (Alsace, France)

WHAT TO COOK	WINE PAIRINGS
MAIN COURSE: Sirloin Steak with "Beurre-Naise" Sauce *(page 173)* VEGGIES: roasted asparagus STARCHES, ETC.: Oven-Crisped Red Potatoes with Thyme and Pumpkinseed Oil *(page 35)*	ONCE-A-WEEK ($–$$): Walter Glatzer Grüner-Veltliner (Austria) Erich Salomon Riesling (Austria) ONCE-A-MONTH ($$$ AND UP): Nigl Riesling (Austria)
MAIN COURSE: pan-seared pork chops VEGGIES: Fennel and Apple Hash *(page 44)* STARCHES, ETC.: walnut bread	ONCE-A-WEEK ($–$$): King Estate Pinot Gris (Oregon) Willamette Valley Vineyard Pinot Gris (Oregon) ONCE-A-MONTH ($$$ AND UP): Weinbach Pinot Gris (Alsace, France)
MAIN COURSE: Plank-Cooked Salmon *(page 45)* VEGGIES: Lucas's Sesame-Ginger Broccoli Florets *(page 80)* STARCHES, ETC.: steamed rice	ONCE-A-WEEK ($–$$): Jacob's Creek Reserve Riesling (Australia) Allan Scott Riesling (New Zealand) ONCE-A-MONTH ($$$ AND UP): Robert Weil Riesling Spätlese Trocken (Germany)
MAIN COURSE: Braised Coq au Riesling with Leeks *(page 46)* VEGGIES: steamed carrots STARCHES, ETC.: crusty bread	ONCE-A-WEEK ($–$$): J&H Selbach "TJ" Riesling (Germany) Kendall-Jackson Vintners Reserve Riesling (California) ONCE-A-MONTH ($$$ AND UP): Grosset Riesling (Australia)
MAIN COURSE: Oatmeal-Crusted Chicken with Gewürztraminer Pan Sauce *(page 48)* VEGGIES: Roasted Brussels Sprouts with Garlic and Sage *(page 165)* STARCHES, ETC.: Sweet Potato Puree with Garlic, Thyme, and Balsamic Vinegar *(page 166)*	ONCE-A-WEEK ($–$$): De Loach Gewürztraminer (California) Columbia Crest Gewürztraminer (Washington State) ONCE-A-MONTH ($$$ AND UP): Martinelli Gewürztraminer (California)

chapter two

SAUVIGNON BLANC

◉

Sauvignon Blanc Sum-Up

HOME REGION
Bordeaux and the Loire Valley in France

———————

OTHER KEY SOURCES
California, Washington State, New Zealand

———————

STYLE
Light- to medium-bodied, pungent

———————

FLAVOR
Fruit flavor from lime to passion fruit, with herbaceous,
"grassy" notes

Chefs love to spark up a dish by tossing in a handful of

herbs. Sommeliers like to do something similar—to boost the flavors in a dish, we will pour alongside it a *glassful* of herbs, in the form of Sauvignon Blanc. This white grape is one of my favorites for pairing with food because it offers so much: pungent and inviting fragrance, tongue-tingling acidity, and truly great value and quality for everything from budget to world-class versions.

Sauvignon Blanc's home base is France, specifically in the Loire Valley and Bordeaux regions. The two styles are quite different. Loire Valley Sauvignon Blanc is the thoroughbred horse to Bordeaux's Clydesdale, each majestic in its own particular way. The Loire thoroughbred is sleek and what the French call *ennervé,* literally "nervous," with taut and lively acidity. The Bordeaux is, by contrast, grand and powerful. Here's why they differ, and what to look for when buying them:

Loire Valley Sauvignon Blanc. This Sauvignon Blanc gets its sleekness from three sources—the chalky soil and cooler climate, which contribute racy acidity, and the vinification. Specifically, winemakers typically ferment the wine in stainless-steel tanks rather than in oak barrels. Unlike oak barrels, stainless tanks are neutral, so they don't contribute character to the wine that would detract from the pure Sauvignon Blanc flavor. In the Loire Valley, that flavor encompasses fresh-cut grass and crushed green herbs, key lime and green apple fruit (the "lean" end of the fruit spectrum we explored in Chapter 1), and a hint of pungency that the English infamously compare to cat pee. At first blush you might think "yuck," but it's rather like cheese. That little bit of funk is actually quite appealing.

The top Loire Valley Sauvignon Blancs are named for their growing regions, Sancerre (sahn-SAIR) and Pouilly-Fumé (poo-YEE foo-MAY), so you do not see the grape on the label. Sancerre's fragrance is more delicate and minerally, and Pouilly-Fumé's a bit more smoky and earthy. Both are usually great values in stores and on wine lists for the quality and complexity you get.

A CLASSIC PAIRING: SANCERRE AND GOAT CHEESE

A *"classic pairing"* is one that's considered to have virtually universal appeal to most tasters. Sometimes the pairing is a commonsense match, like steak and Cabernet Sauvignon, which is logical because the two are on a stylistic par—rich and heavy dish, big and powerful wine. Sometimes a classic pairing trades on contrasts—sweet Port wine with salty-savory English Stilton cheese is a great example. And then some classic matches are regional products whose affinity comes from the fact that they literally "grow up" together, born of the same soil. Spanish sherry and olives is one such example. Goat cheese and Sancerre is another, and it ranks as one of my favorite wine and food pairings in the world. The tangy-chalkiness of the goat cheese and of the wine seem to melt together, bringing out deeper fruit flavors in the wine, and a tender, buttery creaminess in the cheese, lasting long after you've swallowed. The traditional goat cheese choice in this pairing is called Chavignol, which is the name of a village in the Sancerre region. Selles-sur-Cher is another classic Loire goat cheese, but you can choose any good-quality fresh goat cheese for this match. And then spring it on your friends or dinner guests—they will absolutely *love* it, and you will love the no-cook ease.

Bordeaux Sauvignon Blanc. Bordeaux Sauvignon Blanc gets its power from several main sources: barrel fermentation and aging, blending with another white grape called Semillon, and the warmer climate in this region as compared to the Loire Valley. Unlike a stainless-steel tank, a barrel does impact the wine inside it, in several ways. First, it is porous, so it "breathes," allowing the wine to gently oxidize so that the flavors and fragrances deepen and intensify, in the same way that cheese becomes more fragrant and complex after you unwrap it and expose it to air. Second, as the wine rests inside, the barrel's own color and fragrance leach into the wine. The wood color tinges the wine a yellow-gold, and its sweet fragrance (think of the softly sweet scent of freshly sawn wood and sawdust) adds a layer of toasty-vanilla sweetness to the wine's fragrance and its flavor, and makes the wine's texture fuller-bodied. Adding Semillon to the blend lends a waxy-honeycomb scent, and yields a wine with fuller body and lower acidity.

The Sincerest Form of Flattery—French Style in Global Sauvignon Blanc

BOTH THE LOIRE VALLEY and Bordeaux styles have inspired worthy imitators in wine regions worldwide. In general, the steely Loire Valley style is the model for Sauvignon Blanc varietal wines produced in the Southern Hemisphere. Chile's Sauvignon Blancs are crisp, with kiwi and apple flavors, and generally are some of the best budget SBs on the market. New Zealand's Sauvignon Blancs are a must-try, having gained a world-class reputation in their own right due to their distinctive flavors of kiwi and passion fruit, and scents of crushed herbs and grass.

The Bordeaux style of Sauvignon Blanc is the one most commonly copied in North America—specifically California and Washington State. Many are named Fumé Blanc rather than Sauvignon Blanc—just remember that's a tip-off that the wine is most likely made in the fuller, oakier Bordeaux style.

Is your mouth watering? That's what happens when you taste, and cook for, Sauvignon Blanc, one of the liveliest guests you could invite to your (everyday) dinner party!

TANGY WINE + TART FOOD = A TREAT!

You might think that putting vinegar- or lemon-laced dishes with a crisp, tangy wine would result in a nerve-jangling teeth-on-edge acid overdose, but the opposite is true. When you put the two together, the acid components in the dish and the wine actually tone each other down, letting the other flavors in the dish and the fruit in the wine really soar. In fact, these tangy-times-two combinations are some of my favorites, because of the exponential pleasure they yield:

- Ceviche with New Zealand Sauvignon Blanc
- Trout in browned butter with lemon and white French Bordeaux
- Goat cheese and beet salad with California Fumé Blanc
- Lemon chicken with Pouilly-Fumé
- Fried green tomatoes with Sancerre
- Salmon with dill and lemon sauce and Washington State Sauvignon Blanc

SUMMER TOMATO SALAD

SERVES FOUR • Although I do most of my produce shopping at the supermarket, I insist on farm-stand or homegrown tomatoes in August and September, especially for this salad. They are one of life's great pleasures, especially when combined with wine-loving ingredients like pumpkinseed oil and Manchego cheese. With crusty bread, this makes a delicious light lunch. If you can't find Manchego, substitute Parmigiano-Reggiano or aged Monterey Jack. Hopefully you will also find at the farm stand some lovage, a wonderful herb with the sprightly taste of celery. Or grow it yourself—this is one of the most prolific and pretty herbs in my garden!

WINE RECOMMENDATIONS

NEW WORLD SAUVIGNON BLANC

Brancott, Nautilus (New Zealand)

Canyon Road, Ferrari-Carano Fumé Blanc (California)

1 pound ripe homegrown, farm-stand, or heirloom tomatoes

1 tablespoon extra virgin olive oil

1 tablespoon sherry vinegar

2 tablespoons chopped fresh lovage or chives

Pumpkinseed oil

3 ounces Manchego cheese, shaved

1. Core the tomatoes and cut them into irregular chunks over a bowl, to catch all of the juices. Add the chunks to the bowl and stir in the olive oil, vinegar, and lovage or chives. Let stand 15 minutes at room temperature to allow the flavors to marry.

2. To serve, divide the salad among 4 salad plates, drizzle each portion with a little pumpkinseed oil, and shower with the shaved Manchego cheese. Serve immediately.

CRUNCHY HERB SALAD

SERVES SIX • Herbs are used here as if they were salad greens, making for a remarkably flavorful green salad that's also tasty as a bed for simply grilled chicken or fish. It's fun to incorporate other herbs such as mint, chervil, tarragon, or lovage when you have them (I avoid rosemary, thyme, and sage because they're a bit too strong-tasting for this type of preparation). To save time, I sometimes chop the greens and herbs in the food processor instead of by hand (with the exception of the chives, the hollow centers of which may contain moisture, causing the herb to gum up the food processor blade). There is one caveat, though: The food processor is less gentle than hand chopping, and may speed the oxidation of the greens, causing them to darken. I find it's not a problem if I food process the herbs just before dressing and serving the salad. The flavors here are tailor-made for herbaceous Sauvignon Blancs. The final hit of coarse salt is a must—it gives a wonderful taste and texture jolt to the salad.

WINE RECOMMENDATIONS

SAUVIGNON BLANC

Honig, Geyser Peak, Selene (California)

Stoneleigh, Goldwater Dog Point (New Zealand)

4 celery stalks, with leaves

5 ounces mesclun lettuce mixture, torn into very small pieces

1 bunch fresh chives, finely chopped

½ cup fresh basil, thinly sliced (chiffonade)

¼ cup fresh parsley, finely chopped

½ cup fresh cilantro, finely chopped

3 tablespoons extra virgin olive oil

1 tablespoon sherry vinegar, approximately

1 teaspoon coarse sea salt such as fleur de sel, or more to taste

With a vegetable peeler, peel the convex outside of each celery stalk to remove the tough strings. Coarsely grate or finely chop the celery stalks and chop the leaves. Place the celery in a bowl with all the remaining ingredients and toss, adding more sherry vinegar and salt to taste. Serve immediately.

TOMATO-WATERMELON SORBET

SERVES SIX • I adapted this from a frozen gazpacho recipe developed by my chef-instructors at The French Culinary Institute. I replaced their bell peppers and cucumber with watermelon, and substituted roasted shallots for the raw red onion. (Red onion seems to take on a bitterness with wine, while shallots seem to love wine.) I use a very low-tech Donvier ice cream maker—a few cranks and this is a nice consistency within about thirty minutes. When served right out of the machine or after just a short holding time in the freezer, the sorbet is nice and smooth. But, because of the low sugar content, the mixture does freeze hard after an extended stay in the freezer. Not to worry—you can eat as much as you want as a smooth sorbet, freeze the rest, and then break up the frozen mixture with a fork to make a granita. Pour chilled Prosecco sparkling wine over the granita shards in a martini glass for a beautiful and delicious cocktail. The savory-sweet flavors of this sorbet are wonderful with New World Sauvignon Blancs whose herbaceousness is balanced by an extra dollop of ripe fruit flavor.

In cooking school, we were taught not to discard the seedy parts of the tomato but to use them to make vegetable stock. I hate waste of any kind, so I do this at home, too. I place the parts of the tomato that I'm not using in a zipper-lock bag and freeze, so I can add them to the pot the next time I'm making stock.

WINE RECOMMENDATIONS

NEW WORLD SAUVIGNON BLANC

Cain Musqué, Babcock, Voss, Robert Mondavi Fumé Blanc Reserve (California)

2 medium shallots

1 garlic clove

2 tablespoons olive oil, plus more if needed

1 tablespoon apple juice, heated

1 teaspoon unflavored gelatin

½ teaspoon kosher salt

1 pound ripe tomatoes, cored and quartered

1 cup ½-inch dice seedless watermelon

2 tablespoons sherry vinegar

1 tablespoon gin, aquavit, or vodka

2 teaspoons sugar

1. Preheat the oven to 350°F. Peel the shallots and garlic clove, and place on a piece of aluminum foil large enough to enclose. Drizzle with the olive oil, seal the foil around the shallots and garlic, and roast until soft, about 45 minutes. Drain the oil into a small bowl and add additional olive oil to total 2 tablespoons.

2. Place the apple juice in a small metal bowl and sprinkle the gelatin over the juice. Let stand 1 minute to soften. Set the bowl over a small saucepan of barely simmering water; whisk the liquid until the gelatin dissolves, about 1 minute.

3. Combine the shallots and garlic, salt, tomatoes, watermelon, vinegar, gin, and sugar in the workbowl of a food processor and process until very smooth. With the motor running, add the oil and the gelatin mixtures, processing to combine thoroughly. Press the puree through a fine sieve into a bowl, pressing on the solids. Chill the strained mixture until cold, then freeze in an ice cream maker according to manufacturer's instructions. Serve immediately, or store in the freezer until ready to use, up to 1 day. If it freezes hard, thaw slightly and break up with a fork until grainy or slushy, as you prefer.

CODDLED EGGS WITH CAULIFLOWER-POTATO PUREE

SERVES FOUR • Wondering how to put to use some leftover potato and cauliflower puree (soup, really, but it had thickened up overnight in the refrigerator), I came up with this recipe for coddled eggs. The result couldn't be more sophisticated for brunch or for dinner, when served with a barrel-aged Sauvignon Blanc that includes some Semillon in the blend. The nutty richness of barrel aging and the earthiness and creamy texture from the Semillon grape echo the dish's creamy texture and truffly earthiness. I like this dish so much that I now make the puree solely for the purpose of coddling eggs. If you have leftovers, go ahead and use them. About half a recipe will make four servings. If the puree is still too thin after being in the refrigerator, thicken it up by reheating on top of the stove. Here are the directions for the dish starting from scratch. The truffle oil is optional, but, when given that option, I always go for it!

BARREL-AGED SAUVIGNON BLANC

Château La Louvière, Château Carbonnieux (Bordeaux, France)

Ruston Sauvignon Blanc, Simi Sauvignon Blanc (California)

- 1 tablespoon unsalted butter, plus more for buttering the ramekins
- 1 tablespoon olive oil
- 1 small shallot, finely chopped
- 1 head cauliflower (about 1 pound), cored and broken into florets
- 1 pound Yukon Gold potatoes, peeled and cut into 1-inch chunks

- Kosher salt and freshly ground white pepper
- 2 tablespoons white truffle oil, optional
- 4 large eggs
- ¼ cup heavy cream
- ¼ cup freshly grated Parmesan cheese

1. Preheat the oven to 350°F. Butter four ¾-cup ramekins.

2. Heat the olive oil on medium heat in a medium stockpot and add the shallot. Cook, stirring frequently, until soft and translucent, about 5 minutes.

3. Add the cauliflower and potatoes to the pot. Cover with cold water. Turn the heat to high and bring to a boil. Reduce heat and cook at a simmer, uncovered, until the potatoes and cauliflower are tender, 15 to 17 minutes.

4. Remove from heat and drain the potatoes and cauliflower, reserving some of the hot cooking liquid. Use an immersion blender to blend the cauliflower-potato mix-

ture, butter, salt and white pepper to taste, and about ¼ cup of the hot cooking liquid, until smooth. Or puree the mixture in batches in a food processor. Stir in the truffle oil, if desired. Measure about 2 cups of the puree, and set the remainder aside for another use.

5. Spoon ⅓ cup of the cauliflower-potato mixture into each of the prepared ramekins and cool to room temperature. (The ramekins may be covered with plastic wrap and refrigerated overnight at this point. Bring to room temperature before proceeding with the recipe.)

6. Carefully crack an egg into each ramekin and pour a tablespoon of cream onto each egg. Sprinkle with the cheese. Place the ramekins in a large baking pan and pour very hot tap water into the pan so that it comes halfway up the side of each ramekin. Place the baking pan in the oven and bake until the egg whites are set but the yolks are still loose, 16 to 19 minutes. Remove the ramekins from the baking pan with a wide spatula, place on individual serving plates, and serve, reminding guests that the ramekins are hot.

COCONUT MILK–CURRY SHRIMP SOUP

SERVES SIX • The tropical fruit flavor of California and Washington State Sauvignon Blancs complements the coconut and curry flavors of the soup perfectly! Frozen shrimp from the warehouse club are generally of excellent quality and a great buy. They make this dish reasonably priced as well as quick—perfect for a warming weeknight dinner. Thaw the shrimp by placing them in a colander and running cold water over them for about ten minutes.

2 tablespoons vegetable oil

1 medium onion, diced

1 celery stalk, sliced

1 pound large shrimp, peeled and deveined, thawed if frozen

½ pound red potatoes, scrubbed and cut into ½-inch cubes

2½ teaspoons curry powder, or more to taste

Two 14½-ounce cans low-sodium chicken broth

One 14-ounce can unsweetened coconut milk

One 14-ounce can plum tomatoes, with their juice

2 tablespoons freshly squeezed lime juice (about 1 lime)

Kosher salt

Freshly ground black pepper

½ cup chopped fresh cilantro, optional

1. Heat the oil in a large saucepan over medium heat. Add the onion and celery and cook, stirring, until softened and just beginning to brown.

2. Add the shrimp, potatoes, and curry powder, stirring to coat the vegetables and shrimp.

3. Add the chicken broth, coconut milk, and tomatoes, stirring to break up the tomatoes. Bring the soup to a simmer and cook until the potatoes are tender, about 10 minutes.

4. Add the lime juice and salt and pepper to taste. Ladle the soup into bowls, sprinkle with cilantro, if desired, and serve.

SEARED SHRIMP AND CHORIZO BITES

MAKES ABOUT TWENTY • Spanish-style chorizo is a fully cooked smoked sausage. After years of negotiations, the United States is finally allowing real Spanish chorizo into this country. The flavor is wonderful if you can get your hands on some (look in gourmet specialty markets), or substitute a supermarket brand such as Goya. The raciness and delicacy of Loire Valley Sauvignon Blancs (Sancerre or Pouilly-Fumé) are a refreshing contrast to the spiciness of the chorizo and the sweetness of the shrimp. Often I make more than I think I'll need for one meal, so I can chop the cooked shrimp and chorizo and use them the next day, along with some Manchego cheese, to fill an omelet or quesadilla.

Note: Use plain wooden toothpicks to skewer the shrimp, not cocktail picks with plastic frills, as they will melt in the pan.

WINE RECOMMENDATIONS	LOIRE VALLEY POUILLY-FUMÉ Michel Redde, Henri Bourgeois	LOIRE VALLEY SANCERRE Michel Picard, Bailly, Pascal Jolivet	1 medium garlic clove, peeled and crushed 2 tablespoons sherry vinegar ¼ cup plus 1 tablespoon olive oil 1 pound medium shrimp, peeled and deveined ¼ pound chorizo (about two to three 6-inch links)

1. Combine the garlic, sherry vinegar, ¼ cup olive oil, and shrimp in a medium bowl and toss to combine. Cover with plastic wrap and refrigerate for 15 to 20 minutes.

2. Slice the chorizo on an angle into ½-inch rounds. Drain the shrimp, reserving the marinade. With a toothpick, skewer one marinated shrimp through the head and tail (so it won't spin around), and then a piece of chorizo so that it lays flat next to the shrimp. Repeat with the remaining shrimp and chorizo.

3. Heat 1 tablespoon of olive oil in a large, heavy skillet on medium-high. Place the skewers in a single layer in the heated pan, brush with the reserved marinade, and cook, turning occasionally, until shrimp are pink and cooked through and chorizo has crisped slightly, 4 to 5 minutes. If necessary, work in batches to avoid overcrowding the skillet. Serve immediately.

TARRAGON- AND MUSTARD-CRUSTED SCALLOPS

SERVES FOUR AS A MAIN COURSE OR EIGHT AS A FIRST COURSE • This is John's invention and one of our favorite "sear-and-serve" recipes because it's so fast and tastes just dynamite. John loves to "blind taste," which means sampling wines blind, with no knowledge about them, and then trying to identify them based on their look, smell, and taste. (My Master Sommelier colleagues would be impressed—John's hit rate would definitely qualify him for the all-star team of tasters.) Given the tarragon herbaceousness of the dish, I put up several Sauvignon Blancs for sampling blind, and our clear preferences with this dish were the Bordeaux-style Sauvignon Blancs. The richness of both their barrel character and the Semillon grapes in the blend picked up on the sweetness of the scallops, while the grassy/pungent notes kicked in to complement the tarragon and the mustard tang. Our ritual with this dish is that John cooks it, while I set up glasses, go to my wine stash to choose two or three wines to try, and get them open. We're both finished with our "duties" in about the same amount of time! If you can find them, the sear works best with dry-pack scallops, rather than the scallops with water added.

WINE RECOMMENDATIONS	
BARREL-AGED SAUVIGNON BLANC/SEMILLON BLENDS Murphy-Goode Fumé Blanc, Dry Creek Fumé Blanc (California) DeLille Chaleur Estate Blanc (Washington State) Château La Louvière, Château Rahoul (France)	16 large sea scallops, patted dry 3 tablespoons Dijon mustard 3 tablespoons finely chopped fresh tarragon Kosher salt Freshly ground white pepper 1 tablespoon unsalted butter 1 tablespoon olive oil

1. Place the scallops, mustard, tarragon, and salt and pepper to taste in a medium bowl and toss well to combine. Cover the bowl with plastic wrap and refrigerate for 30 minutes.

2. Heat the butter and olive oil in a large skillet over medium-high heat until the butter is foaming. Place the scallops in the skillet in one layer and cook without turning until they are browned and their edges are crisped, 2 to 3 minutes. Turn and cook until the other side is browned, another 2 to 3 minutes. Remove from the pan and serve immediately.

MUSSEL SALAD WITH SEARED AVOCADO DRESSING

SERVES FOUR TO SIX AS AN APPETIZER • The juices that mussels release when steamed in wine create a flavorful broth, upon which the dressing for this salad is built. Cooking the avocado in olive oil colors the oil Day-Glo green and infuses it with rich, wonderful flavor. The avocado and oil give the salad some creamy richness, balanced by the acidity of the tomatoes and lime juice and spiked by some jalapeño heat. I go with ripe-flavored Sauvignon Blancs from California and New Zealand, whose succulence stands up to the richness of the avocado flavor and highlights the inherent sweetness in the mussels. The green and pink color palette of this dish makes it beautiful and festive.

WINE RECOMMENDATIONS

SAUVIGNON BLANC

Rancho Zabaco, Benziger
(California)

Allan Scott, Cloudy Bay
(New Zealand)

---

2 pounds mussels

¾ cup plus 2 tablespoons olive oil

2 medium shallots, finely chopped

2 cups white wine (leftover is fine)

2 sprigs fresh thyme

½ cup diced, seeded plum tomatoes (about 4 tomatoes)

½ cup chopped scallions (5 or 6 scallions)

2 tablespoons chopped fresh chives

½ cup chopped fresh cilantro

1 tablespoon finely chopped jalapeño pepper, optional

1 small ripe Hass avocado, peeled, pitted, and cubed just before cooking

½ cup freshly squeezed lime juice (about 5 limes)

Kosher salt

Freshly ground black pepper

Fresh cilantro sprigs, optional

1. Clean the mussels by scrubbing their shells with a brush while rinsing under cold running water. If necessary, use a paring knife to tug and cut out the weedy beards coming out of the bottom of the shells. Pick through the mussels, discarding any with broken shells and any that are open and don't close when you tap them.

2. Fill a bowl with ice and have ready another bowl that will fit inside the first bowl. Heat the 2 tablespoons of olive oil in a medium saucepan over medium heat. Add the shallots and cook until translucent, 3 to 4 minutes. Add the wine, thyme, and mussels. Cover and cook, shaking the pot occasionally, until all of the mussel shells have opened, about 10 minutes.

3. Transfer the mussels to the empty bowl and place it in the bowl full of ice to stop the cooking. Pick through the mussels and discard any whose shells have not opened. Set the mussels aside to cool, then remove the cooked mussels from their shells and discard the shells.

4. Strain the cooking liquid through a fine sieve to remove the shallots and thyme. Discard the shallots and thyme. Place a coffee filter inside the sieve and strain again to remove any sand and dirt.

5. In a large mixing bowl, stir together the tomatoes, scallions, chives, cilantro, and jalapeños.

6. In a small nonstick pan heat the remaining ¾ cup olive oil. Add the avocado and sauté for 5 minutes. Remove the avocado with a slotted spoon and add it to the bowl with the tomato, herbs, and scallions. Add the cooled, shelled mussels to the bowl.

7. Whisk together the lime juice, the avocado-infused olive oil, and 1 cup of the strained mussel juice (or more to taste) to make the dressing. Season with salt and pepper. Pour the dressing over the salad ingredients and toss well to coat. Chill the salad for 1 hour. Garnish with sprigs of cilantro, if desired, and serve.

Everyday Dinners with
SAUVIGNON BLANC

PASTAS AND OTHER ONE-PLATE DINNERS

WHAT TO COOK	WINE PAIRINGS
Coddled Eggs with Cauliflower-Potato Puree *(page 62)*, salad, toasted country bread	ONCE-A-WEEK ($–$$): Ruston Sauvignon Blanc (California) Simi Sauvignon Blanc (California) ONCE-A-MONTH ($$$ AND UP): Château Carbonnieux (Bordeaux, France)
Coconut Milk–Curry Shrimp Soup *(page 64)*, crispy chow mein noodles or rice	ONCE-A-WEEK ($–$$): Beringer Founders' Estate Sauvignon Blanc (California) Covey Run Fumé Blanc (Washington State) ONCE-A-MONTH ($$$ AND UP): Matanzas Creek Sauvignon Blanc (California)
Mussel Salad with Seared Avocado Dressing *(page 68)*, lettuce leaves or warm corn tortillas for wrapping	ONCE-A-WEEK ($–$$): Rancho Zabaco Sauvignon Blanc (California) Allan Scott Sauvignon Blanc (New Zealand) ONCE-A-MONTH ($$$ AND UP): Cloudy Bay Sauvignon Blanc (New Zealand)

TRADITIONAL (MAIN-AND-SIDES) DINNERS

WHAT TO COOK	WINE PAIRINGS
MAIN COURSE: Churrasco-Style Skirt Steak *(page 112)* VEGGIES: Summer Tomato Salad *(page 58)* STARCHES, ETC.: black beans and rice	ONCE-A-WEEK ($–$$): Brancott Sauvignon Blanc (New Zealand) Canyon Road Sauvignon Blanc (California) ONCE-A-MONTH ($$$ AND UP): Ferrari-Carano Fumé Blanc (California)
MAIN COURSE: Seared Shrimp and Chorizo Bites *(page 65)* VEGGIES: Carrot Slaw with Toasted Pine Nuts and Herbs *(page 39)* STARCHES, ETC.: Spanish rice	ONCE-A-WEEK ($–$$): Michel Redde Pouilly-Fumé (France) Michel Picard Sancerre (France) ONCE-A-MONTH ($$$ AND UP): Pascal Jolivet Sancerre (France)

WHAT TO COOK	WINE PAIRINGS
MAIN COURSE: Tarragon- and Mustard-Crusted Scallops *(page 66)* VEGGIES: steamed spinach STARCHES, ETC.: buttered egg noodles	ONCE-A-WEEK ($–$$): Murphy-Goode Fumé Blanc (California) Dry Creek Fumé Blanc (California) ONCE-A-MONTH ($$$ AND UP): DeLille Cellars Chaleur Estate Blanc (Washington State)
MAIN COURSE: Shrimp Ceviche with Avocado, Cilantro, and Lime *(page 113)* VEGGIES: Tomato-Watermelon Sorbet *(page 60)* STARCHES, ETC.: white rice or tortilla chips	ONCE-A-WEEK ($–$$): Voss Sauvignon Blanc (California) Cain Musqué (California) ONCE-A-MONTH ($$$ AND UP): Robert Mondavi Fumé Blanc Reserve (California)
MAIN COURSE: Plank-Cooked Salmon *(page 45)* VEGGIES: Crunchy Herb Salad *(page 59)* STARCHES, ETC.: Grilled Corn on the Cob with Pumpkinseed Oil *(page 81)*	ONCE-A-WEEK ($–$$): Goldwater Dog Point Sauvignon Blanc (New Zealand) Geyser Peak Sauvignon Blanc (California) ONCE-A-MONTH ($$$ AND UP): Selene Sauvignon Blanc (California)

chapter three

CHARDONNAY

●

Chardonnay Showcase

HOME REGION
Burgundy, France

OTHER KEY SOURCES
California, Washington State, Australia

STYLE
Medium- to full-bodied; ranging from crisp to luscious

FLAVOR
The entire fruit spectrum from lean crisp apple to juicy
peach to lush tropical fruits

You know you love it, and for good reason. Chardonnay is the number-one-selling white wine grape in this country—the go-to by-the-glass choice, the house pour, the default dinner companion—because it's got in spades what we look for in wine more than anything else: fruit. And such a spectrum of fruit! Chardonnay is unique among white grapes in that it's capable of deliciously roaming the entire fruit flavor continuum we explored in Chapter 1, from lean crisp apple flavors, to juicy peach and melon, to lush and tropical mango. Where the flavor style of any particular Chardonnay falls depends on where the grapes were grown. So let's start with the lean end of the fruit spectrum, which brings us to Chardonnay's historic home region, Burgundy, France.

Although its wines aren't labeled with the grape name, white French Burgundy is the original Chardonnay, and all Chardonnay produced worldwide is modeled on its two main styles—stainless steel–fermented and barrel-fermented. Since all French Burgundy is named for the growing region (usually a small village), you need to know which ones are associated with the two different styles:

Stainless steel–fermented French white Burgundies. The French Burgundy region is bookended at its northern and southern tips with districts that specialize in this style. From least to most expensive they are: Macon, St. Véran, and Pouilly-Fuissé at the southern end of Burgundy and Chablis at the northern extreme of the zone. The wines taste of crisp green apples and lemon, with a tangy snap of acidity due to the cool climate. The Chablis district's wines are the most expensive because they are less plentiful, and because their chalky soil lends extra complexity, concentration, and ageability to the wines. The overall style of these wines is light-bodied and elegant.

The wine regions that emulate this style most frequently are Australia and New Zealand, whose Chardonnays—labeled "un-oaked" or "un-wooded" to tip you off to the style—have become quite trendy among wine pros. A handful of California wineries also specialize in this style.

Barrel-fermented French white Burgundies. This is the Chardonnay style emulated more than any other—deep baked-apple fruit flavor framed by toasty, nutty, spicy, and delicately sweet oak scents. The epicenter for it is a district in the Burgundy region called the Côte de Beaune. The most famous wines, named for the villages where they're grown, are Meursault, Chassagne-Montrachet, Puligny-Montrachet, and Corton Charlemagne (named for the village of Aloxe-Corton and its wine's most famous fan, King Charlemagne). These wines are world-renowned for their complexity and ageability. The best of them are medium-bodied and elegant, yet deeply concentrated. It's no wonder they have so many emulators. Here are the main ones, and where their flavors fall on the fruit spectrum:

NEW YORK, ITALIAN, NEW ZEALAND, OREGON, AND WASHINGTON STATE CHARDONNAYS: These regions' climates range from cool to moderate, and the wines' fruit flavor varies accordingly, from lean, crisp apple to juicy peach and melon. The body style of Chardonnay from these regions is light in the cooler zones (New York and Italy) to medium in the moderate zones (the rest). The amount of oakiness usually varies according to price, with the most expensive wines having the most oak character.

OAK: YOU GET WHAT YOU PAY FOR

The amount and intensity of oak character in a wine depends on the age of the barrels used and the length of time the wine rests in the barrel. New barrels impart more oak character than used ones (it's like reusing a teabag—the second cup of tea is weaker than the first), and they also cost more.

Therefore, wines aged in new barrels are usually both oakier and more expensive. The length of time in the barrel is also a factor—the longer in the barrel, the oakier the wine. How do winemakers decide which age of barrels to use and for how long? They base the decision on the flavor intensity of their grapes.

The best grapes from the best vineyard sites have the most fruit intensity, and thus can handle more oak intensity. So as a rule, the popular-priced brands will have less oak intensity than smaller-production premium-priced wines.

SOUTH AMERICAN (CHILEAN AND ARGENTINIAN), SOUTH AFRICAN, CALIFORNIA, AND AUSTRALIAN CHARDONNAYS: These regions' climates span moderate to warm. As such, the wines' fruit flavor ranges from stone fruits (peach, apricot) and melons to tropical flavors like pineapple, papaya, and mango. The fruit intensity of wines from these regions generally supports a generous dose of oak, making these some of the most full-bodied, powerful Chardonnays in the wine world.

Pairing Chardonnay with Food

IN THE 1980S AND '90S it became fashionable among sommeliers to bash most any Chardonnay other than French white Burgundy as "not good with food." To which I felt compelled to ask, "Which food?" After all, isn't that an enormous generalization about a wine that, as we've seen, spans a whole spectrum of body and fruit flavor styles? In my experience, there's a style of Chardonnay out there for just about any food, from the subtlest seafood to the brawniest steak.

The Chardonnay grape is incredibly diverse and deservedly popular. As a sommelier, I've always wanted to arm myself with lots of super matches for America's favorite white grape. So I've experimented extensively with food-and-Chardonnay pairings and come up with several simple pairing principles that you'll see applied in the pages that follow. Here they are.

The prominent acidity and pure, delicate fruit in stainless steel–fermented French white Burgundies:

- Tone down fishy flavors and complement briny seafoods such as oysters and clams

- Flatter tangy sauces like lemon butter and vinaigrette

The lively tanginess and plumped-up, riper fruit in New World (North America and the Southern Hemisphere) un-oaked Chardonnays:

- Launch the sea-sweet flavors of sushi, ceviche, and other super-fresh, minimally handled seafood

- Boost the spicy and fresh flavors in garlic-, chili-, and curry-laced stir-fries

The nutty-toastiness, earthiness, and elegance of French barrel-fermented white Burgundies:

- Harmonize beautifully with mushroom and white or black truffle flavors
- Complement the texture and rich flavors of butter and cream sauces
- Set off the sweetness of delicate shellfish like lobster, scallops, and shrimp
- Showcase the earthy-sweetness of root vegetables such as potatoes, beets, turnips, and sweet potatoes

The tropical fruit and oakiness of warm-climate barrel-fermented Chardonnays:

- Embrace exotic and ethnic flavors such as tropical fruit salsas, coconut milk curries, jasmine rice, Chinese five-spice seasoning, Moroccan tagines, and sweet Asian sauces (hoisin, teriyaki, sesame oil)
- Launch the sweetness and parallel the rich texture of seafoods such as lobster, scallops, cod, and sea bass
- Kick up the sweet taste of corn preparations, from on the cob to chowder to tortillas

You've probably been drinking Chardonnay for years, to the point of practically taking it for granted (which is fine, of course!). Now it's time to start cooking up some everyday dinners with Chardonnay that will remind you of why you fell in love with it in the first place.

YUKON GOLD POTATO AND CAULIFLOWER SOUP WITH TRUFFLE OIL

SERVES SIX • It may seem incongruous to combine humble veggies like potatoes and cauliflower with the luxury of white truffle oil. But the flavors work wonderfully. The earthiness of truffle brings out the best in the earthy spuds and cauliflower. To further showcase that earthiness, I pair this dish with French Burgundy whites—both the stainless steel–fermented and the barrel-fermented styles match nicely. The resulting match is at once earthy and elegant.

WINE RECOMMENDATIONS	STAINLESS STEEL–FERMENTED WHITE FRENCH BURGUNDIES	BARREL-FERMENTED WHITE FRENCH BURGUNDIES	Ingredients
	Louis Jadot Macon, Bouchard Pouilly-Fuissé, Domaine Laroche Chablis St. Martin	Olivier Leflaive Santenay, M. Colin Saint-Aubin, Louis Latour Meursault	1 tablespoon olive oil 1 shallot, finely chopped 1 head cauliflower, cored and broken into florets 1 pound Yukon gold potatoes, peeled and cut into 1-inch chunks 1 tablespoon unsalted butter Kosher salt Freshly ground white pepper 2 tablespoons white truffle oil, for drizzling

1. In a large stockpot, heat the olive oil on medium and add the shallot. Cook, stirring frequently, until soft and translucent, about 5 minutes.

2. Add the cauliflower and potatoes to the pot. Cover with cold water. Turn the heat to high and bring to a boil. Reduce the heat and cook at a simmer, uncovered, until the cauliflower and potatoes are tender, 15 to 17 minutes.

3. Remove from heat and drain, reserving some of the hot cooking liquid. Use an immersion blender to blend the cauliflower-potato mixture, with the butter, salt and pepper, and about ½ cup of the hot cooking liquid, until smooth. (If you don't have an immersion blender, puree the soup in batches in a regular blender.) Add additional liquid as needed to reach the desired soup consistency (I like it fairly loose). To serve, ladle into warm bowls and drizzle each portion with a teaspoon of truffle oil or more to taste.

CHARRED CORN SALAD WITH AVOCADOS AND ORZO

SERVES FOUR AS A MAIN COURSE OR SIX AS A SIDE DISH • This is a beautiful summer salad, perfect alongside grilled chicken or shrimp skewers, or on its own as a light supper, with thick slices of farm-stand (or homegrown) tomatoes. The smoky-sweet flavor of charred corn and the textural richness of the avocados are tailor-made for a luscious barrel-fermented New World Chardonnay.

The avocados are sautéed in olive oil to fix their color, then drained; the delicious cooking oil is then used for the dressing (the recipe makes enough dressing for drizzling over grilled chicken, shrimp, or fish if you like). To free yourself from too much last-minute preparation, you can cook and drain the pasta ahead, toss with 2 teaspoons olive oil to prevent sticking, and chill until ready to mix with the remaining ingredients.

4 ears fresh corn, husked

½ cup plus 3 tablespoons extra virgin olive oil

Kosher salt

Freshly ground black pepper

2 large shallots, finely chopped

1 red bell pepper, stemmed, seeded, and cut into ¼-inch dice

2 zucchini, cut into ¼-inch dice

1 medium garlic clove, finely chopped

1 Hass avocado, peeled, pitted, and cut into ½-inch dice just before cooking

2 tablespoons sherry vinegar

3 tablespoons finely chopped fresh cilantro

⅓ cup orzo pasta, cooked according to package directions until al dente

1. Preheat a gas grill to medium-high (or preheat a grill pan to medium on the stovetop). Brush the corn lightly with 1 tablespoon of the olive oil and season with salt and pepper on all sides. Cook the corn on all sides, turning frequently with tongs, until lightly charred and tender, 10 to 12 minutes on the grill or 12 to 15 minutes on the stovetop. Set aside to cool, then cut the corn from the cobs.

2. In a medium skillet, heat 2 tablespoons of the olive oil on medium-high, and add the shallots and red pepper. Cook, stirring, until just soft, about 2 minutes. Add the zucchini and cook, stirring, 1 minute. Add the garlic and cook, stirring, 1 additional minute. Remove from heat and set aside to cool.

3. In a nonstick skillet, heat the ½ cup olive oil to medium. Add the diced avocado and cook (the oil should be gently bubbling) for 3 minutes to set the color of the avocado and flavor the oil, turning the avocado pieces gently halfway through the cooking. Use a slotted spoon to transfer the avocado pieces to a bowl. Pour the oil into another small bowl (it will be bright green).

4. Add the sherry vinegar to the oil and whisk lightly. Combine the corn, shallot-pepper-zucchini mixture, cilantro, and cooked orzo and fold gently to mix. Pour on about half the vinegar and oil mixture, reserving the remainder for another use, and toss to combine. Season with salt and pepper to taste.

Charred Corn Salsa. Omit the orzo and increase the corn to 6 ears. Serve with grilled fish, stuffed into pita bread with tomatoes and Monterey Jack cheese, or with scrambled egg–stuffed tortillas for an easy and colorful brunch dish.

LUCAS'S SESAME-GINGER BROCCOLI FLORETS

SERVES FOUR AS A SIDE DISH • Toasted, pure sesame oil is the secret ingredient in this kid-friendly broccoli dish that's a favorite of my ten-year-old. But grown-ups enjoy it, too. The nutty-toastiness of the sesame oil makes the broccoli extremely wine-friendly with Australian oak-aged Chardonnays—sesame oil echoes the toasty oak, and the ginger complements the tropical fruit flavors in the wine. A sprinkling of toasted sesame seeds is a nice textural addition, but is optional. (When I am in a hurry, I have found it works great to microwave the broccoli florets on high for about 4 minutes until tender, rather than steaming them.)

WINE RECOMMENDATIONS

AUSTRALIAN OAK-AGED
CHARDONNAY

Rosemount Roxburgh,
Lindemans Reserve,
Yellowtail, Black Swan

1 tablespoon sesame seeds, optional

1 large head broccoli

1 tablespoon Asian sesame oil

2 teaspoons finely grated fresh ginger

Coarse sea salt

1. If using sesame seeds, place them in a small, dry skillet and toast, shaking the pan frequently, until lightly browned. Set aside to cool.

2. Rinse the broccoli and separate the florets from the stalks, reserving the stalks for another use. Arrange the florets in a vegetable steamer basket or steamer insert.

3. Bring about 1 inch of water to boil in a deep, wide pot. Lower the steamer into the pot, making sure it rests above the water. Cover and cook the broccoli until tender, 4 to 5 minutes.

4. Transfer the cooked broccoli to a serving bowl and drizzle with the sesame oil. Add the ginger, sea salt to taste, and sesame seeds, if using, and stir to combine. Serve immediately.

GRILLED CORN ON THE COB WITH PUMPKINSEED OIL

SERVES SIX • The nutty flavor of the pumpkinseed oil and the toasty-charred taste of corn are just fantastic with the toastiness of barrel-fermented Chardonnay. That said, I prefer subtler versions over the big, ripe styles with this dish and have recommended accordingly. Use the oil sparingly—just a drizzle rather than a full coating—to let the corn flavor shine through. If you have some fleur de sel instead of plain table salt or kosher salt for seasoning, use it! The texture and flavor of this special salt when sprinkled on the tender sweet corn are just breathtaking.

WINE RECOMMENDATIONS	CALIFORNIA CHARDONNAY	FRENCH WHITE BURGUNDY
	Macrostie, Edna Valley, Estancia	Faiveley Mercurey, Louis Jadot Puligny-Montrachet, Louis Latour Meursault

6 ears fresh corn, husked

2 tablespoons extra virgin olive oil, plus more if necessary

Kosher salt and freshly ground black pepper

2 tablespoons pumpkinseed oil

Fleur de sel, optional

1. Preheat a gas grill to medium (or preheat a grill pan on medium on top of the stove). Brush the corn lightly with the olive oil, and season very lightly with salt and pepper on all sides. Grill, turning frequently with tongs, until the corn is lightly charred and tender, 10 to 12 minutes on the grill or 12 to 15 minutes on the stovetop.

2. Drizzle the corn lightly with pumpkinseed oil, letting it drip a little and then using a butter knife to spread it around. Serve immediately, with fleur de sel, if using.

SCRAMBLED EGGS WITH CORN TORTILLA STRIPS AND MONTEREY JACK

SERVES FOUR • The toasted corn flavor of the tortillas makes this classic Tex-Mex dish a natural with Australian and New Zealand Chardonnays that have lots of ripe fruit but not too much oak. It just goes to show that even the simplest of dinners can be improved on and enjoyed with wine. Canned chipotle chiles, available at many supermarkets and Latin groceries, give these eggs a hint of smoky heat, but fresh jalapeño may be substituted if you like.

WINE RECOMMENDATIONS

NEW ZEALAND
CHARDONNAY

Brancott, Kumeu River, Cloudy Bay, Kim Crawford "Un-oaked"

AUSTRALIAN
CHARDONNAY

Lindemans Bin 65, Rosemount Diamond Label, Omrah "Un-oaked"

Three 6-inch corn tortillas

1 tablespoon vegetable oil

8 large eggs

½ teaspoon kosher salt

Freshly ground black pepper

½ cup milk

1 tablespoon unsalted butter

1 small shallot, finely chopped

½ canned chipotle chile, finely chopped, or ½ jalapeño pepper, seeded and finely chopped

1 small plum tomato, cored and finely chopped

3 ounces Monterey Jack or mild Cheddar cheese, grated

1 tablespoon finely chopped fresh cilantro leaves, optional

1. Preheat the oven to 375°F. Cut each tortilla in half and then cut each half into 3 triangles. Brush a baking sheet with the vegetable oil. Spread the tortilla wedges in a single layer on the sheet and bake, turning once, until pale golden and just beginning to crisp, 7 to 9 minutes. Remove from the oven and cool slightly. Break up the triangles into smaller bite-size pieces.

2. Crack the eggs into a medium bowl. Add the salt, pepper, and milk and beat with a fork until the eggs are a uniform yellow color with no streaks of white.

3. Heat the butter in a large nonstick skillet over medium-high heat. Add the shallot and chile and cook until softened, about 3 minutes.

4. Reduce the heat to medium. Pour in the eggs and cook, slowly pushing them from one side of the pan to the other with a wooden spoon or rubber spatula, lifting and folding the eggs as they cook. When the eggs begin to form curds, but have not yet cooked through, about 1 minute, stir in the tortilla pieces, tomato, cheese, and cilantro, if desired. Continue to cook until the eggs are solidified but not dry and the cheese is melted, 1 to 2 minutes longer. Serve immediately.

PLANTAIN-CRUSTED CHICKEN

SERVES FOUR • Plantain chips—available at some supermarkets and in ethnic markets—give this pan-fried chicken its sweet crunch (or you can substitute banana chips from the health food store). A little habañero hot sauce and some spices borrowed from Jamaican jerk give it a hint of heat. I pair it with Chardonnays from California's Central Coast, whose tropical fruit flavor and subtle but spicy oak complement the coating's toasty banana and spicy flavors.

WINE RECOMMENDATIONS

CALIFORNIA CENTRAL
COAST CHARDONNAY

Lockwood, Morgan,
Estancia, Byron, Calera,
Au Bon Climat

1 cup plantain chips or unsweetened banana chips

1 tablespoon dry mustard

1 tablespoon dried thyme

¼ teaspoon allspice

¼ teaspoon ground cloves

1½ teaspoons kosher salt

1½ teaspoons freshly ground
  black pepper

1 large egg

1 tablespoon hot sauce made
  with habañero peppers

¼ cup all-purpose flour

4 boneless, skinless chicken breast
  halves (about 1½ pounds), rinsed
  and thoroughly dried

¾ cup vegetable oil

1 lime, cut into wedges

1. Combine the plantain chips, mustard, thyme, allspice, cloves, salt, and pepper in a blender or the workbowl of a food processor and grind. Place in a shallow bowl or pie plate.

2. Whisk the egg and hot sauce to taste in another shallow bowl. Place the flour in a third shallow bowl or pie plate.

3. Trim any fat and remove the tendons from the breasts. One at a time, place them between two sheets of plastic wrap and place on a cutting board. Use a meat pounder or lay the side of a large chef's knife on the breast and pound with your fist to flatten the breasts to a ½-inch thickness.

4. Working with one breast half at a time, press each side of the breast in the flour, shaking over the bowl to remove any excess. Then dip the breast in the egg and let any excess drip back into the bowl. Finally, press each side of the chicken breast half

into the plantain mixture to coat. Place the coated breast on a plate and press on the coating lightly with your fingertips to make sure that the crumbs adhere.

5. Heat the oil in a large skillet over medium-high heat. When the oil is hot, place the cutlets, smooth side up, in the skillet. Cook until brown and crisp on one side, about 3 minutes, checking the underside once or twice to make sure the coating isn't burning. If it is getting too dark, reduce the heat to medium. Turn the chicken and cook until done, another 3 to 4 minutes. Transfer to a paper towel–lined plate to drain briefly, then serve with lime wedges on the side.

TURKEY QUESADILLAS WITH SESAME-SWEET POTATO MOLE SAUCE

SERVES SIX GENEROUSLY • Here's a way to use your Thanksgiving turkey *and* sweet potato leftovers, giving them a Mexican flavor. Traditional moles, which are as subtle and complex as the fanciest French sauces, can contain a dozen ingredients and take hours to simmer. But this one is a simple blender sauce inspired by the mole method taught by chef Rick Bayless in his great Mexican food cookbooks. This quesadilla combination is particularly great with barrel-fermented Chardonnays. The sweet potato richness and sesame nuttiness mirror the toasty scent and extra body contributed by the barrel. The recipe makes a lot of mole because you need a sufficient amount of ingredients in the blender to achieve a smooth texture. Enjoy the sauce leftovers on scrambled eggs, grilled fish, or pork chops.

WINE RECOMMENDATIONS

BARREL-FERMENTED CHARDONNAY

R.H. Phillips Dunnigan Hills, Beringer Napa, Geyser Peak, Kongsgaard

½ cup sesame seeds

2 tablespoons vegetable oil, plus more for oiling the pans and brushing the tortillas

2 medium onions, diced

1 garlic clove, minced

1 fresh or canned jalapeño pepper, roughly chopped

½ cup loosely packed chopped fresh cilantro

½ cup loosely packed fresh flat-leaf parsley leaves

1 cup unsalted chicken or vegetable broth, plus more if necessary

2 large cooked sweet potatoes, peeled and cut into chunks (about 1½ cups)

Kosher salt

Twelve 6-inch flour tortillas

1½ cups bite-size cooked turkey pieces (cooked chicken or pork may be substituted)

5 ounces Monterey Jack or Cheddar cheese, shredded

1. Place the sesame seeds in a small, heavy skillet and heat on medium, stirring, until browned and fragrant. Transfer to a small bowl to cool. Reserve 2 teaspoons of seeds for garnish.

2. In the same skillet, heat the oil on medium. Add the onions, garlic, and jalapeño and cook, stirring, until the onions are just soft, about 7 minutes.

3. Combine the sesame seeds minus the 2 reserved teaspoons, the onion mixture, cilantro, parsley, and 1 cup broth in a blender. Puree until very smooth. This may take several minutes. To test, rub a drop between two fingers. The mixture should be smooth, not gritty.

4. Add the cooked sweet potatoes and blend until the mixture is the consistency of applesauce, adding more broth if necessary. Add salt to taste. (The mole will keep in the refrigerator in an airtight container for several days.)

5. Preheat the oven to 400°F. Place the mole in a medium saucepan over low heat and gently warm while you prepare the quesadillas.

6. Lightly oil 2 baking sheets, and place 3 tortillas on each. Distribute the turkey pieces and cheese evenly on the 6 tortillas, and top with the remaining 6 tortillas. Brush the tops lightly with oil and cover with foil. Bake for 6 minutes. Remove the foil, press down on the tops of the tortillas with the back of a spatula to compact the melting cheese, and bake until the tortillas begin to brown slightly, about 4 minutes longer. Serve immediately, topped with the warm mole sauce and a sprinkle of toasted sesame seeds.

QUESADILLAS AND CHARDONNAY?

At first glance, quesadillas, which in their simplest form are flour tortillas sandwiched together with melted cheese, don't scream out for wine. Maybe a pitcher of margaritas or some cold Coronas, but a glass of Chardonnay? Absolutely!

Like pizza dough, pasta, and chicken breasts, flour tortillas provide a neutral base for many wine-friendly flavors and ingredients. Quesadillas are fun to make and fun to eat, and can be on the table in minutes. To make a basic quesadilla, sprinkle a large flour tortilla with some grated Cheddar or Monterey Jack cheese, and top with another tortilla. Slide it into a skillet and cook until the cheese has melted and the tortillas are pale golden in spots, turning once. Try these add-ons and variations, with wine matches:

- Monterey Jack, shredded leftover chicken, barbecue sauce: Australian Shiraz
- Monterey Jack, chorizo, sun-dried tomatoes: red Zinfandel
- Canned black beans, goat cheese, scallions: Fumé Blanc
- Cheddar, chopped mango, caramelized onion, ham: Chardonnay
- Roasted tomatillos and queso fresco: New Zealand Sauvignon Blanc
- Arugula, prosciutto, mozzarella: Chianti Classico
- Shrimp, smoked mozzarella, basil: Merlot

Take care not to overfill the tortillas. Quesadillas are meant to be flat and relatively spare, so they can be cut into triangles and eaten by hand.

LOBSTER WITH SMOKED MOZZARELLA SAUCE AND CONFETTI VEGETABLES

SERVES SIX • This is a luxurious dish, rich with lobster and heavy cream. I like to serve the lobster and sauce over the Creamy Goat Cheese Polenta from Chapter 4 (page 108). The sweetness of the corn and lobster, the silkiness of the sauce, and the smokiness of the mozzarella are like a love letter to the tropical fruit, creamy texture, and toasty scent of big, oaky California Chardonnays. For this recipe, you will only need the meat from the tail and claws. But the small pieces of lobster meat in the claw joints are also tasty. Don't discard them with the shells. Use a nutcracker and lobster fork to remove this meat, and reserve it for a salad or an omelet. If you want to avoid the expense and extra work of lobster, the sauce and vegetable garnish are wonderful with any sweet-fleshed seafood. Shrimp, scallops, cod, striped bass, and salmon are all good bets.

WINE RECOMMENDATIONS

CALIFORNIA CHARDONNAY

SONOMA

Sebastiani Sonoma County, Château St. Jean, Stonestreet, Chalk Hill

NAPA

Beringer, Robert Mondavi, Merryvale, Franciscan Cuvée Sauvage

2 tablespoons unsalted butter

2 cups fresh corn kernels, or 2 cups best-quality frozen corn kernels, thawed

1 leek, white part only, cut into thin julienne strips

1 red bell pepper, seeds and membrane removed, cut into thin julienne strips

1 large carrot, peeled, ends trimmed, cut into thin julienne strips

Kosher salt and freshly ground black pepper

Four 1½-pound live lobsters

1 tablespoon vegetable oil

1 shallot, finely chopped

1 garlic clove, finely chopped

3 sprigs fresh cilantro, large stems removed

2 sprigs fresh thyme, stems removed

2 cups homemade or canned chicken or vegetable broth

½ cup heavy cream

1½ ounces smoked mozzarella cheese, cut into ½-inch dice

Freshly ground white pepper

Freshly squeezed lemon juice

Creamy Goat Cheese Polenta (page 108)

Finely chopped fresh cilantro, optional

1. Melt the butter in a medium sauté pan on medium heat and add 1 cup of the corn kernels, the leek, red pepper, and carrot. Sauté until vegetables soften. Season with salt and pepper to taste. Cover and keep warm until ready to use or transfer to a

bowl, cover with plastic wrap, and refrigerate for up to 3 hours until ready to serve and then rewarm gently over low heat.

2. Using a large stockpot, completely cover the lobsters with water, add a handful of kosher salt, and place the pot on the stove on high heat. Bring the pot to a boil. Remove from the heat and let rest, covered, for 5 minutes. Drain the lobsters and set them aside until cool enough to shell, about 10 minutes.

3. Shell the lobsters: Working on top of a large cutting board, grasp the tail in one hand and the body in the other, and pull and twist to separate the tail from the body. Grasp the fan-shaped tip of the tail piece and snap it backward to make an opening at the bottom of the shell. Put your fingers in the opening and push the tail meat from the bottom end of the tail, then pull the meat in one piece from the top end of the tail. Use a paper towel to wipe away any residue and set aside until ready to use.

4. To remove the claw meat, hold the fixed side of the claw in one hand, and grasp the hinged, pincer side with the thumb and forefinger of your other hand. Gently crack the base of the pincer's hinge by pulling the pincer first away from you and then toward you, just until you feel it crack and loosen. Carefully wiggle the pincer to loosen the quill of meat inside, and pull the pincer off. Next, put the claw on the cutting board, with the rounded side of the claw's shell turned up and the claw's tip facing away from you. Rap the widest part of the claw's shell with the dull side of a chef's knife. Use care so that you crack the bottom part of the shell without piercing the meat (shell hardness can vary, so start gently and use additional pressure if needed). Carefully pull apart and break off the bottom part of the shell, and gently slide the meat out through this opening. Finally, remove the thin, bony piece in the claw by inserting the tip of a sharp paring knife into the bottom of the claw piece, opposite the pincer. Use the paring knife to create a slit just large enough for you to cut the meat away from the bony piece, so that you can pull it out through the slit. Set aside the shelled lobster meat until ready to use. The lobsters may be cooked, shelled, and kept covered in the refrigerator for up to 3 hours until ready to eat.

5. Make the sauce: Heat the oil in a medium saucepan over medium heat. Sauté the remaining cup of corn kernels, shallot, and garlic until corn is tender, about 3 minutes for fresh kernels, 5 minutes for frozen and thawed kernels. Do not allow the vegetables to color. Add the cilantro sprigs, thyme, and chicken or vegetable broth. Simmer for 20 minutes. Stir in the cream and bring to a boil. Cook for about 15 minutes or until the liquid is reduced by half, stirring occasionally. Garnish with cilantro if desired.

6. Pour the hot corn and cream mixture into a blender or the workbowl of a food processor. Add the mozzarella and process until smooth. Strain through a fine sieve and season to taste with salt, freshly ground white pepper, and lemon juice. Cover and keep warm until ready to use.

7. Slice each lobster tail into ½-inch-thick pieces. Leave claw pieces whole. Add lobster pieces to sauce to reheat briefly. Spoon polenta onto each of 6 warm plates, and place lobster tail pieces atop, dividing them evenly among the plates. Place a claw piece on top of each, scatter the confetti vegetables colorfully around each plate, and spoon additional sauce around the vegetables. Serve immediately.

HERBED SCALLOP AND POTATO "NAPOLEONS" WITH TRUFFLE OIL

SERVES FOUR AS AN APPETIZER OR TWO AS A MAIN COURSE • Although this recipe calls for a bit of handiwork, the steps are simple and it comes together quickly. The sweetness and succulence of the scallops pick up on Chardonnay's luxuriantly juicy fruit, and the toasty, caramelized crunchiness of the potato crust echoes the toastiness of oak in barrel-fermented Chardonnays. The truffle oil takes the match into luxury territory, worthy of the best Chard you can muster. John and I developed this dish for the voluptuous versions from California and Australia, but loved it with the subtler, nuttier, deeply complex classics from Burgundy in France, too.

WINE RECOMMENDATIONS

AUSTRALIAN CHARDONNAY	FRENCH BURGUNDY	
Coldstream Hills, Leeuwin Estate	Vincent Pouilly-Fuissé, Sauzet Chassagne-Montrachet, Matrot Meursault	2 medium Red Bliss potatoes
		8 large sea scallops
CALIFORNIA CHARDONNAY		24 to 32 fresh tarragon or chervil leaves
Acacia, Chalone, Kistler		2 tablespoons olive oil, plus more for brushing the scallops
		Kosher salt
		Freshly ground white pepper
		1 tablespoon unsalted butter
		Truffle oil for drizzling, optional

1. Peel the potatoes and place them in a bowl of cold water to prevent browning. Remove one potato from the water and slice paper-thin with the single-slice blade of a box grater, the slicing disc of a food processor, or a mandoline. Return the slices to the water until ready to use and repeat with the second potato.

2. Select slices about the same diameter as the scallops, trimming if necessary (they need not be exact). Place the trimmed slices in another bowl of water until ready to use, reserving any extra potato slices for another use.

3. Use a sharp paring knife to cut into the side of each scallop, inserting the knife and cutting back and forth so that it creates a pocket but does not pierce through the other sides of the scallop. Stuff each scallop pocket with 3 or 4 tarragon or chervil leaves. Brush both sides of the scallop with olive oil and season with salt and white pepper.

4. Remove the potato slices from the water and pat dry thoroughly with paper towels. Place a potato slice on the top and bottom of each scallop, like sandwich buns. Heat 2 tablespoons olive oil and the butter in a large skillet over medium-high heat. When the butter foams, add the scallops, being careful not to crowd them. Cook until the potato slices are browned and crisp, 3 to 4 minutes. Turn and cook on the other side until the scallops are cooked through, about 3 minutes.

5. Place the scallops on plates, drizzle with truffle oil, if desired, and serve immediately.

CUBAN-STYLE ASADO PORK WITH VINO MOJO

SERVES SIX • In our house, this is a Sunday dish—I put the pork in the fridge to marinate on Saturday, then have the leisurely Sunday afternoon to roast it slowly, until the meat is falling-off-the-bone tender. Like the Chicken Legs Braised in Pinot Grigio Mojo (page 111), this recipe softens the traditional Latin mojo flavors by using wine in place of sour orange juice, and roasted garlic and shallots in lieu of more pungent fresh garlic. Those deeply caramelized flavors and the richness of the meat taste extraordinary with ripe, toasty, barrel-aged New World Chardonnays.

WINE RECOMMENDATIONS

BARREL-FERMENTED NEW WORLD CHARDONNAY

Edna Valley, Beringer (California)

Catena, Chandon Terrazas (Argentina)

- 1½ cups Chardonnay or other oak-aged white wine (leftover is fine)
- 2 large garlic cloves
- 5- to 6-pound bone-in pork shoulder or fresh ham, skin removed and fat intact
- ¼ cup freshly squeezed lime juice (about 2 limes)
- 1 head Roasted Garlic (page 269), squeezed from its skins
- 4 Roasted Shallots (page 269)
- 2 bay leaves, broken
- 1 tablespoon dried oregano
- 2½ teaspoons ground cumin
- 1½ teaspoons kosher salt, plus more for seasoning
- 1½ teaspoons freshly ground black pepper, plus more for seasoning
- Pinch saffron, optional
- ¾ cup olive oil, or more if necessary

1. Bring the wine to a boil in a small saucepan and reduce by half. Cool to room temperature.

2. Cut the garlic cloves into slivers. Make incisions in the pork with a sharp knife and insert a sliver of garlic into each.

3. Combine the cooled wine reduction with the lime juice, roasted garlic, shallots, bay leaves, oregano, cumin, salt, pepper, and saffron, if using, in a food processor and blend until smooth. With the motor running, pour in ¾ cup olive oil in a slow stream to emulsify. Put a plastic zipper-lock bag big enough to hold the pork into a mixing bowl. Put the pork and wine reduction mixture in the bag and close the bag. Let the pork marinate in the refrigerator overnight, turning the bag occasionally.

4. Preheat the oven to 325°F. Remove the pork from the bag, reserving the marinade in the refrigerator. Season the pork all over with salt and pepper. Place in a Dutch oven or roasting pan, fat side up. Cover and cook in the oven for 1½ hours. Turn the pork fat side down, pour the reserved marinade over the meat, and cook for 1½ hours longer or until the meat is almost falling off the bone. Turn the pork back fat side up and uncover the pan. Increase the heat to 375°F and cook for 30 minutes to brown the pork. Remove the pork from the oven and transfer to a cutting board to let rest. Pour the juices from the pan into a gravy separator or a clear glass heatproof container. The fat will rise to the top and the wine "mojo" will sink to the bottom. When the fat has separated, spoon it off and discard. Warm the mojo in a saucepan and serve in a gravy boat with the meat.

Everyday Dinners with
CHARDONNAY

PASTAS AND OTHER ONE-PLATE DINNERS

WHAT TO COOK	WINE PAIRINGS
Yukon Gold Potato and Cauliflower Soup with Truffle Oil *(page 77)*, salad, French bread	ONCE-A-WEEK ($–$$): Louis Jadot Macon (France) Bouchard Pouilly-Fuissé (France) ONCE-A-MONTH ($$$ AND UP): Louis Latour Meursault (France)
Charred Corn Salad with Avocados and Orzo *(page 79)*, crumbled bacon as a garnish	ONCE-A-WEEK ($–$$): Canyon Road Chardonnay (California) Casa Lapostolle Cuvée Alexandre Chardonnay (Chile) ONCE-A-MONTH ($$$ AND UP): Cambria Julia's Vineyard (Santa Barbara, California)
Scrambled Eggs with Corn Tortilla Strips and Monterey Jack *(page 82)*, picante salsa	ONCE-A-WEEK ($–$$): Lindemans Bin 65 Chardonnay (Australia) Kim Crawford "Un-oaked" Chardonnay (New Zealand) ONCE-A-MONTH ($$$ AND UP): Kumeu River Chardonnay (New Zealand)
Turkey Quesadillas with Sesame–Sweet Potato Mole Sauce *(page 86)*	ONCE-A-WEEK ($–$$): Geyser Peak Chardonnay (California) R.H. Phillips Dunnigan Hills Chardonnay (California) ONCE-A-MONTH ($$$ AND UP): Kongsgaard Chardonnay (California)

TRADITIONAL (MAIN-AND-SIDES) DINNERS

WHAT TO COOK	WINE PAIRINGS
MAIN COURSE: Plantain-Crusted Chicken *(page 84)* VEGGIES: Carrot Slaw with Toasted Pine Nuts and Herbs *(page 39)* STARCHES, ETC.: black beans and/or rice	ONCE-A-WEEK ($–$$): Lockwood Chardonnay (California) Estancia Chardonnay (California) ONCE-A-MONTH ($$$ AND UP): Au Bon Climat Chardonnay (California)

WHAT TO COOK	WINE PAIRINGS
MAIN COURSE: Mushroom-Dusted Tuna with Black Bean–Hoisin Sauce *(page 151)* VEGGIES: Lucas's Sesame-Ginger Broccoli Florets *(page 80)* STARCHES, ETC.: white rice or rice noodles	ONCE-A-WEEK ($–$$): Yellowtail Chardonnay (Australia) Black Swan Chardonnay (Australia) ONCE-A-MONTH ($$$ AND UP): Rosemount Roxburgh Chardonnay (Australia)
MAIN COURSE: Cuban-Style Asado Pork with Vino Mojo *(page 94)* VEGGIES: Summer Tomato Salad *(page 58)* STARCHES, ETC.: Grilled Corn on the Cob with Pumpkinseed Oil *(page 81)*	ONCE-A-WEEK ($–$$): Edna Valley Chardonnay (California) Beringer Chardonnay (California) ONCE-A-MONTH ($$$ AND UP): Catena Chardonnay (Argentina)
MAIN COURSE: Herbed Scallop and Potato "Napoleons" with Truffle Oil *(page 92)* VEGGIES: Salad of Fresh Figs with Manchego, Balsamic Vinegar, and Toasted Pine Nuts *(page 162)* STARCHES, ETC.: crusty bread and good butter	ONCE-A-WEEK ($–$$): Robert Mondavi Private Selection Chardonnay ONCE-A-MONTH ($$$ AND UP): Chalone Chardonnay (California) Coldstream Hills Chardonnay (Australia) Matrot Meursault (France)
MAIN COURSE: Lobster with Smoked Mozzarella Sauce and Confetti Vegetables *(page 89)* STARCHES, ETC.: Creamy Goat Cheese Polenta *(page 108)*	ONCE-A-WEEK ($–$$): Château St. Jean Chardonnay (California) Sebastiani Sonoma County Chardonnay (California) ONCE-A-MONTH ($$$ AND UP): Franciscan Cuvée Sauvage Chardonnay (California)

chapter four

CHAMPAGNE, SPARKLING WINES, AND CRISP WHITES

●

Sparkling Sum-Up

CHAMPAGNE
comes from the Champagne *region* in France
Worthy budget bubblies: Spain—**Cava** is the style name
and the grapes are Parellada, Macabeo, and Xarel-lo;
Italy—**Prosecco** is the name of the grape and the style

———————

NEW WORLD
sparkling wines come from California,
Washington State, Australia, Argentina

———————

BRUT
means dry

———————

NONVINTAGE
(abbreviated **NV**) means a blend of multiple vintages

The sparkles enchant, the scent seduces with subtlety, and

the flavor, especially with food, rocks the house. Yes, if I had to choose just one type of wine to have with everyday dinner for the rest of my life, it would be bubbly. I say "bubbly" because for most people, including me, true Champagne isn't affordable for every day. But other great bubblies are. And that's not even their main virtue when it comes to everyday dining with wine. All the classic bubblies share in common a powerful pairing attribute: vibrant acidity. As I discussed in the Introduction, it's the acidity in wine—its tangy, mouthwatering quality—that really pushes the flavor buttons in food, giving more verve to veggies, a souped-up sweetness to seafood, and extra sizzle to spices and even steak.

The recipes in this chapter feature all of those foods, and more, paired with bubbly. And once you try a few of these pairings, my hope is that you'll have some new views on sparkling wine. For one, you'll see that sparkling wine is just that—wine that sparkles. It truly deserves to go from just-for-toasts to table duty. You'll also see that there's great flavor, quality, and style diversity even at budget prices. And when you want to splurge on French Champagne— the benchmark bubbly—you'll be able to cook up some amazing food partners to really set it off.

French Champagne Basics

TO UNDERSTAND THE WHOLE CATEGORY of sparkling wine, it makes sense to start with the genuine article—Champagne from France—because all the world's quality bubblies are modeled on it, in terms of both how they're made and their styles. The classic method, or "Methode Champenoise," is the name for the painstaking process used in Champagne, and in many other wine regions, to get the bubbles (and flavor complexity) into the bottle. Here are the steps:

1. Blending. The grapes used to make Champagne are the red grapes Pinot Noir and Pinot Meunier, and the white grape Chardonnay. Wines made from

each of these grapes are blended to produce a "cuvée," or selection, according to the bubbly style being made (more on the styles below).

2. Second fermentation in the bottle. The completed blend is bottled with a liqueur of yeast and sugar, and is capped with a crown cap (like that on a beer bottle). The liqueur launches a second fermentation in the closed bottle that yields two by-products, carbon dioxide and a yeast deposit or sediment.

3. Aging. The wine is cellared in a cool place, allowing it to pick up wonderful, complex scents and flavors—*yeasty, nutty, toasty, creamy* are some of the descriptors used—from the contact with the yeast.

4. Disgorging. To remove the yeast sediment, the wineries twist and shake each bottle, working the sediment into the neck, in a process called *remuage* or, in English, riddling. The neck of the bottle is then frozen, capturing the sediment in a plug of ice that is popped out when the crown cap is pulled off. The bottle is then topped up, corked, and labeled.

Champagne Styles

As I explained in *Great Wine Made Simple,* Champagne's style has three components:

1. Body, or house, style: light-, medium-, or full-bodied

2. Category: classic or specialty

3. Taste: dry or sweet

Body Style (or "House Style") of Champagne

Style depends upon the winery, in the same way that the styles of other products like beer or cola or ice cream are similar, but vary slightly from one producer to the next. The greater the proportion of red grapes used in the blend, the fuller the body.

Champagne Categories

From most common to rarest, the categories are nonvintage, vintage, blanc de blancs, rosé, and luxury. Here's what they mean:

Nonvintage. You already know that Champagne is usually a blend of three grapes. Nonvintage Champagne, the most common category, refers to the fact that it is a blend of different vintages as well. Blending wines from multiple vintages helps the Champagne producers assure consistency of the house style from one year to the next.

Vintage. When the growing season enjoys particularly good weather, wineries may choose to bottle some of the harvest as vintage (rather than blended) Champagne, to show off the character of that particular year. Since vintage Champagne is rarer than nonvintage, it is more expensive.

Blanc de Blancs. This is white wine from white grapes—a departure, since most Champagne, while white, is blended largely from black grapes (as the industry refers to red wine grapes). Blanc de blancs ("white from whites") means the Champagne is made entirely from Chardonnay, which yields an elegant and tangy style.

Rosé. This is another very rare style, made usually by adding a little bit of still (nonbubbly) red Pinot Noir wine for color. Rosés have the complexity of red wine, so I often pair them with meat dishes.

Luxury. This style, sometimes called Tete de Cuvée (loosely, "cream of the crop"), is the rarest and finest bottling of each house. Most are vintage-dated, and they're usually the most intense or complex of the Champagne styles.

Sweet or Dry?

Brut (rhymes with *root*) on the label means the wine is totally dry, with no sweet taste. That's the usual style of all the categories described here. The other styles, from least to most sweet, are extra dry, sec (dry), demi-sec (off-dry), and doux (sweet).

Ready for your homework assignment? With all these styles to choose from, the easiest way to understand the differences is to taste and compare them. So pool your resources with a few friends, cook up dinner, and do it! See Great Menus with Wine (page 280) for menus and pairings.

Sparkling Wine Steals: The Key to Everyday Dining with Bubbly

I CAN'T STRESS ENOUGH how beautifully sparkling wine sets off food—not just the recipes in this book but most anything you might cook or order up. For example, a sommelier secret is pairing bubbly with, believe it or not, potato

Champagne and sparkling wine are bottled under extreme pressure, enough to cause the cork to eject at high speeds and cause extreme bodily injury as well as breakage to windows, lighting fixtures, and other fragile objects in a room. Having once seen a bartender take out the entire single-malt Scotch section of his back bar by opening a bottle of Champagne with less than the proper amount of care, I follow these steps to safely opening a bottle, and I urge you to do so, too.

1. Never use a corkscrew.

2. Ensure the wine is well-chilled, as this helps to mute the pressure.

3. Always open a sparkling wine bottle pointing away from all people.

4. Remove the foil that covers the wire cage around the cork. Many bottles have pull-tabs to help with this. If your bottle doesn't, cut the foil with the blade of your corkscrew.

5. Have a towel handy.

6. Place your thumb or the palm of one hand firmly over the cork before you begin loosening or removing the wire cage.

7. While maintaining downward pressure on the cork with your thumb or palm, loosen the wire cage with your other hand by grasping the loop and untwisting the wire. Once the wire is loose, *never release your firm grip on the cork.*

8. Holding the cork tightly, gently begin turning the bottle in one direction, and the cork in the opposite (or just hold it steady). The pressure in the bottle will begin to push the cork out. Control the pressure with your grip, slowly easing the cork out.

9. Don't pop the cork. I know people like the festive sound, but a popping cork can be unpredictable and someone might get hurt. You also lose a lot of the carbon dioxide when the cork pops (those are the bubbles for which you paid extra), and sometimes the wine spews forth as well. If you want sound effects, clink glasses for a toast.

chips (you've gotta try it). And these are some of my favorite mind-bending matches for sparkling: popcorn (buttered, air-popped, microwaved—they're all great), sushi, takeout Chinese, and barbecue. To keep it affordable, check out the rest of the world of quality bubbly. I'll list the best of them here, from least to most expensive.

Spanish Cava. Cava is Spain's sparkling wine made in the classic method. It is less expensive (often under $10) because it's more abundant than Champagne. The grapes used are the Spanish grapes Parellada, Macabeo, and Xarel-lo, and also Chardonnay. They are virtually all made in the brut style.

By now you know my mantra: Crisp + tangy = food-versatile. The huge array of distinctive and assertive flavors in this chapter—from wasabi to cilantro to saffron—is testament to my confidence in the power of acidity, one of the major style components in most white wines, to spark up food flavors from everyday to exotic. It makes sense, when you remember that so many of the condiments we use to pump up our meals—relish, mustard, salad dressing, vinegar, to name a few—feature prominent acidity. When you want to let still (not bubbly) wine do the finishing flavor touches on these recipes, look to the other major wine source that's built for food—Italy.

For most people, Italian white wines are a more familiar territory, especially for everyday drinking, than sparkling wine. And well they should be, because they offer lively, refreshing flavor and great value. Also, thanks to their acidity, any leftovers hold up well for enjoying the next day or even the next. When the wines are too far gone for drinking, they're ideal for cooking. Hang on to them and use when a recipe calls for "dry white wine." Here are the everyday Italian whites, from least to most expensive:

PINOT GRIGIO

Can you say "on fire"? This grape's popularity has exploded over the last few years. The flavors are of fresh pear and citrus, typically without any oaky character because the wines generally aren't aged in barrels. Most Italian Pinot Grigio comes from the Veneto, Friuli, and Trentino districts in the north of the country.

VERMENTINO

Check out this up-and-comer, which is grown in Sardinia and in Tuscany. The lemony-creamy scent and flavor are quite complex.

VERNACCIA DI SAN GIMIGNANO

This is Tuscany's top white wine, the Vernaccia (vair-NAH-chee-uh) grape from the town of San Gimignano. It's got a mineral and crisp apple character with a hint of licorice.

Italian Prosecco. This is the Venetian sparkling wine used in the famous Bellini cocktail (Prosecco with peach puree). The grape used is Prosecco, and the wine is often made with the second fermentation taking place in a tank rather than in each individual bottle, a less expensive process that's reflected in the affordable price.

New World Sparkling Wine. California and Washington State, as well as Argentina and Australia (considered New World winemaking countries as opposed to the Old World classic wine regions of Europe), all make quality

ASPARAGUS MEETS ITS MATCH

Among wine pros, asparagus is often unwelcome at the table, because its distinctive taste properties interact with certain wine types in a way that yields a strangely metallic or sweet aftertaste. My asparagus recipe (see page 190) counters this effect with thoughtful preparation (roasting) and wine-friendly accompanying ingredients (cheese). Like roasting, grilling is also a wine-friendly option. In place of cheese, a vinaigrette dressing will boost this vegetable's wine affinity as well. When I want to enjoy the best of spring asparagus au naturel, I've found that Italian white wines make the best match.

sparkling wines using the classic method and with the same grapes used in French Champagne. The prices are generally lower because there's a greater supply (though many of the wineries do offer a limited-edition, pricier bottling). And the quality is high due to great growing-season weather and abundant expertise: Nearly all of the major French Champagne houses have wineries producing sparkling wine in one or more of these regions. It's no surprise, then, that of all the "alternative bubblies," these are the most Champagne-like in flavor and complexity.

A Toast to Your Newest Dinner Companion—Sparkling Wine

ONE OF MY FAVORITE WEEKNIGHT RITUALS is to pour a glass of sparkling wine and get cooking—it's easy and feels instantly festive and special. I've paired specific bubblies with all the recipes in this chapter, but mix and match as you care to; you really can't go wrong. And when you want to splurge and prepare a really special dinner featuring an array of bubblies (as you'll no doubt yearn to do after enjoying some of the everyday dinner pairings in this chapter!), you can turn to Great Menus with Wine (page 280) for a fantastic sparkling-only menu that's one of my favorite holiday traditions.

ROASTED ROOT VEGETABLES WITH OREGANO

SERVES FOUR AS A SIDE DISH • Every one of these vegetables improves in the oven, where excess moisture is removed and natural sugars are caramelized for intense flavor. Roasting the carrots and sweet potatoes brings out their sweetness, so I like to add some peppery turnips and buttery, nutty parsnips for balance. Try this combination of root vegetables instead of your regular old roasted or baked potatoes next time you are cooking a chicken or searing a steak. Definitely a reason to pop the cork on Italian Prosecco, whose slight nuttiness and hint of licorice scent pick up the richness of the vegetables and the headiness of the oregano.

ITALIAN PROSECCO

Mionetto "Il" Prosecco, Nino Franco Prosecco Rustico

ITALIAN VERNACCIA

Strozzi, Falchini

3 medium carrots (about ½ pound)

3 medium parsnips (about ½ pound)

3 medium turnips (about ½ pound)

1 large sweet potato (about ½ pound)

2 tablespoons olive oil

Kosher salt

Freshly ground black pepper

2 tablespoons finely chopped fresh oregano

1. Preheat the oven to 425°F. Peel the carrots and parsnips, trim their ends, and cut into 2-inch lengths. Use a paring knife or heavy-duty vegetable peeler to remove the tough skin from the turnips. Cut the turnips into ½-inch-thick disks. Peel the sweet potato and cut into ½-inch cubes.

2. Combine all of the vegetables in a large bowl, add the olive oil, salt, and pepper, and toss to coat.

3. Spread the vegetables out on an oiled, rimmed baking sheet or in a roasting pan large enough to hold them in a single layer. Roast, stirring several times, until the vegetables are tender and lightly browned, about 45 minutes. Stir in the oregano and serve immediately, or cool slightly and serve warm.

CAULIFLOWER "POPCORN"

SERVES FOUR • I knew John had a special knack for putting together dishes high on wine affinity when he threw this together. Pine nuts add toasty richness that mirrors that quality in fuller house-style sparklers. Caramelizing the florets adds a beautiful glaze and gives them a toothsome texture. And although your kids won't be enjoying the dish with a glass of Roederer Estate, the way you certainly will, they'll love the transformation of a dreaded vegetable into a fun "popcorn" snack. Even Lucas (who's a foodie but not a cauliflower fan) practically inhaled his plateful.

WINE RECOMMENDATIONS

SPANISH CAVA

Mont Marcal Brut, Paul Cheneau Brut

CALIFORNIA SPARKLING WINE

Roederer Estate Brut NV, Piper-Sonoma Brut NV

2 tablespoons pine nuts

Kosher salt

1 head cauliflower, cored and broken into 1-inch florets

2 tablespoons plus 1 teaspoon unsalted butter

1 tablespoon olive oil

Freshly ground black pepper

$\frac{1}{8}$ teaspoon sugar

$\frac{1}{2}$ cup Chardonnay (leftover is fine)

1. Place the pine nuts in a dry skillet. Toast over medium-high heat, shaking the pan frequently, until browned and fragrant, 3 to 5 minutes. Remove from the hot pan and set aside to cool completely. Coarsely chop.

2. Bring a pot of salted water to a boil. Add the cauliflower and boil for 3 minutes. Drain and then transfer to a bowl of ice water to stop the cooking. Drain and pat dry.

3. Combine the 2 tablespoons of butter and the olive oil in a large skillet and heat on medium high until the butter is foaming. Add the blanched cauliflower and season with salt, pepper, and sugar. Cook without stirring for the first 3 to 5 minutes to allow the cauliflower to caramelize on one side, then stir to turn cauliflower and continue cooking until uniformly caramelized, another 3 to 4 minutes. Transfer to a serving bowl.

4. Pour the Chardonnay into the pan, turn the heat to high, and bring to a boil. Boil, scraping up the browned bits from the bottom of the pan with a wooden spoon, until the liquid is reduced by half and slightly thickened. Remove the pan from the heat and swirl in the remaining 1 teaspoon butter. Pour the sauce over the cauliflower and stir to coat. Sprinkle with the toasted pine nuts and serve immediately.

ANGEL HAIR PASTA WITH SMOKED SALMON AND EDAMAME "PESTO"

SERVES FOUR • Edamame are fresh soybeans, flash frozen either in their pods or shelled and then frozen. They are bright green like peas, but have an earthy flavor and texture more like fresh lima or fava beans. They are popular in Japanese cooking and are often served as a simple snack or appetizer, sprinkled with sea salt, at sushi restaurants. Recently, they've become widely available at supermarkets and natural foods stores. I love to keep them in the freezer for quick dinners. They're a great source of protein, very colorful and healthy, and wonderfully versatile. Here is a truly cross-cultural recipe, using Italian pasta, smoked salmon, and soybeans. The combination is unusual but utterly harmonious and quite wine-versatile: I love it with the Italian white Vermentino grape, which enhances the pesto's herbs, and with California sparkling wine, which contrasts the salmon's saltiness and complements the sesame oil nuttiness in the pesto.

WINE RECOMMENDATIONS

ITALIAN VERMENTINO

Sella & Mosca
Vermentino

SPARKLING WINE

Nino Franco Prosecco
(Italy), Iron Horse Russian
Cuvée Sparkling Wine
(California)

1 cup shelled frozen edamame

3 tablespoons freshly squeezed
   lime juice (about 1 lime)

¾ cup tightly packed fresh cilantro
   leaves, stems removed, several
   sprigs reserved for garnish

½ cup tightly packed fresh basil
   leaves

2 small garlic cloves

⅓ cup olive oil

2 tablespoons toasted sesame oil

1 teaspoon kosher salt

¾ pound angel hair pasta

6 ounces presliced smoked salmon,
   cut into ½-inch-by-1-inch pieces

Freshly ground white pepper

Coarse sea salt such as fleur de sel

1. Place the edamame in a microwave-safe bowl. Cover with plastic and cook on high until heated through, 2 to 3 minutes. Alternatively, cook the edamame in salted boiling water for 3 minutes. Set aside ⅓ cup of the edamame for garnish.

2. Combine the remaining ⅔ cup edamame, lime juice, cilantro, basil, ½ cup water, and garlic in a blender or the workbowl of a food processor and process into a paste, scraping down the sides of the bowl once or twice as necessary. With the motor running, slowly pour in the olive oil and then the sesame oil in a thin stream. Scrape the pesto into a bowl and stir in the kosher salt.

3. Bring 4 quarts of water to a boil in a large pot. Salt the water and cook the angel hair according to package directions until al dente. Drain the pasta, turn it into a large pasta bowl, and toss it with the pesto to coat. Stir in the smoked salmon and reserved edamame and toss again to distribute. Garnish with the reserved cilantro sprigs and serve immediately with freshly ground white pepper and fleur de sel to taste.

CREAMY GOAT CHEESE POLENTA

SERVES FOUR AS A SIDE DISH OR TWO AS A MAIN COURSE • The earthy-sweetness of cornmeal, tang of fresh goat cheese, and fragrant herbaceousness of thyme make this simple dish a match with dry (brut) sparkling wine. You can buy quick-cooking instant polenta or grits, but this is one time when I prefer to take the extra time (we're talking less than fifteen minutes here) to cook plain old cornmeal, which makes for a much creamier dish. Serve the polenta on the side with simply sautéed chicken, steak, or chops, or serve it on its own as a warming vegetarian main course.

<table>
<tr><td rowspan="5">WINE RECOMMENDATIONS</td><td>SPARKLING WINE</td><td>Kosher salt</td></tr>
<tr><td></td><td>1 cup yellow cornmeal</td></tr>
<tr><td>Domaine Chandon
Brut (California)</td><td>4 ounces fresh goat cheese</td></tr>
<tr><td></td><td>2 tablespoons unsalted butter</td></tr>
<tr><td>Zenato Prosecco
(Italy)</td><td>½ teaspoon dried thyme</td></tr>
</table>

1. Bring 2 cups water and ½ teaspoon salt to a boil in a heavy, medium saucepan. Slowly whisk the cornmeal into the pot. Turn the heat to low and continue to cook, whisking frequently, until the polenta is thick and creamy, about 15 minutes.

2. Remove from the heat and stir in the goat cheese, butter, and thyme until the cheese and butter are melted. Season with more salt to taste. Serve immediately.

WARM CRISPY GOAT CHEESE CANAPÉS

MAKES ABOUT THIRTY-TWO • This hors d'oeuvre is a lot more exciting than cheese and crackers, and not that much more difficult to accomplish. You may cook them a few at a time as guests arrive so each is served warm (they are tasty after they've cooled, too). Substitute toasted French bread slices for the melba rounds if you prefer. I slice the goat cheese with dental floss to get clean cuts (it's safe enough to delegate to my ten-year-old, too). The warm cheese disks are also a great topping for a mixed green salad, as a first course, or a light dinner. The best bubblies for this dish are tangy, elegant ones, and it's also great with Pinot Grigio.

WINE RECOMMENDATIONS

SPANISH CAVA

Segura Viudas Reserva Heredad Cava

ITALIAN PINOT GRIGIO

Bottega Vinaia, Ecco Domani

One 6-ounce jar oil-packed sun-dried tomatoes, drained

2 cups fine dried bread crumbs

One 16-ounce log fresh goat cheese, room temperature

2 large eggs

Small melba toast rounds

Olive oil, for sautéing

2 tablespoons finely chopped fresh parsley or chives

1. Cut the sun-dried tomatoes into ½-inch-by-1-inch strips and reserve. Place the bread crumbs in a pie plate or shallow bowl.

2. Place the goat cheese on a 20-inch-long piece of plastic wrap. Slice the cheese in half lengthwise using dental floss. Place the cheese halves end-to-end, cut sides down, on the plastic wrap. Roll the plastic over the cheese to cover it tightly and completely. Then roll and shape the cheese to round the cut edges and reform it into one long, thin log, about 16 inches long.

3. Unwrap the plastic and, with dental floss, slice into thirty-two ½-inch-thick rounds.

4. Whisk the eggs and ¼ cup water together to make an egg wash. Dip each goat cheese slice in egg wash, then in crumbs to coat all sides. Place the rounds on a baking sheet or plate, cover with plastic wrap, and refrigerate until ready to cook, up to 2 hours.

CHURRASCO-STYLE SKIRT STEAK

SERVES FOUR • The steaks marinate overnight, so all the work is done ahead of time. Just fire up the grill and cook when you're ready to eat. I love skirt steak, a slightly chewy, super-flavorful cut. But if you prefer you can substitute sirloin steaks; note that they're thicker than skirt steaks and will take a little longer to cook. I pair this dish with dry rosé sparkling wine or Champagne, and the combination is just amazing.

WINE RECOMMENDATIONS

FRENCH ROSÉ CHAMPAGNE

Gosset Rosé

CALIFORNIA ROSÉ
SPARKLING WINE

Gloria Ferrer Rosé

SPANISH CAVA ROSÉ

Freixenet Brut de Noirs
Rosé

⅓ cup olive oil

½ cup sherry vinegar

2½ teaspoons paprika

1 teaspoon cayenne pepper

6 garlic cloves, finely chopped

½ teaspoon freshly ground black pepper

½ teaspoon ground cumin

1 bay leaf

½ teaspoon kosher salt

½ cup chopped fresh parsley

1½ pounds skirt steaks or boneless sirloin steak

1. Combine the olive oil, vinegar, paprika, cayenne, garlic, black pepper, cumin, bay leaf, salt, and parsley in a medium bowl.

2. Place the steaks in a zipper-lock bag and pour the marinade in the bag. Squeeze the air out of the bag and seal. Shake and press the bag, making sure that the marinade covers all of the meat. Refrigerate overnight.

3. Prepare a medium-hot charcoal fire, preheat a gas grill to medium-high, or heat the oven broiler. Lightly oil the grill or broiler pan. Cook the steaks to desired doneness, turning once, about 7 minutes total for medium-rare skirt steaks (sirloin steaks will take a bit longer). Cut steaks into ½-inch slices across the grain and serve.

SHRIMP CEVICHE WITH AVOCADO, CILANTRO, AND LIME

SERVES SIX • Although this dish isn't a true ceviche, since the shrimp are cooked on top of the stove rather than cured in lime juice or another acidic ingredient, it has the Latin flavors and bracing bite reminiscent of such seafood preparations. It's an especially wine-friendly version because the shrimp and coconut milk both have a subtle sweetness, which picks up the fruit in the wine and softens the tang of the lime juice. I pair it with Spanish Cavas and New World sparkling wines, which are riper-tasting than French Champagne, and also with Vermentino, which has some tropical fruit character. Make sure to stir the coconut milk before measuring, since it separates in the can.

WINE RECOMMENDATIONS

SPARKLING WINE

Aria Cava Extra Dry (Spain)

Argyle Brut (Oregon)

ITALIAN VERMENTINO

Antinori

- 1 pound medium shrimp, peeled and deveined
- ½ cup unsweetened coconut milk
- ½ cup dry white wine
- ¼ teaspoon crumbled saffron
- ¾ to 1 teaspoon Tabasco sauce, to taste
- ¼ cup freshly squeezed lime juice (about 2 limes)
- 2 tablespoons shallots, minced
- ½ cup diced, seeded tomato (about 2 medium tomatoes)
- 2 tablespoons chopped scallions
- 2 tablespoons finely chopped fresh chives
- ½ cup finely chopped fresh cilantro, plus extra for garnish
- Pinch kosher salt, or more to taste
- Small, ripe avocado, peeled, pitted, and diced

1. Combine the shrimp, coconut milk, wine, and saffron in a skillet over medium heat. Bring to a simmer and cook, uncovered, until the shrimp are opaque and cooked through, about 7 minutes.

2. Remove the shrimp from the pan with a slotted spoon and place in a bowl. Set the bowl over a larger bowl filled with ice to halt the cooking and cool the shrimp.

3. While the shrimp are cooling, simmer the cooking liquid in the skillet until reduced to ½ cup, about 5 minutes. Set the pan into a bowl filled with ice to cool.

4. Cut the cooled shrimp into bite-size pieces. Whisk together the Tabasco, cooled coconut milk–saffron broth, and lime juice in a large bowl. Stir in the shrimp, shallots, tomato, scallions, chives, cilantro, and salt to taste. Cover and refrigerate for 30 minutes. Gently fold in diced avocado and serve immediately in martini glasses or small bowls, garnished with additional chopped cilantro.

SHRIMPS IN A BLANKET

SERVES SIX • *To die for*—that is, this dish and this match. This isn't a weeknight quickie, but it is a relatively quick appetizer for casual entertaining. You can have the shrimp brined, blanketed, and crisp-cooked in under an hour. The brining ensures that the shrimp won't dry out before their potato blankets are crisped. The "blanketing" is based on a technique developed by star chef Jean-Georges Vongerichten, in which he grates Idaho potatoes in long shreds and wraps the shreds around fish fillets (the recipe can be found in his terrific book *Simple to Spectacular*). John and I adapted the technique to wrap shrimp, and the results are crunchy and scrumptious two-bite wonders that sing with Champagne or sparkling wine. This is a great use for the shelled, frozen, deveined shrimp you buy in big bags at the warehouse club, since most of the hard work is done for you when you buy shrimp this way, and the price is right. Because these are cooked in stages as they're wrapped, they are a good "interactive" appetizer (for whoever wants to help you or watch). A perfect way to start the evening, along with Champagne, talk, and tunes.

WINE RECOMMENDATIONS		
SPARKLING WINE Seaview Brut (Australia) Domaine Ste. Michelle Blanc de Blancs Brut NV (Washington State) **FRENCH CHAMPAGNE** Charles Heidsieck Brut NV	1½ pounds large shrimp ¼ cup packed brown sugar ¼ cup kosher salt, plus extra for seasoning the potatoes 1 bay leaf, broken 12 peppercorns 4 ounces Prosciutto di Parma or di San Daniele, julienned and cut into lengths slightly shorter than the shrimp	3 tablespoons finely chopped fresh rosemary 3 jumbo russet baking potatoes Freshly ground white pepper 3 tablespoons olive oil, plus more if necessary 1 tablespoon unsalted butter, plus more if necessary

1. If the shrimp are frozen, defrost them by placing in a colander in the sink and running cold water over them for 5 to 10 minutes.

2. Combine the brown sugar, salt, and 1 cup of hot water in a large bowl. Stir to dissolve the sugar and salt. Add 3 cups of cold water, the bay leaf, and peppercorns, and refrigerate the brining mixture while you work on the shrimp.

3. With a sharp paring knife, butterfly the shrimp by slicing the outsides (vein sides) almost through from head to tail, leaving the inner curve and tail intact.

4. Stir the butterflied shrimp into the brine and refrigerate for 30 minutes. Drain, rinse, and pat dry with paper towels.

5. Place the shrimp on a baking sheet. Open up each shrimp where it has been cut and lay a strip of prosciutto along the length of the inside of the shrimp. Sprinkle the prosciutto with chopped rosemary, then close up the shrimp. Cover the baking sheet with plastic wrap and refrigerate.

6. Peel the potatoes and place them in a bowl of cold water to prevent browning. Fill another bowl with cold water and lightly season the water with salt and pepper. Remove one potato from the water and, using the large-holed side of a box grater, grate the potato into long shreds by running the entire length of the potato along the side of the grater. Put the shreds in the bowl of seasoned water and repeat with the remaining 2 potatoes.

7. Remove half of the potatoes from the water and place them inside several layers of paper towels and squeeze to remove excess moisture.

8. Heat 1½ tablespoons of the olive oil and ½ tablespoon of the butter on medium heat in 2 large, heavy nonstick skillets. Or cook the shrimp in 2 batches, adding half of the oil and butter to the pan for each batch. With one hand, pick up a filled shrimp. With the other hand, pick up a large pinch of potato strands (about the amount you'd get if you twirled spaghetti onto a large fork) and drape the strands over the middle of the shrimp so that they hang down evenly on either side of the shrimp. Wrap the strands around the shrimp, spreading them out as you wrap so they enclose all but the tip and tail. Patch with additional shreds where necessary.

9. As you finish wrapping each shrimp, place it in the skillet and cook until the potatoes are browned and crisp and the shrimp is cooked through, turning once, 4 to 6 minutes. You will have to keep an eye on the individual shrimp as they cook, adding more oil and butter as necessary. Remove the rest of the potato shreds from the water and dry as in step 7 when needed. Remove the cooked shrimp to a paper towel–lined plate. When all of the shrimp are out of the pan, serve immediately.

ROASTED OYSTERS "ROCKEFELLER CENTER"

SERVES SIX • This recipe, adapted from a signature oyster appetizer we served at the Rainbow Room long ago, is very pretty and not at all difficult. I always make it on New Year's Eve, as it is elegant, seasonally appropriate, and beautiful with bubbly. I set up multiple sheet pans in the refrigerator and roast them one at a time, so that each pan is served warm. They also make a beautiful first course for a sit-down dinner party. Line salad plates with rock salt or seaweed to keep the oysters from tipping, and serve four oysters per guest. Ask your fishmonger for the seaweed, which is used to pack wholesale seafood shipped to retailers.

It's not difficult to shuck your own oysters. Use an oyster knife, which is bent at the end, to pry open the shell at the hinge. Always start with the rounded end down, so you won't lose any precious oyster liquid. Once the oyster is opened, use the knife point to scrape the meat attached to the top shell into the bottom shell, keeping as much liquid in the bottom shell as possible. If you prefer, you may ask your fishmonger to shuck the oysters for you, placing the shucked oysters and liquid in a container and reserving the rounded, cup-shaped side of each shell. Before using the shells, sanitize them by putting them in a large stockpot with water, and bringing it to a boil for an hour. Drain and cool the shells before using.

WINE RECOMMENDATIONS			
ITALIAN PROSECCO SPARKLING WINE	2 tablespoons unsalted butter	One 2-pound box rock salt	
	2 small shallots, finely chopped	Seaweed (enough to make a small bed for each appetizer plate if not using salt—request it from your fishmonger)	
Mionetto Brut, Zardetto	⅓ cup Chardonnay (leftover is fine)		
FRENCH CHAMPAGNE	1 cup heavy cream		
	Pinch white pepper, or to taste		
Pol Roger White Label NV	2 dozen fresh oysters, shucked, "bottom" shells (the rounded, cup-shaped side) reserved		

1. Melt the butter over medium heat in a small saucepan. Add the shallots and cook, stirring, until they are translucent and beginning to soften, about 2 minutes. Add the Chardonnay, bring to a lively simmer, and reduce until only about 2 tablespoons of liquid remains. Add the cream and bring to a boil. Lower the heat to a simmer and reduce to ⅔ cup. Remove from the heat, stir in the white pepper, and set aside.

2. Preheat the oven broiler to 500°F. Arrange the top oven rack so a roasting pan will fit below the heating element. Prepare appetizer plates by putting a loose nest of seaweed on each, to hold the oysters. Distribute the rock salt evenly between two roasting pans large enough to hold the oysters.

3. If the fishmonger shucked your oysters, return the oysters to their cleaned shells one by one, and add about ½ teaspoon of the oyster liquid to each, nesting the shells carefully in the rock salt so the contents don't spill. Otherwise, arrange freshly shucked oysters in the rock salt–filled roasting pans, ensuring that their liquid doesn't spill. Spoon about 2 teaspoons of the shallot-cream mixture on top of each oyster (you want to coat each oyster well, without having the shell overflow with liquid).

4. Put one roasting pan in the oven and broil just until the liquid bubbles and the oysters' edges begin to curl, about 3 minutes, watching closely to prevent burning. Repeat with the other roasting pan. Carefully lift 4 oysters in their shells from the rock salt onto each appetizer plate, nesting them in the seaweed. Serve immediately.

Oysters Baked in Ramekins. Most fishmongers sell shucked oysters in their liquor. If you'd rather not take the trouble to sanitize the shells, you may bake the oysters in ramekins instead. Butter 6 individual 1-cup ramekins and place on a cookie sheet. Place 4 shucked oysters in each ramekin and divide the oyster liquor evenly among them. Spoon the cream mixture atop and place the cookie sheet with the filled ramekins under the preheated broiler to cook as described above. Place the ramekins on small plates so you can handle them, and make sure to let everyone know that the ramekins are hot to the touch.

PAN-CRISPED OYSTERS WITH SESAME SEEDS

MAKES TWENTY-FOUR • A festive, simple appetizer or hors d'oeuvre. The crispy bread crumbs, sweet oysters, and toasty sesame seeds are perfect with crisp-textured, toasty-tasting Champagnes and sparkling wines. Panko, Japanese bread crumbs used in tempura, cook up crispier and fluffier than any other bread crumbs. They are available in many supermarkets and in Asian groceries. Black sesame seeds add a smoky flavor and a pretty, speckled look and can also be found at Asian groceries and through mail-order spice catalogs (see page 286).

WINE RECOMMENDATIONS

CALIFORNIA SPARKLING WINE

Mumm Cuvée Napa, Roederer Estate

SPANISH CAVA

Mont Marcal

½ cup sesame seeds

2 tablespoons black sesame seeds

1½ teaspoons kosher salt

2 cups panko (Japanese bread crumbs)

2 dozen oysters, shucked

1 tablespoon olive oil, plus more if necessary

2 tablespoons unsalted butter, plus more if necessary

1. Place the sesame seeds in a large, dry skillet and cook over medium-high heat, shaking the pan frequently, until they are golden, 2 to 3 minutes. Transfer to a small bowl and cool completely.

2. Combine the toasted sesame seeds, black sesame seeds, salt, and panko in a medium bowl. Roll the oysters in the crumb mixture to coat and remove to a large plate.

3. Heat the olive oil and butter in a large skillet on medium-high until the butter foams. Add the oysters in a single layer and cook until golden brown and crisp, turning once, about 1½ minutes per side. (If the oysters won't all fit in a single layer, cook in batches, adding more oil and butter to the pan as necessary.) Transfer the cooked oysters to a paper towel–lined plate to drain briefly. Serve warm.

CHAMPAGNE-STEAMED MUSSELS

SERVES SIX AS A FIRST COURSE • Here is a festive first course or one-plate meal, simple and fun but special because it's made with bubbly. Mussels and sparkling wine are natural partners: The crispness of the wine brings out the briny-sweet taste of the shellfish. But the mussels are not the only wine-loving ingredient here. A humble garnish of crushed sourdough pretzels toasted in browned butter has a yeasty-toasty flavor, similar to the yeasty-toasty flavor that traditionally made bubbly acquires from aging on yeast cells after the second fermentation.

Considering that mussels are among the least expensive items at the seafood market, you may not want to spend a fortune on bubbly. A value choice is Spanish Cava, a sparkling wine that is especially suited to this dish because its herbaceousness (provided by the Parellada, Macabeo, and Xarel-lo grapes) picks up on the chervil/tarragon in the mussel broth.

WINE RECOMMENDATIONS

SPANISH CAVA

Freixenet Carta Nevada, Paul Cheneau Brut

CALIFORNIA SPARKLING WINE

Domaine Carneros Brut

---

2 pounds mussels

2 tablespoons unsalted butter

½ cup sourdough pretzel crumbs, crushed in a blender or food processor

1 medium shallot, finely chopped

2 garlic cloves, finely chopped

2 plum tomatoes, cored and chopped

1 cup Champagne or sparkling wine

½ cup fish stock or bottled clam juice

1 tablespoon chopped fresh chervil or tarragon

1. Clean the mussels by scrubbing their shells with a brush while rinsing under cold running water. If necessary, use a paring knife to tug and cut out the weedy beards coming out of the bottom of the shells. Pick through the mussels and discard any with broken or open shells that won't close when you tap them.

2. Heat 1 tablespoon of the butter in a small skillet over medium-high heat. When the foam subsides and the butter just begins to brown, add the crushed pretzels and toss to coat. Reduce the heat to medium and cook, stirring, until the crumbs are crisped, about 2 minutes. Remove from the heat and set aside.

3. Heat a large, dry skillet over medium-high heat. Add the mussels, shallot, garlic, and tomatoes and stir to combine. Cook for 2 minutes and then add the Champagne and the fish stock and continue cooking and stirring until the shells open, about another 4 minutes. Transfer the mussels to serving bowls with a slotted spoon and continue to simmer the liquid to reduce it slightly, scraping up any bits stuck to the bottom of the pan with a wooden spoon.

4. Remove the pan from the heat and swirl in the remaining 1 tablespoon butter. Stir in the chervil. Pour the broth over the mussels, sprinkle pretzel crumbs over each portion, and serve immediately.

WASABI PEA-CRUSTED SALMON

SERVES FOUR • This is another drop-dead-delicious, gorgeous dish that's easy, easy, easy. It used to be that you could only get wasabi peas (an addictive snack!) in Chinatown. Now they are in just about every supermarket produce section (near the nuts, dried fruits, and trail mixes). The blender-crushed peas form an amazing crunchy crust for salmon fillets that's wildly flavorful, and beautiful—pink salmon, green pea crust, rosé Champagne . . . awesome. (I've also included some less-expensive sparkling rosé recommendations.)

<table>
<tr><td rowspan="2">WINE RECOMMENDATIONS</td><td>FRENCH ROSÉ CHAMPAGNE

Billecart-Salmon Rosé

CALIFORNIA ROSÉ
SPARKLING WINE

Iron Horse, S. Anderson</td><td>Four 1-inch-thick, 6-ounce salmon fillets

2 tablespoons olive oil, plus more for brushing fillets

½ cup wasabi-crusted peas

2 tablespoons unsalted butter</td></tr>
</table>

1. Brush both the skin and flesh sides of the salmon fillets with olive oil. Whirl the wasabi peas in a blender until they are the consistency of bread crumbs, and spread them on a plate. Dip the flesh side of each salmon fillet into the peas, pressing gently so that the surface is evenly coated with the wasabi crumbs. Set aside and continue with the remaining fillets.

2. In a large, flat-bottomed nonstick skillet, heat the butter and 2 tablespoons olive oil on medium. Place the fillets pea side down in the skillet and cook until the pea crust becomes crisp and starts to brown lightly, about 4 minutes. Lift the edge of each fillet carefully to check the browning, and lower the heat if necessary to prevent burning. Turn the fillets and continue to cook until the fillets are medium rare, about 4 minutes. Remove to a paper towel–lined plate to drain briefly, and then serve immediately.

Everyday Dinners with
CHAMPAGNE, SPARKLING WINES, AND CRISP WHITES

PASTAS AND OTHER ONE-PLATE DINNERS

WHAT TO COOK	WINE PAIRINGS
Champagne-Steamed Mussels *(page 119)*, crusty bread or steamed rice	ONCE-A-WEEK ($–$$): Freixenet Carta Nevada (Spain) Paul Cheneau Brut (Spain) ONCE-A-MONTH ($$$ AND UP): Domaine Carneros Brut (California)
Angel Hair Pasta with Smoked Salmon and Edamame "Pesto" *(page 107)*	ONCE-A-WEEK ($–$$): Sella & Mosca Vermentino (Italy) Nino Franco Prosecco (Italy) ONCE-A-MONTH ($$$ AND UP): Iron Horse Russian Cuvée (California)
Warm Crispy Goat Cheese Canapés *(page 109)* served as the "croutons" atop salad greens dressed with vinaigrette	ONCE-A-WEEK ($–$$): Ecco Domani Pinot Grigio (Italy) Bottega Vinaia Pinot Grigio (Italy) ONCE-A-MONTH ($$$ AND UP): Segura Viudas Reserva Heredad Cava (Spain)

TRADITIONAL (MAIN-AND-SIDES) DINNERS

WHAT TO COOK	WINE PAIRINGS
MAIN COURSE: Chicken Legs Braised in Pinot Grigio Mojo *(page 111)* VEGGIES: Roasted Root Vegetables with Oregano *(page 105)* STARCHES, ETC.: Spanish-style rice	ONCE-A-WEEK ($–$$): Livio Felluga Pinot Grigio (Italy) Monteviña Pinot Gris (California) ONCE-A-MONTH ($$$ AND UP): Teruzzi e Puthod Vernaccia di San Gimignano (Italy)
MAIN COURSE: Churrasco-Style Skirt Steak *(page 112)* VEGGIES: Garlic-Braised Collard Greens *(page 189)* STARCHES, ETC.: Spicy Fruited Couscous *(page 193)*	ONCE-A-WEEK ($–$$): Freixenet Brut de Noirs Cava Rosé (Spain) Gloria Ferrer Rosé (California) ONCE-A-MONTH ($$$ AND UP): Champagne Gosset Rosé (France)

WHAT TO COOK	WINE PAIRINGS
MAIN COURSE: Wasabi Pea–Crusted Salmon *(page 121)* VEGGIES: Cauliflower "Popcorn" *(page 106)* STARCHES, ETC.: Udon noodles with sesame oil	ONCE-A-WEEK ($–$$): Iron Horse Rosé (California) S. Anderson Rosé (California) ONCE-A-MONTH ($$$ AND UP): Billecart-Salmon Rosé (France)
MAIN COURSE: Shrimps in a Blanket *(page 114)* VEGGIES: steamed green beans; romaine lettuce with vinaigrette	ONCE-A-WEEK ($–$$): Seaview Brut (Australia) Domaine Ste. Michelle Blanc de Blancs Brut NV (Washington State) ONCE-A-MONTH ($$$ AND UP): Champagne Charles Heidsieck Brut NV (France)
MAIN COURSE: Shrimp Ceviche with Avocado, Cilantro, and Lime *(page 113)* VEGGIES: Crunchy Herb Salad *(page 59)* STARCHES, ETC.: corn tortilla chips or corn bread	ONCE-A-WEEK ($–$$): Aria Cava Extra Dry (Spain) Argyle Brut (Oregon) ONCE-A-MONTH ($$$ AND UP): Antinori Vermentino (Italy)
MAIN COURSE: Pan-Crisped Oysters with Sesame Seeds *(page 118)* VEGGIES: Tomato-Watermelon Sorbet *(page 60)*	ONCE-A-WEEK ($–$$): Mont Marcal Cava (Spain) Mumm Cuvée Napa (California) ONCE-A-MONTH ($$$ AND UP): Roederer Estate (California)
MAIN COURSE: Roasted Oysters "Rockefeller Center" *(page 116)* VEGGIES: steamed spinach with sesame oil STARCHES, ETC.: Yukon Gold Potato and Cauliflower Soup with Truffle Oil *(page 77)*	ONCE-A-WEEK ($–$$): Mionetto Brut Prosecco (Italy) Zardetto Prosecco (Italy) ONCE-A-MONTH ($$$ AND UP): Champagne Pol Roger White Label NV (France)

The Pinot market is similar to the real estate market when it comes to pricing. Just as you pay more to live in a chichi neighborhood, even for the same size house, you'll pay more for a bottle of Pinot Noir if its grapes came from a prime piece of land. When it comes to Burgundy, the vineyard's soil and exposition (the angle of the slope and the direction it faces) are what define prime real estate. "Park Avenue" in Burgundy terms is called the Côte d'Or, which translates as "golden slope." Within the Côte d'Or the vineyards are ranked in ascending order as *village, premier cru* (first rank), and *grand cru* (top rank). All can be great quality, but as you go up the rankings, less supply (and more demand) and stricter quality controls yield more expensive wines. The top ranks boast some of the most coveted collectibles in the wine world. Although they're hardly everyday wines, I've included some recommendations in case you care to splurge and see what all the excitement's about. I've also included a menu showcasing these wines (see page 282), so you can see how amazingly they pair with great food.

French Red Burgundy. Part of the allure of French red Burgundies is owed to a paradox—the region is tiny, only about sixty-five miles north to south, and a couple of miles wide at its widest point, yet the diversity of wines here, all made from just one grape, is amazing. Because of ancient shifts of the earth's tectonic plates, many different geologic soil strata were brought to the surface at this particular spot. Thus the vineyards are a crazy quilt of varied soil types, all in one small strip of land. You can literally stand in a vineyard with iron-rich soil tinged a rust color, and look across no more than a tractor path to a vineyard whose dirt is whitened by its chalk content. The sight is amazing, and the subtle yet distinctive differences in the wine flavors are, too. As with most classic French wines, Burgundies are named for their district, village, or vineyard, rather than for the grape name. Here are the main ones you'll see in shops, from least to most expensive:

Bourgogne Regional Wines. It's pronounced boor-GOHN-yuh, and is the French term for Burgundy. It's the least expensive because it's the least specific: The grapes can be grown anywhere in the entire Burgundy zone.

Côte Chalonnaise Wines. This area, at the southern end of Burgundy, offers great value because the quality is excellent, but the wines are less well known. On the label, look for the village names Mercurey, Givry, and Montagny.

Côte d'Or Wines. This area is divided into two parts, each named for the main town in it—the Côte de Nuits in the north (named for the town of Nuits St. Georges) and the Côte de Beaune in the south (named for the town of Beaune). The villages in both areas yield wines that are, at their best, earthy-elegant, silky, and concentrated. The Côte de Nuits is known for the most powerful and long aging, yet elegant, wines. The Côte de Beaune's wines are considered more rustic and are less long-lived in the cellar. Here are the major wine names to look for:

CÔTE DE NUITS: Gevrey-Chambertin, Morey St. Denis, Chambolle-Musigny, Vosne-Romanee, Nuits St. Georges

CÔTE DE BEAUNE: Aloxe-Corton, Beaune Savigny-Les-Beaune, Pommard, Volnay, Santenay

As with Chianti in Italy, each of these regional wines is produced by multiple wineries. My recommendations will focus on those that I think are the best and most consistent and available from year to year.

The Burgundy Label

ALL FRENCH RED BURGUNDY is 100 percent Pinot Noir by law. But, unless you've spent time memorizing the Burgundy village and vineyard names, it can be difficult to recognize whether a wine actually *is* Burgundy or some other regional wine. Here's an almost foolproof way to tell: Most Burgundies imported to this country contain these words, on either the bottom of the front label or on the back label: *red Burgundy wine* or *French red Burgundy wine*. So if you see that, you're home free because you know the grape variety is Pinot Noir. Now here's how to recognize the different quality levels of Burgundy wines by their labels (the labeling requirements are set by French law).

BURGUNDY BON APPÉTIT

Although it's expensive, a favorite pastime of many wine pros is to create an all-Burgundy dinner, featuring both the Chardonnay whites that we explored in Chapter 3 and the Pinot Noir reds. See page 282 of Great Menus with Wine for a delicious menu that really sets off these wines.

Village. A village-level wine means the grapes can come from anywhere in the village, and the wines may be labeled with the village name, such as Gevrey-Chambertin or Aloxe-Corton.

Premier Cru. This means the grapes must come only from vineyards ranked premier cru. If the grapes are sourced from several such vineyards, the words *premier cru,* along with the village name, are on the label. If the grapes come from a single premier cru vineyard, the vineyard name plus the village name are on the label, for example, Chambolle-Musigny Les Amoureuses (Chambolle-Musigny is the village, Les Amoureuses is the premier cru vineyard).

Grand Cru. In this case the grapes must come exclusively from a grand cru vineyard, of which there are thirty-two in the Côte d'Or, and the wine is labeled just with the name of the grand cru vineyard, for example, Le Chambertin, Le Corton, or La Tache.

The Taste of Pinot Noir

WHERE DO I START? Pinot is so special, and so versatile with food, because it is complex but not heavy. This complexity of flavor includes elements of earthiness that pros describe in terms such as *mushroomy, forest floor, truffles* (the fungus, not the chocolate kind), *smoky,* and even *barnyard.* As with cheese, the earthiness can be subtle, or downright stinky (for true Pinot-heads like myself, the stinkier the better!).

BARRELS = BUCKS

The oak barrels used for wine generally come from America or France, and range in price anywhere from $300 (American) to about $700 (French). So it's easy to see why "oakier" Pinot Noirs (and other wines, too) are generally more expensive. Using new barrels for their stronger taste and scent means wineries have the expense of replacing them every year. And French barrels, which are preferred for Pinot Noir, are the most expensive of all. Those extra costs get passed along in the price of the wine.

In addition, virtually all Pinot Noirs are aged in barrels, and thus have an element of oakiness. As I described for Chardonnay in Chapter 3, the amount of oakiness in the wine depends on the intensity of the grapes. Grapes from top-quality vineyard sources are given a higher proportion of new barrels, and more time in the barrel, because the fruit can stand up to the stronger oakiness. By contrast, value-priced Pinot Noirs are made from less-intense fruit, and thus are given less oak—either used barrels, or shorter time in the barrel, or both.

Finally, there is fruit flavor, which in red wines ranges across a spectrum, from lean and tangy to juicy and mouthwatering, to lush and ripe-tasting, as follows:

LEAN   JUICY   LUSH

cranberry   red currant   raspberry   strawberry   cherry   black currant   blueberry   blackberry   fig

Pinot Noir's flavors generally fall along the lean and tangy to the juicy zones of the fruit spectrum, depending on the growing region and the harvest weather that year. Cool (compared to the average) vintages yield leaner wines; warm vintages yield juicier, riper ones.

Pairing Pinot: The Best "Food Wine" in the World?

MANY SOMMELIERS AND WINE pros think so, because this grape's got so much going for it: complexity in the form of earthiness, oakiness, and sleek fruit; subtlety, due to its light to medium body and silky tannins; and last but never least from a food-matching perspective, acidity. Since it's grown in cooler climates, harvest-ripe Pinot Noir retains great acidity that, as we've been exploring throughout this book, really helps to launch the flavor of the foods with which it's paired. And talk about versatility! As my Windows on the World mentor Kevin Zraly used to say, Pinot Noir has red wine flavor and complexity, but white wine texture; so it matches nicely with meat, red wine's traditional partner, as well as with fish and seafood, which are often thought of as white wine fare. No wonder sommeliers love it so much: It's a please-all pairing for that table of restaurant guests who've ordered both lamb and fillet of sole and want one bottle of wine!

That said, I choose my Pinot pairings purposefully, because the wonderful sub-

A SPLASH OF COLOR, A TUG OF TANNIN

As the pairings in this book make clear, I'm not a big believer in color coding my wine and food matches. The reason is that it's not the color of the wine that's strictly relevant. Rather, when it comes to pairing red wines with chicken, fish, or meat, a more important match factor is tannin.

True, tannin is closely associated with color, because it comes from the same place, the grape skins. Let me explain: The juice of nearly all wine grapes is clear; the color is in the skins. So to get color in a red wine, vintners let the juice and the skins soak together so that the color can leach into the wine. At the same time, another component of the skins, tannin, infuses the wine. Tannin is an acid that gives red wines the chalky, drying sensation on your tongue, and acts as a preservative to extend the wine's ageability.

The depth and hue of color, and the amount of tannin, varies according to the grape variety. As you'll see when you try the dishes and pairings in this chapter, Pinot Noir has a pale, translucent ruby color and silky tannins. The reason is that the skins of the Pinot Noir grape are relatively thin, and thus have less pigment and tannin to impart to the wine than do other red grapes. Here's what to expect in terms of color and tannin intensity from the other main red grapes covered in this book:

Sangiovese and Tempranillo
(Chapter 8)
Ruby red
Medium, chalky tannin

Merlot (Chapter 6)
Ruby-purple
Medium to full tannin

Cabernet Sauvignon
(Chapter 6)
Ruby-purple
Full, firm tannin

Syrah/Shiraz and Zinfandel
(Chapter 7)
Purple
Full, velvety tannin

Over time, the color and tannin molecules bond together and settle, forming that dark deposit or sediment you may have seen at the bottom of a wine bottle or in your glass if yours was the last one filled. Sommeliers prevent this by decanting the wine—pouring the clear wine into a carafe and leaving the sediment "dregs" in the bottle. Decanting also helps to aerate the wine and to soften and harmonize the tannins, making them seem less drying.

But the main thing that helps to soften the tannin in a full red is, happily, food! Specifically, protein- and fat-rich preparations coat your tongue and shield it from the tannin's drying sensation, letting the wine's fruit shine. So the next time you enjoy a classic match like steak and Cabernet Sauvignon, you'll see that there is common sense in the idea of "red wine with red meat," but because of the wine's tannin, not its color.

tlety of my beloved grape is something I want to showcase and not clobber with overpowering food flavors. So I have some general pairing rules when it comes to Pinot Noir, universal "Pinot Principles," as well as region-specific pairing pointers.

First, the universal pairing principles:

- Pinot Noir is a home-run match with earthy ingredients, including mushrooms and truffles as well as potatoes, beets, and other root vegetables

- Pinot Noir is fabulous with richer fish such as salmon and tuna

- Pinot Noir is wonderful with poultry, from a perfect roast chicken, to duck, to game birds

The region-specific pairing pointers showcase the body and fruit flavor profile of each of the main Pinot Noir regions, as follows:

Burgundy, France. In cool or average years, the fruit flavor is of dried cranberry and red currant, while in the best vintages Burgundy achieves amazing ripe raspberry and black cherry fruit flavor. But because Burgundy's subtleties are so alluring, I keep food matches simple so as not to overpower them. That means simple roasted or seared meats and fish, the earthy flavors of mushrooms and beets to showcase the wine's earthiness, or subtle, firm cheeses that harmonize without overpowering. And of course boeuf bourguignonne is the classic match for Burgundy.

Oregon. These Pinots often have a sweet-savory tomato paste, strawberry-rhubarb character that goes wonderfully with fresh and dried herbs such as thyme, oregano, and marjoram. I also like smoked foods with this style, and Pacific Northwest salmon is a classic match.

New Zealand and California. Both of these regions usually get riper flavors of raspberry and black cherry, laced with a sweet scent like cherry Lifesavers or cola syrup. Those sweetish elements, and the fuller body of these wines, sets them up to handle more assertive fare. For example, I love these wines with the Asian flavors of five spice powder, hoisin, fermented black beans, and teriyaki. They're also great with richer meats like short ribs, lamb, and venison.

Because Burgundy is rare and pretty pricey, you'll see in the recipes that follow that for everyday dinner I look to the other Pinot zones for more affordable options, and there are plenty. But I've got some splurge recipes and wines, too, because Pinot Noir really is worth it!

WARM WILD MUSHROOM SALAD WITH BLACK TRUFFLE VINAIGRETTE

SERVES SIX • This special match brings out the best in both the wine and the food. The tender texture of the mushrooms and their earthy, truffly perfume mirror the succulence of the Pinot Noir fruit, and its earthy-animal scent. I love to start dinner parties with this dish, because it's so impressive guests can't help but get excited about what's to come. The fragrances and textures heighten everyone's senses, so I know that they will enjoy the rest of the pairings to the utmost. (A side note: Vintage Champagne is also a stellar pairing with this dish—no surprise as it's made with a healthy proportion of Pinot Noir, and receives extra bottle age, which gives it a mushroomy fragrance, too. If you want to make this match, try Charles Heidsieck or Pommery vintage Champagne.)

Wild mushrooms may be difficult to find and are expensive. If you'd like, you may substitute any combination of shiitake, button, and cremini mushrooms for some or all of the wild mushrooms, depending on availability and your budget.

WINE RECOMMENDATIONS

BURGUNDY, FRANCE

Bouchard Savigny-Les-Beaune Les Lavières, Tollot-Beaut Aloxe-Corton

OREGON

Argyle Cellars, Chehalem

CALIFORNIA

Pepperwood Grove, BV Coastal, Cambria, Marimar Torres

2 tablespoons sherry vinegar

1½ teaspoons balsamic vinegar

½ teaspoon Dijon mustard

1 tablespoon black truffle juice, optional

¼ cup white or black truffle oil

Kosher salt

Freshly ground black pepper

1 teaspoon unsalted butter

1 pound fresh wild mushrooms, or 1 pound any combination shiitake, button, or cremini mushrooms, wiped clean, tough stems trimmed, and thinly sliced

1 small shallot, peeled and finely chopped

2 tablespoons finely chopped fresh chives

½ pound (about 8 cups) mixed baby lettuces, washed and dried

1. Whisk together the sherry vinegar, balsamic vinegar, mustard, and truffle juice in a small bowl. Slowly whisk in the truffle oil. The emulsified vinaigrette should be thick enough to coat the back of a spoon. If too thick, whisk in more truffle juice or some water, drop by drop, to achieve this consistency. Season to taste with salt and pepper.

2. Melt the butter on medium heat in a medium skillet until it foams. Add the mushrooms and shallot and cook, stirring, until warmed through and slightly tender, 3 to 4 minutes. Transfer to a mixing bowl, add half of the chives, and toss with half of the vinaigrette to coat. Season with salt and pepper to taste and cover to keep warm while preparing greens.

3. In a large bowl, toss the greens with the remaining vinaigrette and chives, and distribute among 6 salad plates. Top with the warm wild mushrooms and serve immediately.

OVEN-ROASTED FENNEL

SERVES FOUR • If you want an example of how roasting can transform a vegetable into a great wine partner, here it is. Just trim and chop the fennel, toss it with olive oil and thyme (wine's favorite herb), and bake. During roasting, the strong licorice flavor of the raw fennel mellows into a wonderful savory sweetness that dances beautifully with the cherry-cola flavors of Sonoma Pinot.

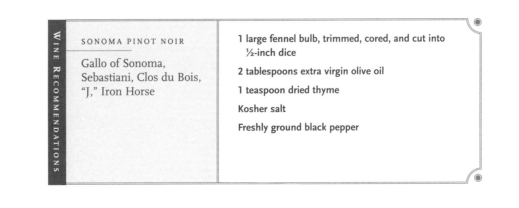

WINE RECOMMENDATIONS

SONOMA PINOT NOIR

Gallo of Sonoma,
Sebastiani, Clos du Bois,
"J," Iron Horse

1 large fennel bulb, trimmed, cored, and cut into
½-inch dice

2 tablespoons extra virgin olive oil

1 teaspoon dried thyme

Kosher salt

Freshly ground black pepper

Preheat the oven to 375°F. Combine the fennel, oil, thyme, salt, and pepper to taste in a large bowl and toss to coat. Place the fennel on a rimmed baking sheet and roast, stirring occasionally, until the fennel is tender, about 40 minutes. Serve immediately.

Shiraz-Poached Pears with Roquefort
and Black Pepper, page 187

Summer Tomato Salad, page 58

Lobster with Smoked Mozzarella Sauce and
Confetti Vegetables, page 89

Pear, Fennel, and Blue Cheese Salad
with Red Wine Glaze, page 221

Roasted Oysters "Rockefeller
Center," page 116

Lemon-Herb-Prosciutto Shrimp,
page 201

Crispy Artichokes and Squid,
page 231

Herbed Scallop and Potato "Napoleons"
with Truffle Oil, page 92

Wasabi Pea–Crusted Salmon,
page 121

Apple, Sage, and Onion Soup with
Cheddar-Bacon Croutons, page 36

Rosemary and Sweet Garlic
Roast Chicken, page 171

Warm Wild Mushroom Salad with
Black Truffle Vinaigrette, page 132

Sirloin Steak with "Beurre-Naise"
Sauce, page 173

Honey- and Lavender-Glazed Fruit,
page 244

Tarte Tatin with Bourbon
and Vanilla, page 254

Cool Balsamic and Black Pepper Strawberries with Warm Toasted Mozzarella Flatbread, page 219

LIGHTENED-UP "CREAMED" SPINACH

SERVES FOUR • John and I love the fresh, earthy taste of spinach, but I'm always cognizant of its texture when matching with wine. Often spinach leaves a drying sensation on your tongue that's similar to the tannin texture of red wine. I think that's why richly creamed spinach is a steakhouse staple—the cream counters the tannins in the spinach and in all the big, tannic reds being served. I wanted a way to get that taste experience, without all the calorie and fat overload. John developed this easy version. It's worth the extra buck or so for the bags of pre-washed baby spinach, whose tender texture requires just a splash of cream to give the desired result (and there are no tough stems to remove, so the dish is quick to prepare). The suppler tannins in Pinot Noir are a great match here since the dish is less fatty than typical creamed spinach. Do not return the pan to the heat once you add the half-and-half—it will curdle. You can also skip the half-and-half in this dish altogether—voilà—sautéed instead of creamed.

<table>
<tr><td rowspan="2">WINE RECOMMENDATIONS</td><td>FRENCH BURGUNDY

Bouchard Bourgogne La Vignée, Groffier Bourgogne, Nicolas Potel Pommard</td><td rowspan="2">Three 9-ounce bags baby spinach

1 tablespoon unsalted butter

1 tablespoon olive oil

1 medium shallot, finely minced

Kosher salt and freshly ground black pepper

Freshly ground nutmeg

1/3 cup half-and-half</td></tr>
<tr><td>OREGON PINOT NOIR

Willamette Valley Vineyards, Sokol-Blosser, Ken Wright</td></tr>
</table>

1. Bring a large pot of water to a rolling boil. Fill a large mixing bowl with cold water and ice. Blanch the spinach in the boiling water in batches, about half a bag at a time, for one minute. Use tongs to remove the spinach to the ice bath to stop the cooking, and then lift the spinach into a colander to drain. Repeat until all the spinach is blanched.

2. Squeeze the spinach hard with your hands to remove as much water as possible. Place the spinach on a cutting board, chop it roughly, and set aside. Heat the butter and olive oil in a large skillet over medium-high until the butter foams. Reduce the heat to medium, add the shallots and cook, stirring, until the shallot softens and begins to brown, 2 to 3 minutes. Add the spinach and season with salt, pepper, and nutmeg to taste. Cook, stirring, until ingredients are combined and the spinach is heated through. Remove from the heat and add the half-and-half, stirring to combine well. Serve immediately.

FETTUCCINE WITH PROSCIUTTO, WILD MUSHROOMS, AND SAGE

SERVES FOUR AS A MAIN COURSE OR SIX AS AN APPETIZER • This recipe is wonderfully adaptable to the seasons. In the spring, I love to add fresh, barely cooked peas or asparagus tips to the skillet along with the cooked pasta. Chunks of diced, roasted butternut or hubbard squash are a wonderful fall addition.

If shiitake mushrooms are unavailable, cremini or button mushrooms may be substituted. Sliced-to-order Italian prosciutto is quite expensive, but in this case the more affordable presliced packaged prosciutto sold in supermarkets works just fine. All of the earthy-heady flavors here call for one of the gamier, barnyardy New World Pinot Noirs. That style isn't specific to a region, but rather to certain producers, including those suggested here.

WINE RECOMMENDATIONS

GAMY NEW WORLD PINOT NOIR

Firesteed, Calera Central Coast, Au Bon Climat, Ponzi

1½ cups vegetable broth, chicken broth, or water

1 ounce dried mushrooms, preferably porcinis or morels

½ pound fresh shiitake mushrooms (button or cremini mushrooms may be substituted)

3 ounces thinly sliced prosciutto

8 to 10 fresh sage leaves

Kosher salt

1 tablespoon extra virgin olive oil

4 tablespoons unsalted butter

1 teaspoon sherry vinegar

8 ounces dried fettuccine

Freshly ground black pepper

1. In a small saucepan, bring the broth to a boil and remove from the heat. Place the dried mushrooms in a heatproof bowl and pour the boiling broth over them. Let stand to soften, about 30 minutes. Drain the dried mushrooms, squeezing out excess liquid and reserving the liquid. Strain the mushroom liquid through a fine sieve lined with a coffee filter, and place it in a small saucepan on medium heat. Simmer until reduced by half, and keep warm. Rinse the reconstituted dried mushrooms to remove any grit, pat dry with paper towels, and chop fine. Transfer to a small bowl and set aside.

2. While the mushrooms are soaking, trim the tough stems from the shiitake mushrooms. Cut into ½-inch slices and set aside. Slice the prosciutto and the sage leaves

into thin slivers, place in small bowls, cover with plastic wrap, and refrigerate until ready to use.

3. Add 1 tablespoon of salt and 1 teaspoon of the olive oil to a large pot filled with 4 quarts of water. Bring to a boil.

4. While the water is coming to a boil, heat 1 tablespoon of the butter and the remaining 2 teaspoons olive oil on medium-high until bubbling. Add the fresh mushrooms and cook, stirring frequently, for 3 minutes. Add the sherry vinegar and chopped dried mushrooms and cook an additional 2 minutes. Remove from the heat and set aside to cool.

5. Add the fettuccine to the pot of boiling water and cook until al dente according to package directions. While the pasta is cooking, finish the sauce.

6. In a skillet large enough to hold the cooked pasta and the mushroom mixture, melt the remaining 3 tablespoons butter on low. Add the prosciutto and sage strips, stir, and remove from the heat. Drain the pasta, reserving 1 cup of the hot cooking liquid, and add the pasta to the skillet along with the mushrooms and warm mushroom liquid. Return the skillet to medium heat and add the reserved hot pasta cooking water. Stir briefly until well combined and heated through. Season to taste with salt and pepper, and serve immediately in warmed pasta bowls or on deep, rimmed plates.

PEARL BARLEY RISOTTO WITH MUSHROOMS AND CARROTS

SERVES SIX • Barley is a great substitute for risotto, especially when you don't have a lot of time to spend stirring the pot. Unlike risotto, which requires constant attention, with barley you can just add the liquid, cook, and give it an occasional stir. It's a little nuttier and chewier, all the better to pair it with the earthy-style Pinot Noirs from Oregon and from the Côte Chalonnaise district of Burgundy, whose mushroomy character echoes the earthy dried and fresh mushrooms.

WINE RECOMMENDATIONS

OREGON PINOT NOIR

King Estate, Rex Hill, Erath, Benton Lane

CÔTE CHALONNAISE BURGUNDY

Joblot Givry, Mercurey "Perdrix," Juillot Mercurey

---

1 ounce dried shiitake mushrooms

1 tablespoon olive oil

1 large onion, chopped

3 medium carrots, peeled and diced (about 1 cup)

1 medium shallot, chopped

6 ounces coarsely chopped button mushrooms

½ cup dry white wine

1½ teaspoons dried thyme

1 cup pearl barley

3 cups canned low-sodium chicken or vegetable broth

3 tablespoons chopped fresh parsley

½ cup grated Manchego or Parmesan cheese

Kosher salt

Freshly ground black pepper

---

1. Place the dried mushrooms in a heatproof bowl and pour 2 cups of boiling water over them. Let stand to soften, about 30 minutes. Line a small strainer with a coffee filter, and strain the mushroom liquid through the filter and into a bowl or measuring cup. Squeeze the mushrooms to extract any excess liquid and strain into the container and reserve. Rinse the reconstituted dried mushrooms under running water to remove any grit, pat dry with paper towels, and chop fine. Set aside.

2. Heat the oil in a large, heavy stockpot over medium heat. Add the onion, carrots, and shallot and sauté 5 minutes. Add the button mushrooms and sauté until tender and beginning to brown, about 10 minutes. Add the chopped dried shiitakes, wine,

thyme, and barley, stirring until the wine is nearly evaporated. Add the broth and 1 cup of the reserved mushroom liquid and bring to a boil. Reduce the heat to medium-low and simmer, stirring occasionally, until the liquid is almost completely absorbed and the barley is almost tender, about 25 minutes. Add the remaining 1 cup mushroom broth and cook, stirring, until the barley is tender and creamy, about 5 minutes. Stir in the chopped parsley and cheese, season with salt and pepper, and serve.

CRISPY CHICKEN AND SHALLOT HASH

SERVES FOUR • John and I had fun "engineering" this recipe—he wanted crispy-yet-moist shredded chicken, I wanted a method whose required effort and turnaround time were realistic for everyday dinner. So we turned to another brilliant technique courtesy of the great chef Jean-Georges Vongerichten, who cooks chicken breasts on top of the stove in a tightly sealed foil pouch. The building heat and pressure cause the chicken to cook very quickly (don't worry, there's no danger of an explosion!), freeing up the extra time needed to shred the chicken and crisp it in the pan with the other ingredients. I contributed the idea of brining the chicken to speed up cooking and to keep it super-moist. John calibrated the mushroom, shallot, and thyme flavors precisely to showcase the elegance and mushroomy earthiness of his all-time favorite wine style—French red Burgundy. We have enjoyed this dish with varietal Pinot Noirs from the Carneros and Central Coast regions of California, too. And for a value choice, Beaujolais Cru, a French Burgundy wine based on the Gamay grape, has a similar earthiness and silky body style to our beloved Pinot Noir, as well as mouthwatering berry fruit.

WINE RECOMMENDATIONS		
BURGUNDY, FRANCE Faiveley Mercurey, Louis Jadot Santenay Clos de Malte, Philippe LeClerc Gevrey-Chambertin **CALIFORNIA** Acacia, Saintsbury Garnet, Kent Rasmussen (Carneros) Morgan, La Crema, Chalone (Central Coast)	**BEAUJOLAIS CRU** Georges Duboeuf Moulin-a-Vent, Jacky Janodet Morgon	½ cup packed brown sugar ½ cup kosher salt, plus more for seasoning 4 boneless, skinless chicken breast halves 6 tablespoons plus 2 teaspoons olive oil 4 medium shallots, sliced Freshly ground black pepper 1 bay leaf, broken 1 teaspoon whole peppercorns 2 teaspoons unsalted butter ½ pound shiitake mushrooms, tough stems trimmed, thinly sliced 1 cup white wine (leftover is fine) 1 tablespoon finely chopped fresh thyme, or 1 teaspoon dried thyme

1. Combine the brown sugar, salt, and 2 cups of hot water in a large bowl. Whisk to dissolve the sugar and salt. Add 3 cups cold water and stir to combine. Place the

chicken breast halves in a single layer in a large, nonreactive baking dish. Pour the brine over the chicken, cover with plastic wrap, and refrigerate for at least 3 hours or overnight.

2. Cut 4 pieces of aluminum foil, each measuring 18 inches square. Place one piece on top of another to make a double layer of foil for one package. Repeat with the remaining foil to make a second double-layered package.

3. Remove the breasts from the brine and pat dry with paper towels. Brush 1 tablespoon olive oil on the center of each foil square, making a patch large enough for 2 chicken breast halves to lie side-by-side. Scatter 2 slices of shallot on each patch of oil. Lay two chicken breast halves side-by-side atop shallots; sprinkle with salt and pepper. Scatter the bay leaf pieces and peppercorns over each set of breast halves.

4. Fold the foil over the chicken onto itself and then crimp the edges as tightly as possible by making 1- or 2-inch folds, one after the other, each sealing the other. Seal the packages very tightly, but leave plenty of room around the chicken. (Chicken packets may be prepared up to 3 hours before cooking and refrigerated until ready to use.)

5. Place 2 skillets large enough to hold 1 package each over high heat. Heat for 1 minute. Add 2 tablespoons olive oil to each skillet, swirl the oil around the bottom of the pans, and then pour off all but a film of oil. Place one package in each skillet (the oil will sizzle). In about 2 minutes, the packages will blow up like balloons; be careful of escaping steam. Cook 5 minutes longer.

6. Remove the packages from the pans very carefully to avoid escaping steam. Let rest for 1 minute, then cut a slit down the length of each packet with a knife. Use a knife and fork to open up the package. Remove the shallots, which will be caramelized, from beneath the chicken to a small bowl. Let the chicken breasts stand in the opened foil to cool slightly.

7. Heat 1 teaspoon of the butter and 1 teaspoon of olive oil in a large skillet. Add the shiitake mushrooms and cook, stirring occasionally, until tender and lightly browned, 5 to 7 minutes, adding ½ cup of the wine after 3 minutes. Season with salt and pepper and stir in the thyme. Remove the pan from the heat and set aside.

8. Shred the chicken breasts with the grain. Heat the remaining teaspoon of olive oil and the remaining teaspoon of butter in a large skillet over medium-high heat. Add the remaining wine and the shredded chicken and sauté until the wine is evaporated, and the chicken is crisp and brown. Stir in the shallots and shiitakes. Warm through and serve.

GRILLED DUCK BREAST WITH RED WINE REDUCTION

SERVES FOUR • Duck breasts are notoriously fatty, which gives them great flavor and juiciness, but makes them tricky to cook. Grilling is a great way to cook them to perfection, giving them a little smoky flavor without filling the house with smoke. Leaving just a narrow strip of skin and fat on the breasts will give you a deliciously crackly piece of duck skin while avoiding grill flame-ups. A simple reduction of red wine and chicken stock increases the duck breasts' succulent texture—the key to its affinity to the silky-textured Pinot Noir. Dried cherries in the sauce are a classic with duck, and great with the cherry flavor of Pinot, but are optional.

WINE RECOMMENDATIONS

NEW ZEALAND PINOT NOIR

Allan Scott, Brancott Reserve, Martinborough

CALIFORNIA PINOT NOIR

Buena Vista, Wild Horse, Dehlinger, Marimar Torres

1 cup chicken stock or canned low-sodium chicken broth

1 cup Pinot Noir (leftover is fine)

1 small shallot, finely chopped

⅓ cup dried cherries, optional

2 whole boneless duck breasts (about 12 ounces each)

Kosher salt

Freshly ground black pepper

1 teaspoon finely chopped fresh sage leaves

1 teaspoon finely chopped fresh thyme leaves

1. Combine the stock, wine, shallot, and cherries, if using, in a small saucepan and bring to a boil. Cook at a lively simmer until the sauce is reduced by half and thickened, 15 to 20 minutes. (The sauce may be made up to 1 day in advance, refrigerated, and reheated before serving.)

2. Preheat the grill to medium-high. Split each duck breast into 2 halves. With a sharp chef's knife, trim away any overhanging skin and fat. Slide your fingers between the skin and breast meat on either side of the breast to loosen both edges of the skin, leaving a strip of skin about 2 inches wide attached to each breast half. Trim away the loosened fat and skin so that only the 2-inch-wide strip remains on each breast.

3. Sprinkle the breast halves on both sides with salt and pepper. Place on the grill, skin side down, and grill, covered, until well browned, about 8 minutes. Turn and continue to grill, covered, until medium rare, 3 to 4 minutes longer.

4. Remove the breasts from the grill, cover loosely with foil, and let stand 5 minutes to rest. Stir the sage and thyme into the sauce and rewarm if necessary. Slice each breast and fan it out on a dinner plate. Serve immediately with sauce on the side.

SHALLOT- AND THYME-RUBBED ROAST TURKEY

SERVES TWELVE • A paste made from sweet roasted garlic, shallots, thyme, and mustard, rubbed between the skin and the meat of the turkey, keeps the bird moist and infuses it with Pinot-loving flavor. The paste's earthy-sweetness complements the earth and fruit of French Burgundies and Oregon Pinot Noirs, while the cut of mustard echoes their firm acidity. This is a great Thanksgiving dinner centerpiece, but I make it other times, too. Going to college in football-frenzied Dallas, my buddies' tailgate roast turkey tradition taught me that it's a festive, simple, wine-friendly dinner for a crowd.

8 medium shallots, peeled and quartered

8 garlic cloves, peeled

6 tablespoons olive oil

2 tablespoons finely chopped fresh thyme leaves

2 tablespoons Dijon mustard

½ teaspoon kosher salt

½ teaspoon freshly ground black pepper

One 15- to 16-pound turkey, neck, gizzard, and heart reserved

1 large onion, coarsely chopped

2 celery stalks, coarsely chopped

2 sprigs fresh thyme

2½ cups dry white wine

5 cups canned low-sodium chicken broth, or more if necessary

2 pounds mushrooms, thickly sliced

⅓ cup Wondra flour

1. Preheat the oven to 350°F. Place the shallots and garlic in a small ovenproof baking dish and drizzle with the olive oil. Cover the dish with foil and bake until the shallots are very tender but not brown, about 1 hour. Uncover and cool 30 minutes. Place the shallots, garlic, and oil in the workbowl of a food processor. Add the chopped thyme, mustard, salt, and pepper. Process until almost smooth. Transfer the paste to a small bowl. (Shallot paste can be covered with plastic wrap and refrigerated for up to 4 days.)

2. Position the oven rack in the bottom third of the oven. If necessary, preheat the oven to 350°F. Rinse the turkey inside and out with cold running water and pat dry. Starting at the neck end, carefully slide your hand between the skin and breast to

loosen the skin. Spread ½ cup of the shallot paste under the skin and over the breast meat. Tuck the wings underneath the body of the turkey and tie the legs together loosely with kitchen twine or dental floss so that the turkey will hold its shape. Place the turkey on a small wire rack set inside a large roasting pan. Spread ½ cup of the shallot paste all over the outside of the turkey, reserving the remaining paste for the gravy. Place the reserved turkey neck, gizzard, and heart and the onion, celery, and thyme sprigs in the pan around the turkey. Bring 1 cup of the wine and 2 cups of the broth to a boil in a medium saucepan. Pour the boiling liquid into the bottom of the roasting pan.

3. Cover the breast loosely with foil, and place the turkey in the oven. Roast for 1½ hours. Add 1 cup of broth and 1 cup of wine to the pan and roast the turkey another 30 minutes. Remove the foil, and add 1 cup broth to the pan. Continue roasting until an instant-read thermometer inserted in the thickest part of the thigh registers 175 degrees, another 1 to 1½ hours. During roasting, cover the exposed parts of the turkey with foil as needed to prevent overbrowning, and add more broth if the pan juices evaporate. Remove the turkey from the oven and transfer to a platter. Tent the turkey loosely with foil and allow to rest 30 minutes (the internal temperature will rise another 5 to 10 degrees).

4. While the turkey is resting, prepare the gravy: Discard the neck, gizzard, and heart and strain the juices from the roasting pan into a bowl, pressing hard on the solids and scraping up any browned bits. Spoon the fat from the top of the juices, reserving 2 tablespoons of fat, or use a gravy separator (available in housewares and kitchen supply stores) to separate the fat from the juices. Strain the juices into a large heatproof measuring cup. Add the remaining ½ cup of wine and enough chicken broth to the turkey pan juices to measure 5 cups.

5. Heat the reserved 2 tablespoons turkey fat in a heavy large pot over medium-high heat. Add the mushrooms and sauté until the mushrooms brown and the juices evaporate, about 18 minutes. Mix in the remaining shallot paste. Gradually sprinkle in the flour, stirring continuously to incorporate, until the flour begins to brown, about 2 minutes. Gradually whisk in the 5 cups of broth mixture. Bring to a boil, scraping up the browned bits. Boil until the gravy coats a spoon lightly, about 8 minutes; season to taste with salt and pepper. Carve the turkey and serve, passing the gravy in a gravy boat.

SEARED PORK TENDERLOIN WITH DRIED FIG AND MUSHROOM SAUCE

SERVES FOUR • This complex-tasting but easy sauce is tailor-made for Pinot Noir. The figs mirror the wine's tender black cherry fruit; the shallots, mushrooms, and thyme its earthiness. The lightness of the sauce, and of pork tenderloin, is in perfect balance with the Pinot's overall delicacy. Demi-glace, a heavily reduced stock that pros use to thicken and flavor sauces beautifully, is increasingly available in supermarkets. This is a dish that warrants the best Pinot you can pull off, either a French red Burgundy or one from the New World's earthier appellations: the Willamette Valley of Oregon or California's Santa Barbara County. If you want to impress a wine lover (or just a lover!), this match will do it. It's great with a bed of mashed Yukon gold potatoes or creamy polenta to soak up the sauce. A note on the shiitake mushrooms: The stems of smaller ones are usually tender enough that you need not remove them—just trim the ends.

WINE RECOMMENDATIONS

FRENCH RED BURGUNDY

Mercurey Le Perdrix, Marquis d'Angerville Volnay, Roumier Chambolle-Musigny, Domaine Dujac Morey-Saint-Denis

WILLAMETTE VALLEY, OREGON, PINOT NOIR

Ken Wright, Archery Summit, Panther Creek, Domaine Drouhin Oregon, Fiddlehead Cellars

SANTA BARBARA, CALIFORNIA, PINOT NOIR

Au Bon Climat, Testarossa, Sanford, Talley

VALUE CHOICES

Willamette Valley Vineyards Whole Berry (Oregon)

Robert Mondavi Private Selection, Echelon, Gallo of Sonoma (California)

½ ounce dried porcini mushrooms

1 cup boiling low-sodium chicken broth or water

2 tablespoons olive oil

3 tablespoons unsalted butter

½ pound shiitake mushrooms, wiped clean and tough stems removed

Kosher salt

Freshly ground black pepper

2 pork tenderloins, trimmed of fat and silverskin, about 1½ pounds

1 large shallot, finely chopped

1 cup red wine

4 dried figs, stemmed and finely chopped

1 tablespoon finely chopped fresh thyme, or 1 teaspoon dried thyme

2 tablespoons veal, duck, or beef demi-glace, optional

Red wine vinegar

1. Place the dried mushrooms in a heatproof bowl and pour the boiling broth over them. Let stand to soften, about 30 minutes. Line a small strainer with a coffee filter, and strain the mushroom liquid through the filter and into a bowl or measuring cup. Squeeze the mushrooms to extract any excess liquid and strain into the container and reserve. Rinse the reconstituted dried mushrooms to remove any grit, pat dry with paper towels, and finely chop.

2. Heat ½ tablespoon of the olive oil and ½ tablespoon of the butter in a medium skillet over medium-high heat. Add the shiitakes and cook until they release their juices and are tender and lightly browned, about 5 minutes. Season with salt and pepper, remove from heat, and set aside.

3. In a large skillet, heat 1 tablespoon of the olive oil and 1 tablespoon of the butter over medium-high heat. Season the pork on all sides with salt and pepper. Add it to the pan and sear, turning it to brown on all sides, 3 to 4 minutes. Reduce the heat to medium, cover, and cook until medium-rare and the internal temperature is 145 to 150 degrees, 10 to 12 minutes. Transfer to a warmed platter and loosely cover with foil to keep warm.

4. Heat the remaining ½ tablespoon olive oil and ½ tablespoon of the butter in a small saucepan over medium heat. Add the shallot and cook until softened, about 5 minutes. Add the wine, reserved mushroom liquid, and chopped figs, bring to a boil, and reduce by half.

5. Add the wine reduction to the skillet used to cook the pork. Bring to a boil, scraping the pan with a wooden spoon to remove any brown bits. Stir in the thyme and demi-glace, if desired. Remove the pan from the heat and swirl in the remaining tablespoon of butter. Add a few drops of vinegar and season with salt and pepper.

6. Cut the pork into 1-inch-thick medallions and return them to the pan to heat through.

7. Briefly return the pan with the mushrooms to the heat to warm.

8. Divide the medallions among 4 dinner plates. Spoon fig and mushroom sauce on top of the medallions and top each portion with a spoonful of shiitakes.

JOHN'S FIRST-DATE SALMON FILLETS

SERVES TWO • The truth is this dish matches beautifully with any red wine, but Pinot Noir—specifically a French red Burgundy—was the match that stole my heart on the first he-cooks-dinner date, and remains our sentimental favorite. The dish is impressive, simple, and fast—allowing you to focus on the date, the wine, or both, as the case may be. This recipe features main-course-sized portions, but John served smaller (4-ounce) portions in a "grazing" menu of many courses, where we cooked, sampled, then cooked some more—it's a wonderfully improvisational, low-pressure, eat-in-the-kitchen program that we've stuck with because it's easy, and brings us back to the thrill of that first date every time.

<table>
<tr><td rowspan="2" style="writing-mode: vertical;">WINE RECOMMENDATIONS</td><td>CALIFORNIA PINOT NOIR</td><td>FRENCH RED BURGUNDY</td><td rowspan="2">¾ pound center-cut salmon fillet, 1 inch thick

1 tablespoon olive oil, plus more for oiling the fish

Kosher salt

Freshly ground black pepper

1½ teaspoons dried thyme

1 tablespoon unsalted butter

Aged balsamic vinegar or Balsamic Vinegar Reduction (page 264), for drizzling</td></tr>
<tr><td>Morgan, Frei Brothers Reserve, Lynmar, Siduri</td><td>Bouchard Savigny-Les-Beaune, René Engel Nuits-St.-Georges, Jadot Santenay Clos de Malte, Domaine Leroy Nuits-St.-Georges</td></tr>
</table>

1. Cut the salmon fillet into two equal portions, and brush both sides of each piece with olive oil. Sprinkle the flesh side with salt, pepper, and the dried thyme.

2. In a large skillet, heat 1 tablespoon olive oil and the butter on medium-high until the butter foams. Carefully place the fillets flesh side down in the skillet. Cook the fish fillets without moving until the edges begin to crisp, about 2 minutes. Decrease the heat to medium and cook until the fillets are golden brown, about 1 minute more. Turn the fillets so they are skin side down and continue cooking until medium-rare and the skin is crisped, 5 to 7 minutes depending on their thickness, adding a few additional drops of olive oil as needed to prevent sticking. Remove the fillets to serving plates and drizzle with balsamic vinegar. Serve immediately.

MUSHROOM-DUSTED TUNA WITH BLACK BEAN–HOISIN SAUCE

SERVES FOUR • Mushroom "dust" is just dried mushrooms (porcinis or cèpes work best) that have been whirled to a dust in the blender. They're also delicious as a dust or crust for scallops, pork chops, or chicken breasts, or sprinkled lightly onto root vegetables before they go into the oven for roasting. And then there's my splurge-out special: Mushroom-Dusted Foie Gras (page 148). How's that for amazing versatility? However you use it, mushroom dust creates an instant, earthy embrace for Pinot Noir–based wines. I choose exotically ripe-tasting California Pinots with spicy oak to complement the sweet spiciness of the hoisin sauce.

WINE RECOMMENDATIONS

CALIFORNIA PINOT NOIR

Meridian, Estancia, Williams-Selyem, "J" Nicole's Vineyard, Morgan Gary's Vineyard, Château St. Jean, Belle Glos, Etude

2 cups homemade chicken stock or canned low-sodium chicken broth

2 cups Quick Mushroom Stock (page 268)

1¼ cups dry red wine

½ ounce dried porcini or cèpes mushrooms

Four 6-ounce tuna loin pieces, 1 inch thick

Kosher salt and freshly ground black pepper

4 tablespoons unsalted butter

2 tablespoons finely chopped shallots

2 tablespoons demi-glace, optional

1½ tablespoons Chinese fermented black beans, finely chopped

1½ tablespoons hoisin sauce

2 tablespoons finely chopped fresh thyme

1. Combine the chicken stock, mushroom stock, and 1 cup of the wine in a medium saucepan. Bring to a boil, reduce the heat to medium, and cook until reduced by three-quarters (to about 1¼ cups).

2. Place the dried mushrooms in a blender and blend to a fine dust. Pour the dust onto a flat plate and spread in a thin layer. Season the tuna pieces on both sides with salt and pepper. Press each side of each piece of tuna in the mushroom dust to lightly coat.

3. Heat 1½ tablespoons of butter in a large skillet over medium-high heat until foaming has subsided. Place the tuna pieces in the pan and cook without turning until

they are nicely seared and crisp on one side, 2 to 3 minutes. Turn the tuna pieces, reduce the heat to medium, and cook until the tuna is medium-rare, 3 to 4 minutes, or to taste. Remove the fillets to a platter and loosely cover with aluminum foil to keep warm.

4. Add ½ tablespoon butter and the shallots to the pan and cook, stirring, until softened and slightly browned, 1 to 2 minutes. Add the remaining ¼ cup red wine and deglaze the pan, scraping the brown bits from the bottom of the pan. Add the stock and wine reduction and the demi-glace, if using, and bring to a boil. Boil until slightly thickened, 1 to 2 minutes. Whisk in the black beans and hoisin and boil another minute. Remove from the heat, stir in the thyme, and swirl in the remaining 2 tablespoons butter to thicken the sauce. Season with salt and pepper to taste. Place the tuna pieces on serving plates, pour the sauce over, and serve immediately.

Everyday Dinners with
PINOT NOIR

PASTAS AND OTHER ONE-PLATE DINNERS

WHAT TO COOK	WINE PAIRINGS
Fettuccine with Prosciutto, Wild Mushrooms, and Sage *(page 136)*, spinach salad	ONCE-A-WEEK ($–$$): Firesteed Pinot Noir (Oregon) Calera Central Coast Pinot Noir (California) ONCE-A-MONTH ($$$ AND UP): Ponzi Pinot Noir (Oregon)
Pearl Barley Risotto with Mushrooms and Carrots *(page 138)*, bacon crumbles, green salad	ONCE-A-WEEK ($–$$): King Estate Pinot Noir (Oregon) Erath Pinot Noir (Oregon) ONCE-A-MONTH ($$$ AND UP): Mercurey "Perdrix" (Burgundy, France)

TRADITIONAL (MAIN-AND-SIDES) DINNERS

WHAT TO COOK	WINE PAIRINGS
MAIN COURSE: grilled pork loin VEGGIES: Warm Wild Mushroom Salad with Black Truffle Vinaigrette *(page 132)* STARCHES, ETC.: Roasted Fingerling Frites *(page 168)*	ONCE-A-WEEK ($–$$): Pepperwood Grove Pinot Noir (California) Argyle Pinot Noir (Oregon) ONCE-A-MONTH ($$$ AND UP): Bouchard Savigny-Les-Beaune Les Lavières (Burgundy, France)
MAIN COURSE: Chicken Breasts with Prosciutto and Sage *(page 227)* VEGGIES: Oven-Roasted Fennel *(page 134)* STARCHES, ETC.: couscous	ONCE-A-WEEK ($–$$): Gallo of Sonoma Pinot Noir (California) Clos du Bois Pinot Noir (California) ONCE-A-MONTH ($$$ AND UP): Iron Horse Pinot Noir (California)
MAIN COURSE: Crispy Chicken and Shallot Hash *(page 140)* VEGGIES: Roasted Root Vegetables with Oregano *(page 105)* STARCHES, ETC.: buttered egg noodles	ONCE-A-WEEK ($–$$): Saintsbury Garnet Pinot Noir (California) Acacia Pinot Noir (California) ONCE-A-MONTH ($$$ AND UP): Philippe LeClerc Gevrey-Chambertin (Burgundy, France)

WHAT TO COOK	WINE PAIRINGS
MAIN COURSE: Rosemary and Sweet Garlic Roast Chicken *(page 171)* VEGGIES: Garlic-Braised Collard Greens *(page 189)* STARCHES, ETC.: Oven-Crisped Red Potatoes with Thyme and Pumpkinseed Oil *(page 35)*	ONCE-A-WEEK ($–$$): Bouchard Bourgogne La Vignée Pinot Noir (Burgundy, France) Willamette Valley Vineyards Pinot Noir (Oregon) ONCE-A-MONTH ($$$ AND UP): Sokol-Blosser Pinot Noir (Oregon)
MAIN COURSE: Grilled Duck Breast with Red Wine Reduction *(page 142)* VEGGIES: Wine-Braised Leeks *(page 167)* STARCHES, ETC.: mashed potatoes	ONCE-A-WEEK ($–$$): Allan Scott Pinot Noir (New Zealand) Buena Vista Pinot Noir (California) ONCE-A-MONTH ($$$ AND UP): Brancott Reserve Pinot Noir (New Zealand)
MAIN COURSE: Shallot- and Thyme-Rubbed Roast Turkey *(page 144)* VEGGIES: Roasted Brussels Sprouts with Garlic and Sage *(page 165)* STARCHES, ETC.: Sweet Potato Puree with Garlic, Thyme, and Balsamic Vinegar *(page 166)*	ONCE-A-WEEK ($–$$): Nicolas Potel Santenay (Burgundy, France) Duck Pond Pinot Noir (Oregon) ONCE-A-MONTH ($$$ AND UP): Cristom Pinot Noir (Oregon)
MAIN COURSE: John's First-Date Salmon Fillets *(page 150)* VEGGIES: Oven-Charred Asparagus with Cheese and Balsamic Vinegar *(page 190)* STARCHES, ETC.: crusty bread	ONCE-A-WEEK ($–$$): Morgan Pinot Noir (California) Frei Brothers Reserve Pinot Noir (California) ONCE-A-MONTH ($$$ AND UP): Domaine Leroy Nuits-St.-Georges (Burgundy, France)
MAIN COURSE: Mushroom-Dusted Tuna with Black Bean–Hoisin Sauce *(page 151)* VEGGIES: sautéed bok choy STARCHES, ETC.: soba noodles	ONCE-A-WEEK ($–$$): Meridian Pinot Noir (California) Estancia Pinot Noir (California) ONCE-A-MONTH ($$$ AND UP): Etude Pinot Noir (California)

Note: The Mushroom-Dusted Foie Gras from this chapter is a special splurge. I've included it in the Sparkling Soirée multicourse dinner-party menu (page 281). I once enjoyed the foie gras toasts as a one-plate meal, over salad greens slicked with extra virgin olive oil and seasoned with coarse salt. Wow!

chapter six

MERLOT AND
CABERNET SAUVIGNON

●

Merlot and Cabernet Sauvignon Info

HOME REGION
Bordeaux, France

———

OTHER GREAT MERLOT AND CABERNET SOURCES
California, Washington State, Chile, Australia

———

STYLE
Medium- to full-bodied; firm tannins

———

FLAVOR
Plums, dark berries (blueberry, blackberry), and figs

Back in 1990 I decided to leave my Wall Street career for the world of

wine. "What a leap!" my friends and family said. But actually the two worlds weren't so far apart. I put in the same long hours at Windows on the World that I did as a financial analyst. Most of our regulars were trader types who came to celebrate or commiserate, depending on the day's market performance. Every day I found myself discussing investments—not in blue chip stocks, but in blue chip wines—with my customers. And more often than not, our talk would turn to Cabernet and Merlot, the ultimate blue chips among wine grapes.

Collectors count on these grapes, like investors count on their shares in a utility company, to stand the test of time and to appreciate steadily in value. But as I tell any wine lover, Wall Street titan or not, wine is first and foremost an investment in pleasure. Sure, for some heavy hitters wine is a commodity, to be bought, cellared, and sold at auction for profit. But for most people the payoff in buying wine is in opening it and enjoying it. Although Cabernet Sauvignon and Merlot have reputations as "investment" wines, most of the bottles on the market are not expensive and are ready to drink right now. As you'll see from the recommendations and pairings in this chapter, you don't need a big-bucks budget and a cellar to enjoy them. These grapes deliver excellent quality and flavor at every price level, from steal to splurge.

Here's the lowdown on getting your pleasure dividends from Cabernet Sauvignon and Merlot, whose similar flavors and body styles dictate similar pairing approaches.

Bordeaux, the Ultimate Blue Chip

NEARLY EVERY MAJOR wine-producing country makes Merlots and Cabernets across the price spectrum. But the home base for these grapes—and the style model for all wines made from them, whether budget or boutique—

is the Bordeaux region of France. Bordeaux's wine fame is owed to its top-of-the-line boutique bottlings, which are called château wines—*château* is the region's traditional name for a wine estate. All of the great Cabernets and Merlots of the world are modeled after Bordeaux and are made using the same winemaking techniques to achieve its big, "blue chip red" style. These are the techniques and how they affect the style, and the price, of the wine:

Vineyard Location Affects the Fruit Intensity

As we explored with Pinot Noir in Chapter 5, vineyards with the best soil and location—whether at a top Bordeaux château or a prime spot in one of the New World's best growing regions—yield the best-quality grapes, with the greatest fruit and flavor concentration. The reputation of these wines puts them in high demand, and thus pushes up their price. The best vineyard sites in Bordeaux are labeled with the village name. Margaux, St.-Julien, Pauillac, St.-Estèphe, St.-Emilion, Pomerol, and Pessac-Léognan are the top towns. Less prestigious vineyard sites, usually labeled simply "Bordeaux," yield everyday styles, with prices to match.

Blending the Grapes Impacts the Wine's Flavor and the Amount of Tannin

In Bordeaux, Cabernet Sauvignon and Merlot wines are nearly always blended, with each other and/or the local red grapes Cabernet Franc, Malbec, and Petit Verdot. This practice, which adds complexity, is emulated worldwide for Cabernet Sauvignon and Merlot varietal wines. The dominant grape in the blend determines the fruit flavor and tannin level, as follows:

MOSTLY MERLOT. Plum and dark cherry fruit, medium body, big but smooth tannins, best wines capable of medium-term aging

MOSTLY CABERNET SAUVIGNON. Black currant, blackberry, and fig fruit, full body, gripping tannins, best wines capable of longer-term aging

The other blending grapes are used to add earthiness and fragrance (Cabernet Franc), spice (Malbec), and inky color (Petit Verdot).

It is easy to tell whether Cabernet or Merlot is the dominant grape in most varietal wines, because the wine will be named for that grape. But in Bordeaux, a particular grape dominates depending on the type of soil in a par-

MERITAGE—RHYMES WITH "HERITAGE"

Meritage is a term developed by the California wine industry to describe wine blends based on the Bordeaux grape varieties: Cabernet Sauvignon, Merlot, Cabernet Franc, Malbec, and Petit Verdot for reds; Sauvignon Blanc, Semillon, and Muscadelle for whites. It is used by some, though not all, wineries for blends that do not have the required minimum for varietal labeling, which is 75 percent of the named grape. Using this term gives wineries the flexibility to change their blends from one year to the next according to the fruit quality of that year's harvest. Some wineries apply this practice of blending but, instead of using the term *Meritage*, give their wines a proprietary name. Famous examples include Insignia, Opus One, and Dominus.

ticular village. Cabernet Sauvignon rules in Margaux, St.-Julien, Pauillac, and St.-Estèphe. Merlot does better in Pomerol and St.-Emilion. Pessac-Léognan is roughly an equal mix of the two. Wines simply labeled *Bordeaux* are usually dominated by Merlot. When it comes to price, supply and demand have more impact than the dominant grape in the blend. However, Cabernet wines do sometimes command higher prices than Merlots because their higher tannin levels and fuller body make them capable of longer aging.

Barrel Aging Gives the Wine "Oakiness"

As we've discussed in the context of other grapes, the amount of oakiness a wine will have depends on the fruit intensity of the grapes. The more intense the grapes, the oakier, and more expensive, the wine.

Merlot and Cabernet Sauvignon on the Fruit Flavor Spectrum

FROM THE PRECEDING fruit flavor descriptions of Merlot and Cabernet Sauvignon, you can see that these grapes generally inhabit the juicy and mouthwatering to ripe and exotic range of the red wine flavor spectrum, depending on whether they're grown in a moderate climate like Bordeaux, or in a warm climate

CABERNET (AND MERLOT) COMPATRIOTS: THE CABERNET FRANC, MALBEC, AND CARMENERE GRAPES

If you are looking for something new but similar to Merlot and Cabernet Sauvignon, check out these other originally-from-Bordeaux grape varieties whose family resemblance to Bordeaux's two big guns means they'll pair nicely with the dishes in this chapter.

CABERNET FRANC

I dearly love this grape, which is rare as a varietal on its own, but worth the search for its spicy mint-and-tobacco fragrance and elegance on the palate. Aside from a few specialty producers in California (recommended in these pages), the place to find it is the Loire Valley, where it is the dominant grape in the regionally named wines called Chinon and Bourgueil.

MALBEC

European immigrants brought this grape to Argentina, and now tango country has taken over Bordeaux as a Malbec specialist. It is similar in body and smoothness to Merlot, but with lots of smoky aromatic complexity.

CARMENERE

I love the story of this "lost and found" grape. It was "lost" to its original home of Bordeaux, where it fell out of favor compared to the other red grapes. At some point it was brought to Chile with European immigrants, and subsequently "lost" there to vineyards planted with the more-popular Merlot . . . Or so it was thought, until a French grape specialist recognized that much of what was planted in the Merlot vineyards was in fact the Carmenere grape after all. Although it hasn't been easy in the face of Merlot's popularity to introduce wine consumers to the previously unheard-of Carmenere, Chile has stuck with its serendipitous specialty, and I am thrilled! You will be, too, once you try it. The wine's smoky, heady, almost meaty-balsamic character is an absolute love letter to food.

like California's Napa Valley. As I've explained before, the fruit flavor in one region can vary from one year to the next depending on harvest weather. For example, even though Bordeaux's climate is moderate, in a fabulous (meaning warm and dry) vintage, the fruit flavor can get really intense and exotic.

But as with the other wines we've explored, there's more to the taste of Merlot and Cabernet Sauvignon than just fruit, and it's the subtle complexities in the wines' flavor that makes them such fun to pair. Specifically, both grapes share a flavor and scent characteristic that I love to showcase with food. It is really a family of flavors and scents that wine pros describe as "vegetal," meaning akin to vegetables and other plants. It's ironic, since we generally think of these wines as major meat partners. But those very vegetal notes, which can range from a hint of green pepper to scents of savory herbs or toasted coffee beans, let the wine serve as a "seasoning" for meat and cheese, while harmonizing beautifully with side dishes and sauces that either feature or are flavored by vegetables and herbs. Consequently, you'll see herbs and earthy vegetables such as mushrooms, potatoes, and other root vegetables making appearances in the recipes in this chapter.

Around the World and on the Table

HERE ARE THE other major sources of Merlot and Cabernet Sauvignon, and their flavor and pairing profiles:

Washington State's Columbia Valley. Many pros describe the Merlots and Cabernets from this region as being the most "Bordeaux-like," and I tend to agree. The region occupies about the same latitude as Bordeaux, but has more reliable, sunnier harvest weather. So you get some of the Bordeaux subtlety, yet New World fruit intensity, with flavors of huckleberries and black cherries, and lots of sweet spice—clove and cinnamon—from the oak barrels used. The vegetalness in these wines is subtle, too—hints of toasted coffee bean and tobacco that harmonize nicely with the sweet-savory taste of root vegetables and with the syrupy flavor of balsamic vinegar.

Chile. Chile is one of the great sources for Merlot and Cabernet Sauvignon, offering a lot of character for the money across the price spectrum. Along with deep plum and blackberry fruit, Chilean wines bring to the table a very distinctive herbal-smokiness that complements an incredible array of flavors, including the char of the grill, pungent cheeses, garlic, and savory herbs.

California. Merlot and Cabernet are grown successfully all over California, but the most famous regions for these grapes are Napa and Sonoma, where the fruit achieves incredible ripeness and intensity, plump velvety tannins, and layers of spice and earth. In the Merlots, the vegetal character comes through as a dusty earthiness that pairs beautifully with the earthy tastes of potatoes and mushrooms. In the Cabernets, the vegetal character includes notes of cedar, mint, and green pepper that match well with bitter greens, pungent herbs like thyme, basil, rosemary, and sage, and olives and garlic.

CABERNET, CHE BELLA!

In the last thirty years, Cabernet Sauvignon has been a growing force in Italy's Tuscany region, introduced there by winemakers who saw the grape's potential to improve the power and intensity of their Chiantis (which are based on the lighter Sangiovese grape). The results are excellent and, in some cases, awesome, with some Tuscan Cabernet-based wines—which go by the unofficial moniker "Super Tuscans"—easily the equal of top French Bordeaux and California Cabernets. *Magnifico!*

Australia. Because of its warm climate, Australia's Merlots and Cabernets tend to have some of the ripest flavors—blackberry and fig—and lots of sweet-scented, spicy oak to match all that fruit intensity. Australia also pioneered the blending of Cabernet Sauvignon with the Shiraz grape, a combo that consumers have embraced, and for good reason: The result is Cabernet Sauvignon fruit intensity together with Shiraz spiciness. These wines stand up to the "biggest" flavors—braised and grilled meat and game, pungent cheeses, olives, and rosemary.

If you're thinking that these wines sound like a meal-in-a-glass, you're right. I hope you're also thinking, "Time to get cooking!" If you're in a hurry, you could throw together the simple linguine recipe or the easy steak with "beurre-naise" in time for dinner tonight. When you have more time, these special grapes are fun to explore in depth. Check out the menus on pages 282 and 283, which are designed for just that: An all-Bordeaux menu that includes the whites and dessert wines from that region and an "Old World–New World" Cabernet menu to let you taste and compare.

SALAD OF FRESH FIGS WITH MANCHEGO, BALSAMIC VINEGAR, AND TOASTED PINE NUTS

SERVES SIX • The cheese softens the tannins of New World Cabernets and Merlots, the fig flavor mirrors their fruit, and the toasted nuts echo their oakiness. Bingo!

<table>
<tr><td rowspan="4" style="background:black;color:white">WINE RECOMMENDATIONS</td><td>NEW WORLD REDS</td><td>½ cup pine nuts</td></tr>
<tr><td>Kunde Merlot, Gallo of Sonoma Merlot (California)</td><td>1 pint ripe fresh figs, preferably black Mission</td></tr>
<tr><td>Casa Lapostolle Cuvée Alexandre Merlot (Chile)</td><td>3 ounces Manchego cheese

Aged balsamic vinegar or Balsamic Vinegar Reduction (page 264)</td></tr>
<tr><td>Penfolds Koonunga Hill Cabernet-Merlot (Australia)</td><td></td></tr>
</table>

1. Heat a small, dry skillet on medium and add the pine nuts. Cook, shaking the pan constantly, until they are fragrant and lightly browned, about 5 minutes. Remove to a plate and cool completely. Coarsely chop.

2. Remove the tough stems from the figs and cut them into quarters. Divide them among 6 salad plates. Sprinkle the chopped pine nuts over the figs. Use a vegetable peeler to shave the cheese over the figs and pine nuts. Drizzle with balsamic vinegar to taste. Serve immediately.

WILD MUSHROOM PHYLLO PURSES WITH PUMPKINSEED OIL DRIZZLE

MAKES SIX • The purses can be filled and formed one day ahead, up to the point of baking. Cover and refrigerate, then bake and garnish with pumpkinseed oil just before serving. These are great in a multicourse dinner-party menu, or as a light lunch or supper dish. Their earthy mushroomy flavor is fantastic with the earthiness (think autumn leaves) of Merlot- and Cabernet Franc–based wines from the Bordeaux region of France.

WINE RECOMMENDATIONS

FRENCH RED BORDEAUX

B&G Merlot, Château Tayac, Château Simard, Château Figeac

1 medium head garlic, unpeeled

4 large shallots, quartered

4 tablespoons olive oil

Kosher salt and freshly ground black pepper

½ pound cremini mushrooms, wiped clean with a paper towel

1 ounce dried mushrooms, preferably porcini

½ cup boiling beef broth, vegetable broth, or water

½ cup (1 stick) plus 1 tablespoon unsalted butter

½ pound button mushrooms, wiped clean with a paper towel, finely chopped

½ teaspoon dried thyme

Nine 17-x-13 sheets frozen phyllo dough, thawed

2 tablespoons plain dried bread crumbs

6 fresh chives

Pumpkinseed oil for drizzling

1. Preheat the oven to 375°F.

2. Make the filling: With a sharp knife, slice off top third of the garlic head, opposite the root end. Place the shallots and garlic, cut side up, on a 12-inch square of foil, drizzle with 3 tablespoons of the olive oil, and sprinkle with salt and pepper. Fold foil around the garlic to form a tightly sealed packet and bake until the garlic and shallots are soft and brown, about 1 hour. Remove from the oven and let cool completely inside the foil.

3. Meanwhile, trim any tough stems from the cremini mushrooms and place them in an ovenproof dish. Drizzle with remaining tablespoon olive oil, sprinkle lightly with salt and pepper, and cover with foil. Place in the oven to roast until tender, about 20 minutes. Remove and set aside to cool.

4. While the garlic, shallots, and creminis are roasting, place the dried mushrooms in a heatproof bowl and pour the boiling broth over them. Let stand to soften, about 30 minutes. Drain the dried mushrooms, squeezing out excess liquid. If desired, strain the liquid through a coffee filter and reserve for another use. Rinse the reconstituted dried mushrooms to remove any grit, pat dry with paper towels, and chop fine.

5. In a medium skillet, melt 1 tablespoon butter on medium heat, and add the chopped button mushrooms. Season with salt and pepper and cook, stirring occasionally, until the mushrooms are soft and the liquid that accumulates in the pan has evaporated. Remove from heat and set aside to cool.

6. Detach 6 garlic cloves from the roasted head, reserving the remaining cloves for another use. Squeeze the soft garlic cloves out of their papery skins. Chop the roasted garlic and shallots fine and add to the button mushrooms. Add the chopped dried mushrooms and thyme and stir to blend.

7. Form the purses: Melt the remaining ½ cup butter and cool slightly. Place phyllo sheets on a work surface. Cut sheets in half crosswise to form eighteen 13-x-8½-inch rectangles and stack them. Using an 8-inch-diameter plate as a guide, trace a circle on the top phyllo sheet with the tip of a paring knife. With the paring knife, cut all phyllo sheets into circles, forming eighteen 8-inch-diameter rounds. Cover the rounds with plastic wrap and then a clean, damp kitchen towel to prevent drying.

8. Place 1 phyllo round on a work surface, keeping the others covered. Brush with some melted butter. Top with a second phyllo round and brush the second round with melted butter. Top with a third phyllo round and again brush with melted butter. Sprinkle with 1 teaspoon bread crumbs. Place 1 heaping tablespoon of the button mushroom mixture in the center of the phyllo. Top with 1 large or 2 small cremini mushrooms. Gather the edges of the phyllo together and twist to form a purse. Repeat with the remaining phyllo rounds to make a total of 6 purses. Brush the purses with the remaining melted butter. Place on a buttered baking sheet, cover with plastic wrap, and refrigerate until ready to bake, up to 1 day.

9. Preheat the oven to 400°F. Bake the phyllo purses until golden and heated through, 12 to 15 minutes. Carefully tie a chive around the twisted section of each phyllo purse and knot. Transfer 1 phyllo purse to each of 6 plates. Drizzle the purse and the plate lightly with squiggles of pumpkinseed oil, and serve. Or let the purses come to room temperature before plating, garnishing, and serving.

ROASTED BRUSSELS SPROUTS WITH GARLIC AND SAGE

SERVES SIX • This is *such* a delicious red wine dish—the deep, slightly bitter-charred flavor of the roasted Brussels sprouts and the pungency of the sage pick up the leafy-earthy-smoky flavors of wines based on the Cabernet Franc grape (a cousin to Cabernet Sauvignon), and Old World Cabernet-based wines from Bordeaux in France, and from the Tuscany region. And with all this wine-friendly flavor, would you believe that it's easy to make?

WINE RECOMMENDATIONS	CABERNET FRANC	CABERNET SAUVIGNON	
	Lang & Reed, Pride Mountain (California)	Château Greysac, Château Tayac (Bordeaux, France)	2 pounds Brussels sprouts, trimmed and halved
			2 tablespoons olive oil
	Olga Raffault Chinon Rouge, Charles Joguet Chinon Rouge (Loire Valley, France)	Ornellaia Le Volte, Banfi Cum Laude (Tuscany, Italy—these wines include other grapes such as Sangiovese in the blend)	2 garlic cloves, finely chopped
			Kosher salt
			Freshly ground black pepper
			1 tablespoon balsamic vinegar
			2½ tablespoons finely chopped fresh sage

1. Preheat the oven to 450°F. Combine the Brussels sprouts, olive oil, garlic, salt, and pepper in a large mixing bowl and toss to coat. Spread the Brussels sprouts out on an oiled, rimmed baking sheet. Roast, stirring occasionally, until the Brussels sprouts are tender and lightly charred, 17 to 20 minutes.

2. Remove the baking sheet from the oven and transfer the Brussels sprouts to a serving bowl. Stir in the vinegar and sage, tossing to coat. Serve immediately.

SWEET POTATO PUREE WITH GARLIC, THYME, AND BALSAMIC VINEGAR

SERVES FOUR TO SIX • Wow. This dish shows the power of the "making the bed" principle (page 192), particularly if the wine is something quite special. When considering how to get the most out of that exceptional bottle, many sommeliers, myself included, would advise you to keep the food simple and let the wine be the star. Thus a bed of this sweet potato puree is the perfect place for a great Cabernet, Merlot, or Bordeaux blend to cozy up with some simply cooked meat: a great steak or roast, duck or game hens, lamb rack, or pork or venison loin. The garlic and thyme pick up the earthiness of wines made from these grapes, the gentle sweetness of the potatoes echoes the sweetness of the wine's ripe fruit, and both the balsamic vinegar and the wine share the aromatic richness and palate mellowness imparted by oak aging (aged balsamic vinegar is best here, but regular supermarket vinegar can be used in a pinch, if you reduce it as described on page 264 to concentrate its flavor). Simple as it is, this type of meal is worthy of any top Cabernet, Merlot, or Meritage blend based on these grapes. I could name a gazillion great options, but will only mention some of my favorites.

WINE RECOMMENDATIONS

CABERNET SAUVIGNON

Veramonte (Chile)

Geyser Peak, Mt. Veeder, Estancia Meritage (California)

1½ pounds sweet potatoes, peeled and cut into 1-inch cubes

4 small garlic cloves, sliced thin

Approximately 3 cups low-sodium chicken or vegetable broth

3 tablespoons chopped fresh thyme, or 1½ teaspoons dried thyme

2 tablespoons unsalted butter

Kosher salt

Freshly ground white pepper

2 tablespoons aged balsamic vinegar or Balsamic Vinegar Reduction (page 264)

1. Place the sweet potato cubes and garlic in a saucepan and pour in the chicken or vegetable broth to within ½ inch of the top of the potatoes. Boil until very soft (the potatoes will sink down into the liquid as they cook), 12 to 15 minutes.

2. Drain, reserving the cooking liquid. Return the potatoes to the saucepan and mash with a potato masher. Slowly add some of the cooking liquid, stirring, until you get the consistency of a loose puree. It need not be perfectly smooth. Stir in the thyme and butter, adding more to taste if needed, and season with salt and white pepper to taste. Keep warm in a double boiler. Drizzle aged balsamic vinegar over each portion just before serving.

WINE-BRAISED LEEKS

SERVES SIX • This dish illustrates a major principle of wine-friendly cooking that I pointed out in my pairings book *Great Tastes Made Simple*—namely, the wonderful wine affinity of vegetables in the allium family (garlic, shallots, onions, and leeks) when they've been long-cooked or braised to bring out their earthy sweetness. Braised in Merlot, these leeks are a perfect vegetable side dish for the two steak recipes in this chapter. The wine matches have been chosen to mirror the leeks' earthy sweetness. But you could also use chicken stock or white wine to braise these leeks, and serve them alongside roast chicken or game hens, or as a bed for flaky-fleshed fish fillets such as sea bass or cod. (Season the fish with salt and pepper and add to the pan before you cover the leeks for the final stage of cooking; add a little more liquid if necessary, and extend the cooking time until the fillets flake easily with a fork.)

WINE RECOMMENDATIONS		
CABERNET SAUVIGNON Blackstone, Clos du Bois, Benziger, Clos du Val	3 large leeks	
	1 tablespoon unsalted butter	
	1 tablespoon olive oil	
	Kosher salt	
	Freshly ground black pepper	
	½ cup Merlot, or more if necessary (leftover is fine)	

1. Trim off the tough green leaves of the leeks, leaving about ½ inch of green. Quarter the leeks lengthwise and rinse well under cold running water to remove all grit.

2. In a skillet large enough to hold the leeks in one layer, heat the butter and olive oil on medium heat. Add the leeks, cut sides down, and season with salt and pepper. Raise heat to medium-high and cook until the leeks just begin to brown, about 2 minutes.

3. Sprinkle in about ½ cup Merlot, and cover the pan. Reduce heat to medium-low and braise about 5 minutes. Turn and stir the leeks, adding a few drops of additional liquid if needed to loosen any browned bits. Cover and cook an additional 4 minutes, until just tender-crisp. Serve immediately.

ROASTED FINGERLING FRITES

SERVES SIX • Potatoes as a wine match? Yes! As I revealed in *Great Tastes Made Simple,* my "diet" regimen after I've been traveling a lot or eating too much fancy fare is to simplify and make a meal of these potatoes, a green vegetable, and a glass of Cabernet Sauvignon. I used to be a little embarrassed about my potato passion, until I read an interview with Julia Child, where she said that her favorite food was the baked potato. Francophile that she was, I just bet she enjoyed a glass of red Bordeaux along with it.

Fingerling potatoes lend themselves to this "faux frites" preparation because of their long thin shape. Just slice them lengthwise in half (or into quarters if they are on the large side) and you've got rustic French fry shapes. Oven-fried potatoes aren't as crispy as deep fried, but they're a lot simpler and less messy. And these potatoes have their own great texture and flavor—earthy and herby, perfect with these wines.

WINE RECOMMENDATIONS	
CABERNET SAUVIGNON Dynamite, Wente (California) Los Vascos Reserva, Viña Santa Carolina, Concha y Toro Don Melchor Reserva (Chile)	2 pounds fingerling potatoes ⅓ cup olive oil ¼ cup fresh thyme leaves, removed from their stems 2 tablespoons fresh rosemary leaves, removed from their stems Sea salt Freshly ground black pepper

1. Preheat the oven to 450°F. Wash and dry potatoes. Slice them in half lengthwise, or into quarters if they are large.

2. Combine the sliced potatoes, oil, thyme, and rosemary in a large bowl and toss to coat.

3. Place the potatoes on a large rimmed baking sheet. Spread them out evenly so that they are not crowded. Sprinkle lightly with salt and pepper. Roast until tender and brown, 35 to 40 minutes, stirring once after 15 minutes and then again after 25 minutes, for even cooking.

4. Transfer the potatoes to paper towels to drain. Sprinkle with sea salt and serve immediately.

LINGUINE WITH WALNUTS, ARUGULA, AND OLIVES

SERVES FOUR • This is another John creation—simple pasta not sauced with a loose liquid, but rather "spiked" with a few intense ingredients for texture and flavor, and bound together with a bit of olive oil, some of the starchy pasta cooking liquid, and a grating of cheese. Everything comes together quickly, and some finishing salt such as fleur de sel adds the final "pop" of texture and flavor. This dish brings out the earthy, slightly herbaceous notes that are a hallmark especially of well-made California and Washington State Cabernets. The toasty walnuts and arugula highlight the toastiness of oak in the wines, while the vegetal flavors of the olives and arugula pick up Cabernet's cedary-tobacco-minty notes. This is a great vegetarian (though not vegan) meal that lets you pull out the biggest and "meatiest" of reds.

<table>
<tr><td rowspan="4">WINE RECOMMENDATIONS</td><td>CABERNET SAUVIGNON</td><td>¾ pound linguine fini or other thin, flat noodle</td><td>¼ cup extra virgin olive oil, plus more for drizzling</td></tr>
<tr><td>Raymond Napa, Estancia Meritage (California)</td><td>⅓ cup walnut pieces</td><td>⅓ cup pitted, chopped black olives</td></tr>
<tr><td></td><td>2 tablespoons olive oil</td><td>¼ cup grated Manchego or Parmigiano-Reggiano cheese</td></tr>
<tr><td>Chateau Ste. Michelle, DeLille Cellars Chaleur Estate (Washington State)</td><td>3 large garlic cloves, finely chopped

2 cups tightly packed baby arugula leaves, washed and dried</td><td>Freshly ground black pepper

Coarse sea salt such as fleur de sel</td></tr>
</table>

1. Add a tablespoon of salt to a large pot filled with 4 quarts of water. Bring to a boil. Add the pasta and cook according to package directions until al dente.

2. While the pasta is cooking, place the walnuts in a large dry skillet over medium heat, shaking the pan frequently, and cook until browned and fragrant, 3 to 4 minutes. Set aside to cool slightly, then chop roughly and reserve.

3. In the same skillet heat the 2 tablespoons olive oil on medium and add the garlic. Cook, stirring, until the garlic begins to soften and turn golden, about 2 minutes. Remove from the heat and set aside.

4. Drain the pasta, reserving ½ cup of the pasta water, and transfer it to the skillet with the garlic. Turn the heat to medium. Stir in the arugula and the ¼ cup extra virgin olive oil and toss to coat the pasta with the oil and wilt the arugula. Stir in the

15 minutes. Turn it on its other side and roast 15 minutes longer. Turn the chicken on its back and roast until the skin is brown and crisp and the cavity juices run clear, 25 to 30 minutes. (The chicken will be cooked through when an instant-read thermometer inserted into the breast registers 160 degrees and in the thigh registers between 165 and 170 degrees.) Transfer to a platter, loosely cover with foil, and let rest 10 minutes.

4. While the chicken is resting, make the gravy: Pour the liquid from the roasting pan into a gravy separator and pour off and discard the fat. Return the juices to the pan. Set the roasting pan on the stovetop over high heat and when the juices sizzle, add ½ cup of water and any accumulated juices from the chicken platter and boil for 2 minutes, scraping the bottom of the pan with a wooden spoon to loosen any browned bits. Season with salt and pepper. Carve the chicken and serve with the sauce.

SIRLOIN STEAK WITH "BEURRE-NAISE" SAUCE

SERVES FOUR • John and I both love the classic combinaton of steak with béarnaise sauce . . . for about two bites, at which point the thick, eggy sauce becomes too rich and cloying. In addition, the sauce's vinegary base gives it a piercing flavor that overpowers many wines. (Not to mention that making the sauce is time-consuming and tricky, too, because you have to whisk egg yolks into an emulsion.) So I decided to play around with an alternative that would solve these problems, yet still give us a similar flavor profile. I call it "Beurre-Naise" because it's based on the classic French sauce beurre blanc, made by whisking butter into a reduction of shallots and white wine vinegar. Eliminating the egg yolk step yields a simpler, quicker, and lighter sauce. To soften the sauce's acidity and increase the wine affinity, I substitute white wine for a substantial portion of the vinegar in the reduction. Adjust the amount of tarragon to your taste. And substitute your favorite cut of steak for the sirloin if you prefer. This dish goes beautifully with traditional Cabernets from all the best areas for that grape—California, Bordeaux in France, Chile, and Australia.

WINE RECOMMENDATIONS

CABERNET SAUVIGNON

Beringer Founders' Estate, Kendall-Jackson Vintner's Reserve (California)

Los Vascos Reserva, Escudo Rojo, Concha y Toro Don Melchor Reserva (Chile)

1½ pounds boneless sirloin steak, 1 inch thick

Kosher salt

Freshly ground black pepper

1 cup dry white wine such as Chardonnay (leftover is fine)

2 tablespoons white wine vinegar

1 small shallot, minced

1 tablespoon olive oil

6 tablespoons unsalted butter, 1 tablespoon set aside and the remaining 5 tablespoons cut into small pieces and chilled

2 tablespoons finely chopped fresh tarragon

1. Preheat the oven to 400°F. Season the steak on both sides with salt and pepper and refrigerate.

2. Combine the wine, vinegar, and shallot in a small saucepan and bring to a boil. Reduce the heat to medium-low and simmer until the mixture is reduced to 2 tablespoons, 15 to 20 minutes.

3. Meanwhile, heat a large, heavy, ovenproof skillet over medium-high heat. When it's hot, add the oil and the 1 tablespoon of butter. When the butter is melted, add

the steak and sear for 1 minute. Reduce the heat and continue to cook until the first side is golden brown and beginning to crisp, about 3 minutes longer. Turn the steak with tongs and sear the other side until well-browned, 2 to 3 minutes.

4. Place the pan in the oven and finish cooking, turning once, 6 to 8 minutes for medium-rare. Transfer the steak to a platter and loosely cover with foil to keep warm.

5. To finish the sauce, put it through a fine strainer, pressing on the shallots. Whisk the 5 tablespoons of cold butter a few pieces at a time into the warm reduction until you have a creamy sauce. Stir in the tarragon to taste and season with salt and pepper.

6. Slice the steak into ½-inch-thick slices across the grain, spoon the sauce on top, and serve.

"RED AND BLUE" SHORT RIB RAGÙ WITH PAPPARDELLE

SERVES SIX • If you've read my book *Great Tastes Made Simple* then you've seen this recipe featuring red meat, red wine, and the most amazing blue cheese garnish. It was inspired by one of Chef Michael Lomonaco's signature dishes at Windows on the World and is such an astounding match with big, chewy Merlots and Cabernets that I had to include it here. The meaty-rich texture melts the tannins in red wine, bringing out the fruit, which in turn creates a sense-jolting contrast with the saltiness and pungency of the blue cheese. You can braise the ribs a day ahead, pull out the bones, and refrigerate the ragù to let the flavors marry overnight. Then skim off the excess fat and reheat on the stovetop as you are cooking the pasta. I have substituted lamb shanks (one per person) for the short ribs, with excellent results. Go for quality when buying blue cheese—Maytag Blue, Roquefort, and Gorgonzola are my picks. Basic crumbly/dry supermarket blue cheeses can taste salty and harsh with big red wines.

WINE RECOMMENDATIONS

MERLOT

Sagelands, Canoe Ridge (Washington State)

CABERNET SAUVIGNON

Wynn's Coonawarra, Leeuwin Estate (Australia)

3 tablespoons olive oil

4½ pounds beef short ribs

Kosher salt

Freshly ground black pepper

6 large garlic cloves, finely chopped

4 large shallots, diced

2 large carrots, diced

2 celery stalks, diced

1 tablespoon all-purpose flour

½ cup tomato paste

3 cups red wine

1½ cups beef stock or canned low-sodium beef broth

2 sprigs fresh rosemary, plus more for garnish

1 bay leaf

1 teaspoon dried thyme

1 pound wide egg noodles or pappardelle

4 ounces Maytag Blue cheese from Iowa or other high-quality blue cheese

1. Preheat the oven to 325°F. Heat the olive oil in a large Dutch oven over medium-high heat. Sprinkle the ribs on both sides with salt and pepper. Brown them on both sides, turning often. Remove ribs to a plate and set aside.

2. Turn the heat down to medium and add the garlic, shallots, carrots, and celery to the pan. Sauté until the shallots are translucent, 5 to 6 minutes. Sprinkle in the flour

and add the tomato paste. Stir to combine. Slowly pour in the red wine and beef stock, stirring to break up any lumps of tomato paste. Add the rosemary, bay leaf, thyme, and a generous grinding of black pepper.

3. Return the short ribs to the Dutch oven, along with any juices from the plate, and stir them into the sauce. Cover the pot and place in the oven. Bake until the meat is tender and nearly falling off the bones, about 2½ hours.

4. Remove and discard the rosemary sprigs and bay leaf. Remove the meat from the bones and discard the bones, return the meat to the Dutch oven, and stir to break up the meat a little. (The short rib ragù may be covered and refrgerated overnight. Gently reheat over low on top of the stove.)

5. Bring 4 quarts of water, a splash of olive oil, and 1 teaspoon salt to boil in a large pot. Add the noodles and cook according to the package instructions, until al dente. Drain and divide among 6 serving plates. Top with some short rib ragù and sprinkle with the blue cheese. Garnish with a sprig of rosemary, if desired, and serve immediately.

SEARED FILET MIGNON WITH MERLOT AND MUSHROOM *JUS*

SERVES SIX • For a sit-down multicourse dinner party, I like to precede this dish with Wild Mushroom Phyllo Purses (page 163). They go wonderfully together, and the left-over mushroom stock from the purses can be used in the *jus* for the steak. Wine-Braised Leeks (page 167) and Sweet Potato Puree with Garlic, Thyme, and Balsamic Vinegar (page 166) are simple but perfect accompaniments, especially when served with one of the wines recommended below.

WINE RECOMMENDATIONS	
MERLOT Columbia Winery, St. Francis, Bogle CABERNET SAUVIGNON Frei Brothers, Markham	Six 6-ounce filet mignon steaks, 1 inch thick Kosher salt Freshly ground black pepper 2 teaspoons olive oil 1 tablespoon unsalted butter ½ cup Quick Mushroom Stock (page 268) ½ cup canned low-sodium beef broth ½ cup Merlot or other dry red wine

1. Season the steaks all over with salt and pepper. Heat the oil and butter in a heavy skillet large enough to hold all of the steaks in one layer. Add the steaks all at once and sear on both sides until lightly browned, about 2 minutes per side. Remove steaks to a platter, cover with foil, and let rest.

2. Preheat the broiler to 500°F. Place the browned steaks on a lightly oiled broiler pan or clean, ovenproof skillet, pouring any accumulated juices into the skillet used to cook the steaks. Broil the steaks on the top rack to desired doneness, turning halfway through the total cooking time: about 5 minutes total for rare, 7 minutes total for medium-rare, 9 minutes total for medium.

3. While the steaks are cooking, add the mushroom stock, beef broth, and wine to the skillet used to brown the steaks, and bring to a gentle boil, scraping up any brown bits stuck to the bottom of the skillet with a wooden spoon. Cook until liquid is thickened slightly and reduced to about ½ cup. Season the *jus* to taste with salt and pepper.

4. Place steaks on warmed plates, spoon some of the *jus* over each, and serve.

Everyday Dinners with
MERLOT AND CABERNET SAUVIGNON

PASTAS AND OTHER ONE-PLATE DINNERS

WHAT TO COOK	WINE PAIRINGS
Salad of Fresh Figs with Manchego, Balsamic Vinegar, and Toasted Pine Nuts *(page 162)*, toasted and garlic-rubbed country bread	ONCE-A-WEEK ($–$$): Penfolds Koonunga Hill Cabernet-Merlot (Australia) Gallo of Sonoma Merlot (California) ONCE-A-MONTH ($$$ AND UP): Casa Lapostolle Cuvée Alexandre Merlot (Chile)
Linguine with Walnuts, Arugula, and Olives *(page 169)*	ONCE-A-WEEK ($–$$): Raymond Napa Cabernet Sauvignon (California) Chateau Ste. Michelle Cabernet Sauvignon (Washington State) ONCE-A-MONTH ($$$ AND UP): DeLille Cellars Chaleur Estate (Washington State)
Wild Mushroom Phyllo Purses with Pumpkinseed Oil Drizzle *(page 163)*, green salad	ONCE-A-WEEK ($–$$): B&G Merlot (Bordeaux, France) Château Tayac (Bordeaux, France) ONCE-A-MONTH ($$$ AND UP): Château Figeac (St.-Emilion, France)

TRADITIONAL (MAIN-AND-SIDES) DINNERS

WHAT TO COOK	WINE PAIRINGS
MAIN COURSE: Rosemary and Sweet Garlic Roast Chicken *(page 171)* VEGGIES: Garlic-Braised Collard Greens *(page 189)* STARCHES, ETC.: couscous	ONCE-A-WEEK ($–$$): J. Lohr 7 Oaks Cabernet Sauvignon (California) Château Poujeaux (Bordeaux, France) ONCE-A-MONTH ($$$ AND UP): Shafer Cabernet Sauvignon (California)
MAIN COURSE: pot roast VEGGIES: Roasted Brussels Sprouts with Garlic and Sage *(page 165)* STARCHES, ETC.: mashed potatoes	ONCE-A-WEEK ($–$$): Château Greysac (Bordeaux, France) Olga Raffault Chinon (Loire Valley, France) ONCE-A-MONTH ($$$ AND UP): Banfi Cum Laude Super Tuscan (Tuscany, Italy)

WHAT TO COOK	WINE PAIRINGS
MAIN COURSE: Seared Filet Mignon with Merlot and Mushroom *Jus (page 177)* VEGGIES: Charred Tricolore Salad *(page 186)* STARCHES, ETC.: crusty bread	ONCE-A-WEEK ($–$$): Columbia Winery Merlot (Washington State) Bogle Merlot (California) ONCE-A-MONTH ($$$ AND UP): St. Francis Merlot (California)
MAIN COURSE: Sirloin Steak with "Beurre-Naise" Sauce *(page 173)* VEGGIES: watercress or steamed green beans STARCHES, ETC.: Roasted Fingerling Frites *(page 168)*	ONCE-A-WEEK ($–$$): Beringer Founders' Estate Cabernet Sauvignon (California) Los Vascos Reserva Cabernet Sauvignon (Chile) ONCE-A-MONTH ($$$ AND UP): Concha y Toro Don Melchor Reserva Cabernet Sauvignon (Chile)
MAIN COURSE: "Red and Blue" Short Rib Ragù with Pappardelle *(page 175)* VEGGIES: green salad STARCHES, ETC.: egg noodles	ONCE-A-WEEK ($–$$): Sagelands Merlot (Washington State) Wynn's Coonawarra Cabernet Sauvignon (Australia) ONCE-A-MONTH ($$$ AND UP): Leeuwin Estate Cabernet Sauvignon (Australia)
MAIN COURSE: John's First-Date Salmon Fillets *(page 150)* VEGGIES: steamed spinach STARCHES, ETC.: Sweet Potato Puree with Garlic, Thyme, and Balsamic Vinegar *(page 166)*	ONCE-A-WEEK ($–$$): Veramonte Cabernet Sauvignon (Chile) Geyser Peak Cabernet Sauvignon (California) ONCE-A-MONTH ($$$ AND UP): Estancia Meritage (California)
MAIN COURSE: pan-seared pork chops VEGGIES: Wine-Braised Leeks *(page 167)* STARCHES, ETC.: Oven-Crisped Red Potatoes with Thyme and Pumpkinseed Oil *(page 35)*	ONCE-A-WEEK ($–$$): Blackstone Cabernet Sauvignon (California) Frei Brothers Reserve Cabernet Sauvignon (California) ONCE-A-MONTH ($$$ AND UP): Clos du Val Cabernet Sauvignon (California)

chapter seven

SHIRAZ, RHÔNE-STYLE REDS, AND ZINFANDEL

•

Syrah/Shiraz Summary, Zinformation

HOME REGION

Syrah/Shiraz: Rhône Valley, France; Zinfandel: although it's considered "America's grape," experts have determined it is the Primitivo grape of Italy's Apulia region

---

OTHER KEY SOURCES

Syrah: Australia, North America; Zinfandel: no major plantings outside the United States

---

STYLE

Both are full-bodied, with rich, chewy-velvety tannins

FLAVOR

Spicy, with bold dark berry and fig fruit

As my wine mentor Kevin Zraly would say, among true

wine geeks, "All roads lead to red." I happened to get on my personal wine road just as the ride toward red was getting really interesting.

In 1990 I left Wall Street for wine, and before the year was out I was working the floor at Windows on the World, where the idea of premium wine by the glass (as opposed to no-name house wine) was in its infancy, guests had just begun to discover the Chardonnay grape, and white wine comprised about 75 percent of our sales. All of this changed literally overnight, a testament to the power of television. On a sleepy Sunday evening in 1991, Morley Safer presented a *60 Minutes* segment on the so-called French Paradox, the theory that the French have a substantially lower incidence of heart disease because of their everyday dinner *with red wine* routine. The very next night we sold out of most of our Cabernets and began recommending its sister Bordeaux grape, Merlot (which has since unseated Cabernet as the top-selling red varietal). And it wasn't just us. The whole wine industry sprang to life, invigorated by Americans' piqued interest in red wine.

And the thirst for new and different reds has endured. California red Zinfandel, formerly used mostly in generic red blends, has joined Cabernet as a cult-wine phenomenon, with boutique bottlings bearing hip names like Earthquake and Jackass pulling down fancy prices at wine auctions. The juggernaut that is Shiraz (a.k.a. Syrah) has morphed from a mild-mannered French classic into a marketing marvel driven by one of the newest kids on the global wine block—Australia.

To me, the ascendance in this country of red Zinfandel, Syrah/Shiraz, and French Rhône reds (the original Syrahs) makes perfect sense when you consider what they share: deep fruit and bold spice. For all the barbecued, blackened, flame-broiled, crusted, salsa-ed, smoked, and sizzled fare with which Americans are so smitten, these spicy "super reds" are just what the sommelier ordered.

The Rhône Range

FOR PILGRIMS ON the red wine route, the Rhône Valley in France is a mecca of exciting flavor and food affinity, as well as excellent value. It's also the inspiration behind the sea of Syrah and Shiraz wines being produced worldwide. Here's what you need to know about classic French Rhône wines, and the Rhône-*style* wines they inspire.

THE FRENCH RHÔNE RED GRAPES—SYRAH, GRENACHE, MOURVÈDRE

Although there are many red grapes indigenous to the Rhone, this trio is the region's A-team for quality and variety—the array of styles and price points can literally cover any meal situation, from soup-and-sandwich supper to sumptuous feast. The grapes themselves are distinctive: Syrah is known for powerful fig fruit, peppery spice, and ample tannins; Grenache is beloved for its lively, soft juiciness and pomegranate flavor; and Mourvèdre is the exotic one, with blueberry fruit and sweet spices (allspice, clove).

Divide and Conquer

The easiest way to understand the Rhône region is to divide it in two, the Northern Rhône and the Southern Rhône, because they differ in a key way. The Northern Rhône's reds are based on just one grape, Syrah. By contrast, the Southern Rhône's reds are traditionally blends of several different grapes, including Syrah as well as Grenache, Mourvèdre, and other local grapes. Throughout the Rhône, the wines are labeled for the growing region or village, in the French tradition. These are the key appellations (wine names):

Northern Rhône. The top-of-the-line appellations are Hermitage and Côte Rôtie. They are powerful, brawny wines with lots of raisiny, dried fig fruit and a peppery, leathery-smoky scent. They're also the models for the most ambitious Syrah and Shiraz varietal wines from the New World (notably Australia and the United States). A step down the ladder, but similar in style and more affordable, are the Syrah-based wines of Cornas, St. Joseph, and Crozes-Hermitage.

Southern Rhône. The flagship appellation of the Southern Rhône is Châteauneuf-du-Pape, an amazingly diverse wine because up to thirteen different grape varieties, including the "big three" described here, are permitted in the blend. That said, I've never had a bad one, and most that I've tasted were utterly exciting, with savory pomegranate and wild berry flavors, tobacco and spice cabinet scents, and tongue-gripping tannins that are a great foil for food.

Côtes du Rhône. Côtes du Rhône is the name of the overall regional appellation for the Rhône, meaning the grapes for Côtes du Rhône wines can be sourced from anywhere in the zone. In my opinion, Côtes du Rhône is the best everyday-priced red on the market. You just can't beat it for complexity—lots of juicy-savory berry fruit, smoke and spice—and food versatility.

The American "Rhône Rangers"

FRENCH RHÔNE WINES were the inspiration for a group of California winemakers who, having seen the success of the French Rhône grapes in Australia, branched out from Cabernet Sauvignon and Merlot to experiment with Rhône grapes in California vineyards. These pioneers were dubbed "Rhône Rangers" by the wine press because their heroic efforts truly paved the way to success for this category in the state. Nowadays, Syrah/Shiraz or a "Rhône Rangers" category often commands its own section in wine shops and on wine lists.

American Syrah/Shiraz wines, as well as blends and varietals based on the Grenache and Mourvèdre grapes, are grown throughout California (Mourvèdre varietals are sometimes labeled as Mataro). They typically yield vibrant fruit but, to my taste, less earth-spice-leather than the French and Australian versions. The same is true for Syrah grown in Washington. With plantings increasing, it's well on its way to becoming a signature for the state. I hope that as the vines mature, winemakers will be able to capture the spice of Syrah as well as the bold fruit. The California and Washington State recommendations in this book are for wines that I think do capture both savory funk and sweet fruit, the way the French Rhône benchmarks do.

Down Under, On Top

THERE'S PROBABLY NO more sizzling "right place, right time" story in wine than Aussie Shiraz, their signature red that's so hot it's poised to unseat Merlot as consumers' go-to grape. There's good reason for its ascendance. Quality for the money is high at every price point. But it's not an overnight success story. Long before the Rhône Ranger era in California, Australia had a well-established tradition of growing and producing varietal and blended Grenache, Shiraz, and Mourvèdre. In fact, some of the earliest vineyards are still producing, yielding intense "old vines" bottlings that are coveted among wine collectors.

Every Australian state makes wine, but the major sources for quality Shiraz and Rhône-style reds are:

South Australia. Key subregions include Coonawarra, Barossa, McLaren Vale, and Clare Valley.

New South Wales. The Hunter Valley is its best-known subregion.

Western Australia. This is an up-and-coming district with lots of great boutique producers. Look for the subregions Margaret River, Frankland, and Great Southern.

Many of the largest Shiraz brands carry the regional designation South Eastern Australia, which means the grapes can be sourced from anywhere in the country's southeastern states—Victoria, South Australia, and New South Wales.

Zinfandel—America's Red

I CALL THEM Zin-heads; they're grape groupies whose passion is red Zinfandel. If you feel the same way about this grape, you can literally join the club—Zinfandel Advocates and Producers (ZAP)—*www.zinfandel.org*—and avail yourself of events and tastings around the country that celebrate Zinfandel, California's specialty red. What's so great about it? As with the Rhône-style wines, big fruit and big spice. The style can range from medium-bodied, with juicy berries-and-pepper flavors, to lush and full-bodied with intense blueberry, licorice, chocolate, cinnamon, and clove flavors and scents. Many of the best Zin vineyards are pre-Prohibition plantings that, due to the vines' age, produce tiny quantities of incredibly intense, complex wine. Along with their bold fruit and full body, Zinfandels are usually oaky—a little or a lot, depending, as with the other grapes we've explored, on the intensity of the grapes used. The grape intensity is a function of the vineyard—its age and its location. Many of the top Zinfandel regions—including Sonoma (especially its Dry Creek Valley and Russian River Valley subdistricts), Napa, Amador, and the Sierra Foothills—yield wines worthy of cellaring. The value Zinfandel bottlings are usually labeled simply as California or as Lodi—a region in the Central Valley.

If all this talk of spice is making you hungry, that's the idea. In my wine and food pairing classes at The French Culinary Institute in New York, we have such fun with these wines. Their spicy complexity pairs thrillingly with some pretty far-flung flavors—not just the sweet (allspice, clove, cinnamon) and savory (pepper, cumin, fennel) spices, but also the flavors of the grill, game, the pungent tastes of cured meats, the entire garden of herbs including the more pungent ones like rosemary and sage, fruit flavors, and cheeses from subtle to stinky. The recipes and pairings in this chapter will let you explore all of that, and more.

THE NEW AMERICAN CHEESE

In recent years, the idea of "American cheese" has come to mean something far beyond the cellophane-wrapped singles of our youth. Great makers of handcrafted, small-batch cheeses in the European tradition have sprung up across the country, and are creating amazing Camembert, but also some completely original cheeses.

In my classes at The French Culinary Institute, we've been working hard (ha!) "researching" these cheeses and the wines to pair with them. In the course of our labors, we have returned time and again to the big, bold flavors of red Zinfandel and Rhône-style wines, which have the body and intensity to stand up to the amazing flavors and textures of these cheeses. Here are some of our favorite American cheese and wine pairings:

GOAT CHEESE
Capriole Farms Wabash Cannonball (Indiana) with Qupé Syrah; Cypress Grove Humboldt Fog (California) with Jade Mountain Mourvèdre

DRY-AGED
Vella Bear Flag Dry Jack

(California) with Shafer "Relentless" (Syrah blend); Love Tree Farm Tradelake Cedar (Wisconsin) with Ridge Geyserville

CREAMY
Old Chatham Sheep's Milk Camembert (New York) with Joseph Phelps Syrah; Teleme (California) with Monteviña Terra d'Oro Zinfandel

BLUE
Maytag Blue (Iowa) with St. Francis Old Vines Zinfandel; Bingham Hill Blue (Colorado) with Grgich Hills Zinfandel

CHARRED TRICOLORE SALAD

SERVES SIX • This is a wine-friendly variation on the popular endive, arugula, and radicchio salad. The warm charred endive and radicchio are tossed with the arugula to wilt it. Charring the lettuces gives the salad a slightly smoky flavor that's lovely with the charred smokiness of Northern Rhône Syrah-based reds. And here is another dish where using a coarse finishing salt like fleur de sel adds a great final note of flavor and texture.

WINE RECOMMENDATIONS		
NORTHERN RHÔNE REDS	CÔTE RÔTIE	3 large heads radicchio, cored and quartered
CROZES-HERMITAGE	Delas, Guigal	3 large endives, halved lengthwise
Alain Graillot, Albert Belle		1 recipe Balsamic Vinaigrette (page 265)
CORNAS		¼ cup fresh oregano leaves, finely chopped
Jaboulet, Alain Voge, Clape		1 bunch fresh arugula

1. Preheat a gas grill to medium-high, or preheat a grill pan on top of the stove to medium. Place the radicchio and endive in a large bowl and add the vinaigrette and oregano. Toss to coat.

2. Grill the radicchio and endive, uncovered, until they begin to wilt and char but are still holding their shape, 5 to 7 minutes, turning occasionally and brushing with the dressing left in the bottom of the mixing bowl.

3. Place the grilled radicchio and endive in a large salad bowl. Add the arugula and toss to combine. Serve immediately.

SHIRAZ-POACHED PEARS WITH ROQUEFORT AND BLACK PEPPER

SERVES SIX • You can use leftover Shiraz to roast the pears, but to drink with the dish, try a big, gamy Australian Shiraz. I like the blends with Cabernet, or with Grenache and Mourvèdre (two French Rhône red grapes that are often blended with Shiraz both in France and in Australia), because they offer a lot of complexity for the money. I typically serve this as a cheese course in a multicourse meal, which is the point at which I'd serve the biggest wine of the night. (If you'd like to go all French, I've included some Rhône recommendations, too.)

If good-quality French Roquefort is not available, Stilton and Maytag Blue are good alternatives. The pears may be poached in advance, removed from their liquid, and stored in an airtight container for a day. Refrigerate the poaching liquid in a separate airtight container. To serve, bring the pears to room temperature before stuffing with the cheese, and reheat the poaching liquid before spooning it around the pears.

WINE RECOMMENDATIONS		
SHIRAZ-CAB BLENDS Penfolds Koonunga Hill, Penfolds Bin 389 SHIRAZ-GRENACHE-MOURVÈDRE BLENDS D'Arenberg Red Ochre, Rosemount GSM	FRENCH RED CÔTES DU RHÔNE Jaboulet Parallele 45, Guigal, Chapoutier	2 cups Shiraz 2 tablespoons balsamic vinegar ½ cup sugar ½ teaspoon freshly ground black pepper 6 small, ripe pears such as Forelle, French butter, or Bosc 1½ ounces Roquefort, or other creamy blue cheese

1. Combine the wine, vinegar, sugar, and pepper in a medium saucepan and bring to a boil. Reduce heat and simmer until the liquid is reduced by half.

2. While the liquid is reducing, using a sharp paring knife or a vegetable peeler with a swivel blade, cut in a circle around the blossom end of each pear deeply enough to remove the core while leaving the pear intact.

3. Place the pears upright in the poaching liquid. The liquid should come about halfway up the sides of the pears. Return to a simmer, and poach until the bottoms

OVEN-CHARRED ASPARAGUS WITH CHEESE AND BALSAMIC VINEGAR

SERVES FOUR • Asparagus is reputedly the enemy of wine, because its flavor properties can, when paired with wine, create a strangely sweet or metallic aftertaste. This recipe is designed to counteract that effect. The lemon peel, charred flavors, and the saltiness of the cheese all tame that tendency and bring a wonderful flavor yin-yang—herbaceous against smoky-rich—that complements those same contrasts in Rhône-style wines.

The best way to trim asparagus is not with a knife, but by holding the end of the spear in one hand, the other end in the other hand, and snapping. The spear will naturally break at the point where the asparagus is too tough to eat.

SYRAH

Jade Mountain La Provencal, R.H. Phillips EXP, Edmunds St. John, Andrew Murray (California)

1 pound asparagus, tough ends snapped off

1 tablespoon olive oil, plus extra for oiling the pan

½ teaspoon finely grated lemon zest

Kosher salt

Freshly ground black pepper

1½ ounces Manchego, aged Monterey Jack, Asiago, or other firm cheese

2 tablespoons Balsamic Vinegar Reduction (page 264)

1. Preheat the oven to 500°F. Oil a heavy baking sheet or spray with nonstick cooking spray.

2. Place the asparagus on the baking sheet and drizzle with 1 tablespoon of olive oil; then sprinkle with the lemon zest, ½ teaspoon of salt or more, to taste, and a few grinds of black pepper. Toss with your hands to coat.

3. Roast, stirring occasionally, until crisp-tender and lightly charred, about 12 minutes.

4. Remove from the oven and place on serving plates. Shave the cheese over each plate with a vegetable peeler, drizzle with Balsamic Vinegar Reduction, and serve immediately.

TOASTED CHICKPEAS WITH CRISPY SAGE

SERVES FOUR TO SIX • Crisping up canned chickpeas by baking them in the oven is an unusual but fantastic way to improve their flavor and texture. The outsides of the beans gain toasty flavor and crunch from cooking; the insides remain creamy. Tossing the toasted chickpeas with crispy sage transforms them into the perfect bite to go along with the herbaceousness of the Southern Rhône reds in this chapter. I also love them with Amador Zinfandels, whose earthiness echoes the earthiness of the chickpeas.

WINE RECOMMENDATIONS		
SOUTHERN RHÔNE REDS Brusset Gigondas, La Vieille Ferme Rouge, Château la Nerthe, Châteauneuf-du-Pape, Clos des Papes Châteauneuf-du-Pape	**AMADOR ZINFANDEL** Monteviña, Renwood Grandpere	One 15-ounce can chickpeas, drained and rinsed 3 tablespoons extra virgin olive oil 2 tablespoons finely chopped fresh rosemary Kosher salt Freshly ground black pepper Oven-Crisped Sage Leaves (page 270)

1. Preheat the oven to 475°F. Combine the chickpeas, olive oil, rosemary, salt, and pepper in a medium bowl and toss to coat.

2. Spread the chickpeas out in one layer on a rimmed baking sheet and bake, stirring occasionally, until browned and crispy, 15 to 20 minutes.

3. Transfer the warm chickpeas to a bowl, stir in the sage leaves (they will break up into pieces as you do), and serve immediately.

COOKING WITH WINE IN MIND:

MAKING THE BED . . . A NICE CUSHY PLACE WHERE YOUR WINE CAN MAKE ITSELF COMFORTABLE

This is one of John's "guy-cooking" principles that makes so much sense for everyday dining with wine. The idea is to make a flavorful, starchy bed for any center-of-the-plate protein, and then pair the wine with the side dish. I'm sure I'm not the only busy mom who stocks the freezer with chicken breasts, veggie burgers, pork chops, and other main-dish staples when they're on special at the supermarket so that I can cobble together dinner on a busy weeknight. But rather than using retro convenience products like Shake 'n Bake or dried onion soup to transform "fuel" into "fare," I'd rather make a super-simple, powerfully flavored bed on which to place the plain chicken, chop, or salmon fillet. The wine, then, cozies up to the flavors in the bed, giving you a lot of choices to keep weeknight cooking and pairing both simple and scrumptious. Here are some favorite beds:

COUSCOUS

So quick! For 4 to 6 servings, follow the package directions, but give the couscous a Mediterranean flavor by adding a splash of extra virgin olive oil, a pinch each of dried sage and thyme, a spoonful of chopped capers, 2 tablespoons of chopped sun-dried tomatoes, and several cranks of black pepper along with the salt and water before cooking as directed.

Best with: Seared pork chops or broiled salmon.

Pair with: Castello di Gabbiano Chianti Classico or Candido Salice Salentino (Italy), Montecillo Rioja Crianza (Spain), La Vieille Ferme Côtes du Ventoux red or Georges Duboeuf Côtes du Rhone red (France)

MASHED SWEET POTATOES

Quick-cooking, lower in carbs, plush flavor . . . what's not to love? For 4 to 6 servings, peel and cube 2 pounds of sweet potatoes. Place in a saucepan, pour in ½ cup orange juice, and then pour in homemade or canned chicken broth to within ½ inch of the top of the potatoes. Boil until very soft (the potatoes will sink down into the liquid as they cook). Drain, reserving the cooking liquid. Return the potatoes to the saucepan and mash with a potato masher. Slowly add some of the cooking liquid, stirring, until you get the consistency that you want. Season with a pinch of brown sugar, salt, freshly ground pepper, and butter to taste.

Best with: Turkey breast, corned beef, or pork roast.

Pair with: White! Tropical fruity California Chardonnay such as Meridian, Lockwood, or R.H. Phillips; or Gewürztraminer such as Fetzer (California), Hogue (Washington State), or Pierre Sparr (Alsace, France)

QUICK-COOKING POLENTA

Toasty-sweet, earthy cornmeal kissed with a swirl of fresh cheese for tanginess, and thyme for fragrance and a flavorful finish. For 4 to 6 servings, follow package directions. When the polenta is ready, stir in 1 tablespoon butter, 2 ounces fresh goat cheese or mascarpone cheese, and ½ teaspoon dried thyme. Serve immediately.

Best with: Sautéed cod, scrod, bass, or shrimp.

Pair with: Mediterranean whites hit all the fruit, herb, and tang flavor notes of the polenta. Try Sella and Mosca Vermentino or Teruzzi e Puthod Vernaccia (Italy), Chapoutier Côtes du Rhône white (France), or Marques de Riscal Rioja Blanco (Spain)

SPICY FRUITED COUSCOUS

SERVES SIX • This lends some excitement to a weeknight meal of simple grilled chicken, pork chops, or Portobello mushrooms. The sweet hint from the dried fruit and the toasted nuttiness of the couscous pairs perfectly with the deep berry flavors and sweet oak in Sonoma Zinfandels, while the snap of the cilantro picks up their herbal grace note. Try this couscous as a bed for "Brick-Roasted" Chicken Breasts (page 197).

WINE RECOMMENDATIONS

SONOMA ZINFANDEL

Dry Creek Reserve, Seghesio, Gallo of Sonoma, Clos du Bois

1 tablespoon unsalted butter

1 tablespoon olive oil

1 medium onion, finely chopped

1 tablespoon curry powder

2 cups plain couscous

¼ cup dried cranberries

¼ cup dried apricots, finely chopped

¼ cup chopped roasted, salted almonds

⅓ cup finely chopped fresh cilantro

Kosher salt

Freshly ground black pepper

1. Heat ½ tablespoon of the butter and ½ tablespoon of the oil in a heavy, large saucepan over medium heat. Add the onion and sauté until soft, about 5 minutes. Add the curry powder and continue to cook, stirring constantly, 1 minute. Add 3 cups of water and bring to a simmer. Simmer gently for 10 minutes.

2. Meanwhile, heat the remaining butter and olive oil in a heavy, large pot over medium-high heat. Add the dry couscous and sauté, stirring constantly, until the color darkens slightly and the couscous is toasted, 3 to 5 minutes.

3. Stir the simmering curry water into the couscous. Remove the pot from the heat and cover. Allow couscous to stand, covered, for 10 minutes to absorb the liquid. Add the cranberries, apricots, almonds, and cilantro, and season with salt and pepper. Stir with a fork to fluff the couscous and distribute the ingredients. Serve immediately.

POACHED EGGS WITH ROASTED TOMATOES AND CRISPY SAGE

SERVES SIX • Like its European cousins the Spanish tortilla and the French omelet, this dish makes something great out of a half-dozen eggs. The crispy sage leaves and oven-dried tomatoes make the match between the eggs and rustic French Rhône reds, whose acidity complements the tomatoes' tanginess and whose earthy-herbal scent showcases the crispy sage. For extra excitement, drizzle some pumpkinseed oil on top of the eggs before topping them with the sage leaves.

I poach the eggs gently, so that the soft yolks spread sauce-like around the plate once pierced with a fork. Frying the eggs produces the same result, if that's easier for you. In either case, serve with crusty bread to soak up the yolks. If you have concerns about eating lightly cooked eggs, you can scramble them and spoon them over the roasted tomatoes.

WINE RECOMMENDATIONS

RHÔNE REDS

Vidal-Fleury Crozes-Hermitage, Guigal Crozes-Hermitage, Duboeuf Côtes du Rhône, Perrin Reserve Côtes du Rhone, Domaine Santa Duc Gigondas

½ cup distilled white vinegar

6 large eggs

12 Oven-Dried Plum Tomatoes (page 272), at room temperature

Freshly ground black pepper

Oven-Crisped Sage Leaves (page 270)

Coarse finishing salt such as fleur de sel

Pumpkinseed oil for drizzling, optional

1. Fill a bowl with cold water and place it near the stove. Bring 2 quarts of water and the distilled white vinegar to a boil in a large, straight-sided pot. Lower the temperature to a bare simmer (180 degrees on an instant-read thermometer).

2. Break 1 egg into a small ramekin. Carefully hold the ramekin just above the water's surface and tip it toward the water, sliding the egg in. Repeat with the remaining eggs. The whites will begin to coagulate immediately. Don't worry if there are trailing tendrils of egg white; you can trim them before serving.

3. Cook each egg until the white is firm but the yolk is still soft, about 4 minutes. With a slotted spoon, remove each cooked egg to the cold water to stop the cooking, then place the eggs on a paper towel–lined plate to drain. Trim any ragged edges with a paring knife, if desired.

4. When ready to serve, bring 2 quarts of salted water to a simmer. While the water is heating, arrange 4 oven-dried tomato halves in a flower or starburst pattern on each of 6 serving plates. Reheat 1 egg in the hot water for 20 seconds, remove with a slotted spoon, and place at the center of a tomato "flower." Repeat with the remaining eggs. Grind black pepper over each egg to taste. Top with a generous shower of the crispy sage leaves, a sprinkling of sea salt, and a drizzle of pumpkin-seed oil, if desired, and serve immediately.

INCREDIBLE EGGS

When I was growing up, I loved it when my mom went back to school because her study nights meant Dad took dinner duty, and that often meant breakfast (still his favorite meal) for dinner. I was in heaven when I got to Europe: scrambled eggs were a dinnertime bed for truffles in Italy, omelets were our favorite lunch as *vendangeurs* (grape-pickers) in France, and wedges of Spanish tortilla (a frittata-like egg cake) were a bar snack. All of those experiences have broadened my grown-up breakfast-for-dinner repertoire. Now I look at the idea of eggs with mix-ins as the world's most convenient wine-friendly dinner; toasted country bread and salad complete the meal. Here are some of my favorite mix-ins, and wine matches for them:

- Smoked salmon, cream cheese, and fresh chives: Domaine Ste. Michelle Brut sparkling wine
- Goat cheese, dried thyme, and sun-dried tomatoes: Honig Sauvignon Blanc
- Gruyère, ham, and fresh sage: Chapoutier Côtes du Rhône
- Tomatoes, onions, and olives: Montecillo Rioja Crianza
- Prosciutto, Parmesan, and dried oregano: Ecco Domani Chianti
- Mushrooms and truffle oil: Gallo of Sonoma Pinot Noir
- Avocado and chopped cooked shrimp: R.H. Phillips Chardonnay
- Spinach and smoked mozzarella: Bogle Merlot

BRINING FOR FLAVOR AND JUICINESS

Brining in salted water mixed with sugar and spices is a simple way to infuse poultry, meat, and seafood with flavor and make sure that they stay juicy during cooking. Obviously, smaller pieces of meat will take less time to absorb the brine than a fifteen-pound bird, and a whole turkey will need a larger quantity of brining solution than will a cut-up chicken. Delicate seafood like shrimp needs just a quick dip in brine to plump it up. Thicker fillets like salmon, swordfish, and mahi mahi take a little bit longer. Following are some brining times and quantities. If you'd like, substitute some wine for water as I've done in the recipe for Fast-Track Baby Back Ribs (page 50). Place the food and brining solution in either a zipper-lock bag or a larger pot or bucket, depending on size, and then refrigerate until ready. Rinse well under cold running water before cooking.

FOUR BONELESS, SKINLESS CHICKEN BREASTS: ½ cup salt, ½ cup sugar, 2 cups water; 45 minutes

ONE CUT-UP CHICKEN (2 TO 3 POUNDS): ½ cup salt, ½ cup sugar, 2 quarts water; 1½ hours

ONE WHOLE CHICKEN (3½ TO 4 POUNDS): ½ cup salt, ½ cup sugar, 2 quarts water; 2 hours

ONE WHOLE TURKEY (12 TO 14 POUNDS): 2 cups salt, 1 cup sugar, 2 gallons water; 12 hours or overnight

2 POUNDS PORK CHOPS OR PORK TENDERLOINS: ½ cup salt, ½ cup sugar, 2 quarts water; 1½ hours

2 POUNDS MEDIUM SHRIMP: ½ cup salt, ½ cup sugar, 2 quarts water; 30 minutes

FOUR ½-POUND PIECES FIRM FISH FILLETS OR STEAKS SUCH AS SALMON, SWORD-FISH, OR MAHIMAHI: ½ cup salt, ½ cup sugar, 2 quarts water; 45 minutes

"BRICK-ROASTED" CHICKEN BREASTS

SERVES SIX • This showstopper recipe is surprisingly easy to make. Several steps guarantee great flavor. Brining the breasts before cooking ensures they'll remain succulent and juicy (see page 196 for more on brining). Roasting them "under a brick" (or just a heavy pan) gives them a crusty, golden skin. The oregano leaves inserted between the meat and skin make a pretty design and flavor the meat. Most any red loves the taste of oregano, but I especially love red Zinfandel and red Côtes du Rhône with this dish.

CALIFORNIA RED ZINFANDEL	FRENCH CÔTES DU RHÔNE RED	
Rancho Zabaco Heritage Vines, St. Francis, Rafanelli Dry Creek Valley	Jean-Luc Colombo Les Abeilles, Coudoulet de Beaucastel	½ cup packed brown sugar ½ cup kosher salt 6 chicken breast halves, bone in, with skin (about 2 pounds) 2 tablespoons olive oil, plus more for oiling the pan 1 small bunch fresh oregano Salt and freshly ground black pepper

1. Combine the brown sugar, kosher salt, and 1 cup of hot water in a large bowl. Stir to dissolve the sugar and salt. Add 3 cups of cold water and stir to combine. Place the chicken breast halves meaty side down in a single layer in a large, nonreactive baking dish. Pour the brine over the chicken, cover with plastic wrap, and refrigerate for at least 3 hours or overnight.

2. Preheat the oven to 450°F. Remove the breasts from the brine, rinse well under cold running water, and pat dry with paper towels. Brush a large grill pan or a heavy baking dish large enough to accommodate the chicken breasts with olive oil. Wrap another heavy baking dish of the same size in a large sheet of heavy-duty aluminum foil so that the outside bottom of the dish is completely covered. Oil the foil-covered bottom of the baking dish, or spray with nonstick cooking spray, to prevent sticking. Set aside, upside down, until ready to use.

3. Place the 2 tablespoons of olive oil in a small bowl. Gently loosen the skin of the chicken breasts by sliding your fingers under the skin and moving your fingers back

and forth to create a pocket. Moisten your fingers and a small branch of oregano with some olive oil and insert it under the skin. Insert 4 small branches under the skin of each breast half, arranging them so the leaves show through the skin, and sprinkle the breasts all over with salt and pepper.

4. Place the oiled pan in the preheated oven for 5 minutes. Remove the pan from the oven and place the breasts skin side down on the hot pan (they will begin to sizzle). Place the foil-covered baking pan, oiled side down, on top of the chicken and place the pans on the middle rack of the oven, weighing the top pan with another heavy ovenproof dish such as a skillet or heavy casserole. Roast for 17 minutes.

5. Remove the weighting pan and the top pan, turn the chicken so that it is skin side up, and continue to roast, unweighted, until the skin is crisp and the meat cooked through, 5 to 7 minutes depending on the size of the breasts. Remove the plates and serve immediately.

CUMIN-CRUSTED LAMB

SERVES TWO • I've always loved the pappadum wafers served as a predinner snack at Indian restaurants. When I found a source for mail-order pappadums (see page 286), I immediately stocked up. I've discovered that they last for months in a zipper-lock bag in the pantry. To crisp them up, just pop them into the microwave for a few seconds.

Nowadays you can buy rack of lamb, a favorite in my family, at the supermarket perfectly "Frenched" (meaning the excess fat has been removed and the bones scraped clean) and ready for cooking (I watch for it to go on sale). In looking for something different from the usual mustard-and-herb-crusted rack of lamb I'd learned in culinary school, I thought it would be great to make a crust of crushed pappadums instead. The savory spices and crunchy texture of the crust further enhance the wine-affinity of lamb, making it a mind-bending match with the sweet spice of a red Zinfandel, or the pepperiness of Rhône red.

WINE RECOMMENDATIONS

CALIFORNIA RED ZINFANDEL

Rosenblum Vintners Cuvée, Cline Cellars, Marietta, Monteviña Terra d'Oro

RHÔNE RED

Alain Graillot Crozes-Hermitage, Chapoutier Hermitage La Sizeranne

3 pappadum wafers

1 teaspoon black mustard seeds

1½ tablespoons cumin seeds

1 teaspoon dried thyme

½ teaspoon freshly ground black pepper

½ teaspoon freshly ground white pepper

½ teaspoon kosher salt

1 tablespoon olive oil

One 7- or 8-bone rack of lamb, trimmed and Frenched (1¼ pounds)

1. Preheat the oven to 475°F. Place one of the pappadum wafers on a paper towel and microwave on high until crisp, 30 seconds to 1 minute depending on the power of your oven. Remove and let cool. Repeat with the remaining 2 pappadum wafers.

2. Break up the crisped pappadums and place them in a blender or the workbowl of a food processor. Add the mustard seeds, cumin seeds, thyme, black pepper, white

pepper, and salt. Process until the mixture is the texture of fine crumbs. Transfer the mixture to a shallow plate and spread into an even layer.

3. Heat 1 tablespoon of olive oil over medium-high in a heavy skillet. Add the lamb rack, fat side down, and sear until well-browned, about 3 minutes. Grasp the meat with tongs, hold the bones upright and vertical, and sear the top meat until well-browned, another 3 minutes. Turn again and sear the bone side until well-browned, another 3 minutes. Transfer the lamb to a rimmed baking sheet and let cool slightly.

4. When the rack is cool enough to handle, roll it in the pappadum mixture so that it is well coated. Place the coated rack back on the baking sheet, bone side down, and roast to the desired doneness, 15 to 20 minutes for medium-rare. Turn the oven to broil to crisp the crust, 1 to 2 minutes (watch carefully so the crumbs don't burn).

5. Remove the lamb from the oven and loosely cover with foil. Let stand for 5 minutes. Cut the lamb between the bones to separate into chops and serve.

LEMON-HERB-PROSCIUTTO SHRIMP

MAKES TWENTY-FOUR • It's the herbs, black pepper, and heady ham that make this dish a super match for a peppery Shiraz or Syrah. I like this hors d'oeuvre for entertaining. I prepare the shrimp for cooking ahead of time and keep them refrigerated until my guests have arrived. Then I pour some wine and we start cooking and eating them while we talk and hang out in the kitchen. The smell as they're cooking gets everyone's mouth watering, and it's fun and delicious to eat them piping hot from the pan.

WINE RECOMMENDATIONS

SHIRAZ

Black Opal, Wyndham, Cape Mentelle (Australia)

SYRAH

Cline, BV Coastal (California)

24 large shrimp, tails on, peeled and deveined

½ cup fresh herbs, finely chopped (rosemary, sage, thyme, or a combination)

1 tablespoon freshly grated lemon zest

½ cup sherry or white wine

½ cup olive oil, plus more for cooking the shrimp

Pinch saffron threads, broken, optional

Pinch kosher salt

Freshly ground black pepper

8 paper-thin slices prosciutto or Serrano ham

1. With a sharp paring knife, butterfly the shrimp by slicing the outsides (vein sides) almost through from head to tail, leaving the inner curve and tail intact. Place the shrimp, ¼ cup of the herbs, 1½ teaspoons of the lemon zest, the sherry, ½ cup olive oil, the saffron, salt, and pepper in a nonreactive bowl. Stir to combine. Cover with plastic wrap and marinate in the refrigerator 30 minutes.

2. Remove the shrimp to a paper towel–lined plate to drain, and sprinkle with the remaining herbs and lemon zest. Cut each ham slice lengthwise into thirds (you should have ribbons of ham about 1 inch wide). Place a shrimp flat (wings open) on each ham slice, and wrap the ham snugly around the center. Skewer each shrimp horizontally with a toothpick to hold it flat while cooking.

3. Preheat a lightly oiled grill pan or heavy skillet on medium-high. Cook in batches, until shrimp is opaque and ham is crispy, turning once, about 1½ minutes per side. (Shrimp may also be cooked under a broiler, turning once, 1½ minutes per side.)

4. Remove to a platter and serve warm.

SPICE-PAINTED SALMON

SERVES FOUR • Whether I'm poaching or "painting," cooking is definitely my artistic outlet. Painting the flesh of the fish with this spicy glaze and then sautéing it paint side down and undisturbed in a hot skillet caramelizes the paint, intensifying the spices and giving a hint of smoky sweetness, both of which echo the flavors and scents in New World Syrah and Shiraz.

Whole spices that you toast and grind yourself give the paint a truer, more intense spiciness than would jarred preground spices. Use a spice grinder for the whole spices if you have one, or use a small coffee grinder, which works just as well. (I suggest you designate one grinder for spices only to avoid commingling the coffee and spices.) I highly recommend that you buy a rasp-like grater for the orange zest if you don't already own one. This tool, which came on the market just a few years ago, is a true miracle worker. Not only does it grate the finest zest effortlessly and instantly, but it grates hard cheeses like Parmesan very quickly and with equal ease.

WINE RECOMMENDATIONS

SYRAH

McDowell, Alban, Andrew Murray (California)

SHIRAZ

Rosemount, Penfolds Kalimna Bin 28 (Australia)

FOR THE "PAINT"

2 teaspoons black peppercorns

¼ teaspoon whole cloves

¼ teaspoon coriander seeds

2½ tablespoons brown sugar

¼ cup soy sauce

¼ cup dark rum

2 teaspoons finely grated orange zest

2 teaspoons balsamic vinegar

4 center-cut salmon fillets, about 6 ounces each

1 tablespoon olive oil

Fresh cilantro leaves for garnish, optional

1. Combine the peppercorns, cloves, and coriander seeds in a dry skillet and toast over medium-high heat, moving the spices around in the pan constantly, until fragrant, about 1 minute. Transfer to a spice grinder and grind coarsely.

2. Combine the brown sugar, soy sauce, rum, orange zest, and vinegar in a saucepan with the ground spices. Reduce the mixture over medium heat until ¼ cup remains, about 10 minutes. Remove from the heat and set aside to cool.

3. Use a pastry brush to paint the salmon on the non-skin side with the spice mixture. Heat the olive oil in a large, heavy, nonstick skillet on medium. Carefully place the fillets paint side down in the preheated skillet. Cook the fish fillets without moving to allow the paint to caramelize to a dark color, about 2 minutes. Increase the heat to medium-high, and immediately turn fillets skin side down. Continue cooking until medium-rare and the skin is crisped, 5 to 7 minutes, depending on their thickness, adding a few drops of olive oil as needed to prevent sticking. Place fillets paint side up on serving plates, garnished with a few cilantro leaves, if using, and serve immediately.

WHOLE FISH BAKED IN A SALT CRUST

SERVES FOUR • It's hard to believe that a dish this spectacular is quick and easy enough for everyday dining, but it is. Given the delicacy of the fish, it's also surprising that its best matches are big, spicy reds like Zinfandel, Syrah, and French Rhône blends. In this case, the match takes advantage of the breathtaking synergy between Mediterranean herbs and big, rustic red wines that I described at the beginning of this chapter. More proof of how seasoning, rather than what is being seasoned, often guides the best wine match.

For a fun variation, change the herbs to tarragon, chervil, and lovage, and try the dish with a white wine based on the Sauvignon Blanc grape (Sancerre, Pouilly-Fumé, white Bordeaux, or Fumé Blanc would all be great choices). Or get really wacky and try it with chilled Spanish Manzanilla sherry (La Gitana, Barbadillo, or Lustau). Spain's sherry country was where I first tasted salt-baked fish. I'll never forget how the flavor of the fish sprang to life, as if the salty crust and briny-crisp wine made the fish feel back at home in the sea.

WINE RECOMMENDATIONS

CÔTES DU RHÔNE

Alain Voge, Chapoutier, Brusset

RED ZINFANDEL

Bonny Doon Cardinal Zin, Peachy Canyon, Fetzer Valley Oaks, Ridge Geyserville

SYRAH

Columbia Winery (Washington State)

McDowell (California)

Zaca Mesa (California)

2 pounds kosher salt, plus more for seasoning the fish

One 2-pound whole red snapper, pink snapper, or black sea bass, cleaned, leaving head and tail intact

Freshly ground black pepper

5 tablespoons finely chopped fresh oregano, sage, or thyme, or a combination

Half a lemon, sliced crosswise

Extra virgin olive oil for drizzling

Spanish sherry vinegar, optional

1. Preheat the oven to 450°F. Position a rack in the middle of the oven. In a bowl, stir together the salt and 1 cup of water until the salt is evenly moistened.

2. Score both sides of the fish, cutting ⅛-inch-deep slits just through the skin to expose a little of the flesh.

3. Sprinkle the inside cavity of the fish lightly with salt and a few grinds of black pepper. Rub 2 tablespoons of the herbs into the cavity, and insert the lemon slices. Rub 1 tablespoon chopped herbs onto each side of the fish, pressing the herbs into the slits.

4. Spread half of the salt mixture in an oval just larger than the fish on a large baking sheet. Set the fish on top of the salt. Pat the remaining salt mixture over the fish to cover completely, scooping the bottom layer of salt mixture up to mold around the curves of the fish. It's okay for the tail to stick out a little bit. Bake for 30 minutes.

5. Remove the baking sheet from the oven and rap around the edges of the salt crust to loosen it. Lift the crust from the fish. It's okay if the skin comes away with the crust.

6. To serve, use a spatula to cut the exposed side of the fish into 2 portions and place on 2 warmed dinner plates. Lift the tail to remove the bones in one piece and expose the other side of the fish. Cut that side into 2 portions, lift it from the bottom salt crust, and place on warmed plates. Drizzle each portion with extra virgin olive oil and a splash of sherry vinegar, if desired. Sprinkle with the remaining herbs and serve immediately.

Everyday Dinners with
SHIRAZ, RHÔNE-STYLE REDS, AND ZINFANDEL

PASTAS AND OTHER ONE-PLATE DINNERS

WHAT TO COOK	WINE PAIRINGS
Poached Eggs with Roasted Tomatoes and Crispy Sage *(page 194)*, biscuits or sourdough bread	ONCE-A-WEEK ($–$$): Perrin Reserve Côtes du Rhône (France) Vidal-Fleury Crozes-Hermitage (France) ONCE-A-MONTH ($$$ AND UP): Domaine Santa Duc Gigondas (France)
Oven-Charred Asparagus with Cheese and Balsamic Vinegar *(page 190)*, toasted country bread drizzled with olive oil and sprinkled with sea salt	ONCE-A-WEEK ($–$$): Jade Mountain La Provencal (California) R.H. Phillips EXP Syrah (California) ONCE-A-MONTH ($$$ AND UP): Andrew Murray Syrah (California)
Shiraz-Poached Pears with Roquefort and Black Pepper *(page 187)*, prosciutto slices and spinach leaves sprinkled with extra virgin olive oil	ONCE-A-WEEK ($–$$): Jaboulet Parallele 45 Côtes du Rhône (France) D'Arenberg Red Ochre Shiraz blend (Australia) ONCE-A-MONTH ($$$ AND UP): Rosemount GSM (Grenache-Shiraz-Mourvèdre) (Australia)

TRADITIONAL (MAIN-AND-SIDES) DINNERS

WHAT TO COOK	WINE PAIRINGS
MAIN COURSE: Lemon-Herb-Prosciutto Shrimp *(page 201)* VEGGIES: steamed broccoli or spinach STARCHES, ETC.: noodles with olive oil and garlic	ONCE-A-WEEK ($–$$): Wyndham Shiraz (Australia) Cline Syrah (California) ONCE-A-MONTH ($$$ AND UP): Cape Mentelle Shiraz (Australia)
MAIN COURSE: Whole Fish Baked in a Salt Crust *(page 204)* VEGGIES: Pear, Fennel, and Blue Cheese Salad with Red Wine Glaze *(page 221)* STARCHES, ETC.: Roasted Fingerling Frites *(page 168)*	ONCE-A-WEEK ($–$$): Fetzer Valley Oaks Zinfandel (California) Bonny Doon Cardinal Zin (California) ONCE-A-MONTH ($$$ AND UP): Ridge Geyserville Zinfandel (California)

WHAT TO COOK	WINE PAIRINGS
MAIN COURSE: Spice-Painted Salmon *(page 202)* VEGGIES: Lucas's Sesame-Ginger Broccoli Florets *(page 80)* STARCHES, ETC.: Thai-style rice noodles	ONCE-A-WEEK ($–$$): McDowell Syrah (California) Greg Norman Shiraz (Australia) ONCE-A-MONTH ($$$ AND UP): Penfolds Kalimna Bin 28 Shiraz (Australia)
MAIN COURSE: Cumin-Crusted Lamb *(page 199)* VEGGIES: Warm Wild Mushroom Salad with Black Truffle Vinaigrette *(page 132)* STARCHES, ETC.: rice pilaf	ONCE-A-WEEK ($–$$): Marietta Zinfandel (California) Alain Graillot Crozes-Hermitage (France) ONCE-A-MONTH ($$$ AND UP): Chapoutier Hermitage La Sizeranne (France)
MAIN COURSE: "Brick-Roasted" Chicken Breasts *(page 197)* VEGGIES: Roasted Root Vegetables with Oregano *(page 105)* STARCHES, ETC.: buttered orzo pasta	ONCE-A-WEEK ($–$$): Jean-Luc Colombo Les Abeilles Côtes du Rhône (France) Rancho Zabaco Heritage Vines Zinfandel (California) ONCE-A-MONTH ($$$ AND UP): Rafanelli Dry Creek Valley Zinfandel (California)
MAIN COURSE: Churrasco-Style Skirt Steak *(page 112)* VEGGIES: Charred Tricolore Salad *(page 186)* STARCHES, ETC.: white rice	ONCE-A-WEEK ($–$$): Clape Cornas (France) Jaboulet Cornas (France) ONCE-A-MONTH ($$$ AND UP): Guigal Côte Rôtie (France)
MAIN COURSE: Seared Shrimp and Chorizo Bites *(page 65)* VEGGIES: marinated mushrooms or roasted red peppers STARCHES, ETC.: Toasted Chickpeas with Crispy Sage *(page 191)*	ONCE-A-WEEK ($–$$): La Vieille Ferme Rouge (France) Monteviña Zinfandel (California) ONCE-A-MONTH ($$$ AND UP): Renwood Zinfandel (California)
MAIN COURSE: barbecued chicken VEGGIES: Carrot Slaw with Toasted Pine Nuts and Herbs *(page 39)* STARCHES, ETC.: Spicy Fruited Couscous *(page 193)*	ONCE-A-WEEK ($–$$): Gallo of Sonoma Zinfandel (California) Seghesio Zinfandel (California) ONCE-A-MONTH ($$$ AND UP): Dry Creek Reserve Zinfandel (California)

chapter eight

ITALIAN AND
SPANISH REDS

Italy: Rosso Rundown

KEY REGIONS FOR RED
Tuscany (Chianti, Brunello, Vino Nobile), Bolgheri (Super Tuscans), Piedmont (Barolo, Barbaresco, Dolcetto, Barbera)

STYLE
Ranging from easy-drinking and spicy for basic styles to powerful, tannic, and ageable for riservas and Super Tuscans

---

FLAVOR
Bright cherry to dark berry fruit, licorice notes, savory spice from oak

---

REGIONS TO WATCH
Apulia, Sicily

Spain: Tinto Tally

KEY REGIONS FOR RED
Rioja, Ribera del Duero, Priorat

STYLE
Ranging from soft and easy-drinking for Crianza to powerful, tannic, and long-lived for Gran Reserva and all Priorat wines

---

FLAVOR
Ranging from spicy-cherry for basic styles to fig and licorice for Priorat to leathery-toffee for Gran Reserva styles

---

REGIONS TO WATCH
Navarra, Toro, Jumilla

If passion had a home address, it would be Italy. In my book, Spain would share the same zip code.

It's true that the two countries have their own unique cooking traditions and wine styles. But the food and wine of both cultures are crafted with similar boldness and spontaneity. Italy's been seducing us for years with its pasta, sauces, and wines. It is only recently, however, that Americans have been lured by Spain's siren song to her flavor frontier. While it's unlikely you'll add labor-of-love dishes like paella and roast suckling pig to your everyday dinner repertoire, I guarantee that once you try them, Spanish wines will become regulars at your table. Why? Because Spain's wines join Italy's in consistently delivering quality and value across all price points, from budget to boutique.

They also deliver in a big way on food affinity, no matter what you like to eat. In my experience, a lot of people underestimate this, thinking of Italian wines only when they are having pasta or pizza, and Spanish wines even less (most of us don't make paella or tapas very often). But the reality is that these wines are chameleons, as I discovered while working at Wild Blue, the exquisite wine-pairing restaurant-within-the-restaurant at Windows on the World. The chef, Michael Lomonaco, changed the menu daily, drawing from the entire cornucopia of regional American flavors, from Tex-Mex to Chinatown to California farmer's market. As the cellar team experimented with the dishes and wines (with our guests as willing taste-testers!), we marveled again and again at how often the Italian and Spanish reds emerged as our favorites to pair. It's really no surprise when you remember the food-fanatical cultures behind them. Italian and Spanish vintners don't think market share or a critic's score when they make wine. They think dinner.

In my book, good cheese is the busy everyday dinner chef's best friend. At least once a week, I enjoy (tremendously!) a dinner of wine, some good cheese, bread, and a simple fruit or vegetable preparation. Prep and cleanup are a breeze, and the flavors in my favorite cheese supper combinations are to die for. Here they are:

- Blue cheese (Roquefort, Gorgonzola, or Cabrales), fresh pears, nut bread: red Zinfandel

- Pecorino cheese, olives, balsamic vinegar, extra virgin olive oil, and croutons over torn salad greens: Chianti

- Manchego cheese, toasted almonds, and wilted spinach with raisins: Rioja Reserva

- Muenster cheese melted onto sourdough bread chunks, Granny Smith apple slices: Alsace Gewürztraminer or Riesling

- Fresh goat cheese spread onto toasted baguette slices, topped with chopped green herbs, fresh tomato slices, cracked black pepper, and coarse salt such as fleur de sel: Sauvignon Blanc

- Brin d'Amour cheese folded into pita bread with roasted peppers and jarred marinated artichokes: Côtes du Rhône red

mushrooms, and cheese dishes, and leather-spice that's delicious with slow-cooked or cured meats.

GRAN RESERVA. Only the top grape sources are used, and the wines are given long barrel aging. This style—deep fig and raisin fruit, sweet toffee-spice scent, and powerful, mouth-coating texture—is fabulous with grilled food, prime meats, roasted birds, and artisan cheeses. While some of the bottlings can get expensive, there are quite a few excellent under-$20 versions that are great for once-a-month (or so) special weekend dinners.

Ribera del Duero. As in Rioja, the main Ribera del Duero grape is Tempranillo. The wine style, though, is more powerful, tannic, and oaky. Due to a small supply and high quality, most bottlings aren't priced for every day, but are affordable for an occasional trade up. For example, if you've invested in great steaks, a fine rack of lamb, or are having a dinner party and want a great red for a cheese course, Ribera del Duero is perfect.

Succumb to the Seduction of Italian and Spanish Reds

WHEN IN ROME (or Madrid!), as they say . . . Actually, even when you're not, you can still thoroughly enjoy yourself like a native Italian or Spaniard with the food and wine pairings that follow. Let dinner at your house be the occasion that it is every night in these exuberant Mediterranean locales. I often give myself up to this pleasure, even on busy weeknights, by opening a couple of Italian and/or Spanish reds, one to go with a simple salad, pasta, or main course, and another to go with some cheese. It's not more time-consuming than opening a single bottle, and it's a lot more fun. You don't have to finish all the wines, because Italian and Spanish red wine leftovers generally keep well for several days. You *do* have to sit down with your loved ones and talk—lots! (That's part of the formula.) And when you want to put together a really special dinner party, these wines will do you proud. See Great Menus with Wine (page 280) for menu and pairing ideas.

THE BIGGER THEY ARE, THE HARDER THEY PAIR . . .

Wine critics and sommeliers are giving Priorat wines, named for their growing region near Barcelona, a lot of attention—because they demand it. The wines, based mostly on the Tempranillo, Cabernet Sauvignon, and Garnacha grapes, are huge: powerful, inky-purple, oaky, and intense. The most coveted collector bottlings are expensive and built for the cellar. Personally, I'm not convinced they're built for the table, and not just because of the price. I find that such strong flavors are hard to match with most anything other than strong cheeses. It's not that the matches taste bad, but the wines are so big they tend to clobber a lot of food flavors.

In addition, their alcohol level is often so high that more than a sip or two exhausts my palate, and that misses the whole point of wine with dinner. If you want to try Priorat wines, I suggest the biggest game meat dish you can muster, or a big cheese such as Camembert, Spanish Cabrales, or Italian Parmigiano-Reggiano.

ROSÉ-COLORED WINEGLASSES

It's time to ditch your snobbery about rosé wines. If you haven't already heard, all that blushes is not sweet. The Mateus and Lancer's of the 1970s were just a side trip on the classic rosé wine route, which wends its way through some of the sunniest, most savory territory in Europe. Southern France, Italy, and Spain all produce juicy, refreshing, spicy rosés that are bone dry and tailor-made for an amazing array of foods.

Rosé wines are made by soaking the juice of red grapes with their skins for a short amount of time, so the juice picks up just a hint of pale pink or salmon color. Unlike white Zinfandel and its blush brethren, rosés are fermented totally dry, so they retain the red wine character of the grapes from which they're made. Yet they have the refreshing quality for which rosés are celebrated. Here are some of the best rosés to look for, and classic pairing ideas:

ITALY

Rosato is the Italian word for rosé. Italy's *rosatos* are, like all her wines, built for food. Chianti's *rosato*, based on the Tuscan Sangiovese grape, is juicy with fresh strawberry flavor and a bit of white pepper spiciness that matches wonderfully with pizza and spicy, red-sauced pastas. The Sicily region also makes wonderful rosés whose crisp acidity is tailor-made for seafood, spicy stuff like wings, and fried foods.

FRANCE

Southern France is awash in delicious, bargain-priced rosés. My favorites are the Côtes du Rhône and Côte de Ventoux rosés. They're wonderful with Niçoise and Greek salads, olives and tapenade, and tuna fish. Provence is also well known for rosés from the Côtes de Provence appellation. Try them with goat cheeses and grilled vegetables.

SPAIN

The Navarra region of Spain is famous for *rosados* (Spanish for rosé) made from the Garnacha grape. Their watermelon scent and crisp, mouthwatering pomegranate flavor are wonderful with tapas-style fare—garlicky mushrooms and shrimp, chorizo and other sausages, cured hams such as Serrano, and egg dishes such as frittatas, omelets, and the Spanish egg dish called *tortilla*.

ROASTED TOMATO SOUP WITH LEEKS AND CARROTS

SERVES FOUR TO SIX • The natural sweetness and earthiness of the roasted vegetables, and the scented savoriness of fresh basil, are gorgeous with the sweet fruit and savory spiciness of the Sangiovese grape. Pairing them with everyday Chianti shows the genius in Italian thinking when it comes to wine and food: simple + simple = scrumptious!

- 4 tablespoons olive oil, plus more or nonstick cooking spray
- 1 shallot, thinly sliced
- 2 pounds tomatoes, cored and halved, or quartered if large
- 1 pound carrots, sliced ½ inch thick
- 4 garlic cloves, unpeeled
- 2 leeks, white parts only, trimmed and rinsed thoroughly of grit, sliced ½ inch thick
- Kosher salt and freshly ground black pepper
- ½ cup fresh basil, cut into thin chiffonade strips

1. Preheat the oven to 400°F. Oil two 9-x-13-inch baking pans or spray with nonstick cooking spray. Arrange shallot, tomatoes, carrots, garlic, and leeks in the prepared pans. Drizzle each pan with 2 tablespoons olive oil and sprinkle with salt and pepper. Roast until vegetables are tender and brown, stirring once or twice to ensure even cooking, about 45 minutes. Cool slightly, squeeze roasted garlic cloves from their skins, discarding the skins, and transfer the garlic and other vegetables to a bowl.

2. And ½ cup water to each of the baking pans and scrap up any browned bits. Combine half of the vegetables and the liquid from one of the pans in the workbowl of a food processor and process, adding more water a tablespoon at a time if necessary, to achieve a smooth consistency. Transfer the puree to a large saucepan and repeat with the remaining vegetables and cooking liquid. Stir in another 1 to 1½ cups of water to thin the puree.

3. Bring the soup to a gentle simmer and cook for 10 minutes to blend the flavors. Season with salt and pepper. Just before serving, stir in half the basil. Ladle into soup bowls and sprinkle some of the remaining basil over each portion of soup.

utes; or, place pita quarters directly on the grill and close the lid until the cheese is puffy, about 2 minutes. The cheese may get a few toasty-brown spots, but watch carefully to prevent overbrowning.

4. Meanwhile, finely chop the basil leaves and stir gently into the strawberries.

5. When the pita quarters come out of the oven or off the grill, spoon the strawberry mixture over the cheese and serve immediately.

PEAR, FENNEL, AND BLUE CHEESE SALAD WITH RED WINE GLAZE

SERVES SIX • Like a balanced wine, this salad has elements of harmony and contrast that come together beautifully—crunchy fennel, juicy pears, creamy cheese—plus flavors that range from sweet to savory to earthy. Both Chianti and Rosso di Montepulciano have tangy fruit to contrast the salty cheese, and oakiness that echoes the licorice scent of the fennel. This makes a fabulous first course, a light lunch, or a flavorful salad/cheese course to follow a main course.

<table>
<tr><td rowspan="2" style="writing-mode: vertical">WINE RECOMMENDATIONS</td><td>CHIANTI</td><td>1⅓ cups balsamic vinegar</td><td>2 tablespoons extra virgin olive oil</td></tr>
<tr><td>Frescobaldi Chianti Rufina, Castello di Ama Chianti Classico, Rocca delle Macie</td><td>½ cup dry red wine, such as Chianti (leftover is fine)

2 tablespoons packed light brown sugar

1 medium bulb fresh fennel, trimmed and cored</td><td>Kosher salt

6 pears, such as Bosc or Anjou

3 ounces Cambazzola, or other good-quality blue cheese

Freshly ground black pepper</td></tr>
</table>

ROSSO DI MONTEPULCIANO

Avignonesi, Dei, Boscarelli

1. Combine the vinegar, wine, and sugar in a heavy, large saucepan. Bring to a boil over medium heat, stirring to dissolve sugar. Boil until syrupy and reduced to ½ cup, about 20 minutes. Remove from the heat and set aside to cool.

2. Slice the fennel bulb paper thin, using a mandoline, a very sharp knife, or a food processor slicing disc. Toss the fennel with the olive oil, and salt to taste.

3. To serve: Spread a bed of fennel evenly on each of 6 salad plates. Quarter and core the pears and arrange the quarters on each plate. Distribute pieces of the cheese equally among the plates. Grind fresh black pepper liberally over each plate, and drizzle with the red wine glaze. Serve immediately.

SPANISH-STYLE SCRAMBLED EGGS WITH CHORIZO AND MANCHEGO *FRICOS*

SERVES TWO • A *frico* is a crisp, lacy cheese wafer, usually made by melting grated Montasio or Parmesan cheese in a nonstick skillet, then sliding it out and letting it cool. Here I use Spanish Manchego instead, because it goes so well with spicy chorizo and eggs. This is one of my favorite "breakfast for dinner" dishes.

<table>
<tr><td>WINE RECOMMENDATIONS</td><td>SPANISH RIOJA

Montecillo Rioja Crianza

Marques de Arienzo Rioja Crianza, Muga Rioja Reserva</td><td>3 ounces Manchego cheese, shredded
One 4-inch piece Spanish-style chorizo (about 3 ounces)
1 small yellow onion, finely chopped
6 large eggs
3 tablespoons finely chopped fresh parsley
Freshly ground black pepper and sea salt</td></tr>
</table>

1. Heat a medium nonstick skillet over medium heat. When it is hot, sprinkle half of the cheese evenly over the bottom of the skillet. Cook, shaking the pan occasionally to ensure an even distribution of the cheese over the pan bottom, until the edges are lacy and toasted, about 4 minutes. Remove the pan from the heat and allow the cheese to set for about 30 seconds. Use a large heatproof spatula and tongs to carefully flip the *frico* over and cook until the other side is golden, another 2 minutes. Slide the *frico* out of the pan and onto a paper towel–lined plate. Repeat with the remaining cheese. Let stand while you prepare the eggs.

2. Cut the chorizo into ½-inch dice. Heat a nonstick skillet to medium-high, and add the chorizo. Once the fat from the chorizo has started to render, after about 1 minute, add the onion and stir. Reduce the heat to medium and cook, stirring often, until the onion is soft and the onion and chorizo have browned slightly. Pour off all but 1 tablespoon of the fat.

3. Whisk the eggs to break up the yolks, and add to the skillet. Add the parsley to taste. Reduce the heat to low and cook, stirring and scraping the bottom often (this yields a soft, fluffy texture). Spoon the scrambled eggs onto plates and season to taste with pepper and salt (keep in mind that the *fricos* are salty, and the chorizo is peppery). Break the *fricos* into approximately 3-inch pieces, and serve with the eggs.

CHEESE GRITS WITH SHRIMP AND CHORIZO

SERVES FOUR • This recipe marries two of my favorite dishes—low-country shrimp and grits, and the Spanish tapa of shrimp and chorizo bits sizzled together with garlic. Using Manchego cheese in the cheese grits keeps with the Spanish theme, and contributes enough richness that you don't need cream or milk in the grits or sauce—so while it's not spa cooking, this dish isn't as heavy as traditional shrimp and grits. The earthy corn taste of grits is great with the earthiness of old style, spicy Spanish Riojas and Ribera del Dueros. Quick-cooking grits, smoked sausage, and quick-cooking shrimp make this dish a great weeknight choice. For extra convenience, I use the frozen bags of peeled and deveined uncooked shrimp sold at supermarkets and club stores.

<table>
<tr><td rowspan="2">WINE RECOMMENDATIONS</td><td>SPANISH RIOJA

Marques de Riscal Rioja Reserva, El Coto Rioja Reserva

SPANISH RIBERA DEL DUERO

Pesquera Ribera del Duero, Abadia Retuerta Sardon de Duero</td><td>4 ounces chorizo, cut into ¼-inch dice

½ teaspoon kosher salt, plus more to taste

1 cup quick-cooking grits or instant polenta

2 tablespoons unsalted butter

1 pound medium shrimp, peeled and deveined</td><td>2 medium garlic cloves, finely chopped

½ cup grated Manchego cheese

Freshly ground black pepper

2 tablespoons finely chopped fresh chives, optional</td></tr>
</table>

1. Cook the chorizo in a heavy, medium skillet over medium heat until it is crisp, 2 to 3 minutes. Transfer the chorizo to a paper towel–lined plate to drain. Pour off all but a thin film of fat from the skillet.

2. Bring 4 cups of water and ½ teaspoon salt to boil in a medium saucepan. Slowly stir in the grits. Reduce the heat to low and cook about 5 minutes, whisking occasionally, until the grits are thick and smooth.

3. While the grits are cooking, add 1 tablespoon of the butter to the skillet and heat over medium-high until the butter is foaming. Cook the shrimp until just pink, turning once, about 3 minutes. Stir in the chorizo and the garlic and cook, stirring constantly, until the garlic is fragrant, about 30 seconds longer.

4. Stir the remaining tablespoon butter and the cheese into the grits and season with salt and pepper. Spoon the grits into 4 warmed bowls and top with the chorizo and shrimp mixture. Sprinkle with chives, if desired. Serve immediately.

OLOROSO SHERRY–GLAZED PORK CHOPS WITH MUSHROOMS

SERVES SIX • This assertively flavored one-skillet dish is perfect for weeknights. The sherry caramelizes with the garlic and pan drippings to make a delicious, clingy sauce for quick-cooking pork chops. (Oloroso sherry is an amber-colored, nutty-tasting Spanish fortified wine.) The recipe was inspired by the *chuletas* (bone-in chops) I ate while visiting Spain's Rioja wine district, and that's indeed my pairing. I've also included some up-and-comers from Spain's emerging wine regions, because you can't beat the values.

<table>
<tr>
<td>

WINE RECOMMENDATIONS

SPANISH RIOJA

Finca Allende Rioja Crianza

Herencia Remondo Rioja Reserva, Dominio de Conte Rioja Reserva

SPANISH EMERGING WINES

Osborne Solaz Tempranillo Penedes, Las Rocas Calatayud

</td>
<td>

Six ½-inch-thick bone-in or boneless pork loin chops

Kosher salt

Freshly ground black pepper

6 garlic cloves, finely chopped

3 tablespoons olive oil, plus more if necessary

¾ cup Spanish oloroso sherry

½ pound white button mushrooms, thinly sliced

</td>
</tr>
</table>

1. Rinse the chops under cold running water and pat dry with paper towels. Season liberally on both sides with salt and pepper. With your hands, spread and firmly pat the minced garlic evenly onto both sides of the chops.

2. Heat 3 tablespoons of olive oil on medium-high in a heavy skillet large enough to hold all of the chops in one layer. When the oil is shimmering, add the chops and cook until the meat begins to brown and the garlic to caramelize, about 4 minutes. Turn and brown on the other side, about 2 minutes longer, scraping up any loose pieces of garlic so that they don't burn. Reduce the heat to medium-low and cook the chops, turning occasionally until cooked through, about 12 minutes more. Add

more oil to the pan as necessary to keep the chops from sticking and losing their browned crusts.

3. Add ½ cup of the sherry, increase the heat to medium, and cook, scraping the pan to loosen and mix the browned bits with the wine. Cook, shifting the chops around as necessary, until the wine and pan drippings have thickened to a syrup consistency, about 2 minutes. Remove the chops to a warmed platter and cover with foil to keep warm.

4. Add the mushrooms and the remaining ¼ cup sherry to the same pan, and season to taste with salt and pepper. Increase the heat to medium-high and cook, stirring, until the mushrooms release their liquid and begin to brown, 3 to 5 minutes. Return the chops to the pan with the mushrooms to reheat briefly. Serve immediately.

QUICK PAN SAUCES FOR SAUTÉED CHICKEN OR CHOPS

Boneless chicken

breasts and boneless pork chops—when they're on sale, I stock up and freeze them, because they're the ultimate base for the "make a pan sauce" technique described in the Introduction. The reason is that they caramelize nicely when seared, giving great texture and flavor, and they release just enough fat and meat juices to thicken a bit of liquid and some aromatics into a light but tasty pan sauce. The different permutations and combinations of liquid and aromatics give you tons of choices for wine pairings. Here are some quick pan sauce/wine combinations for weeknight chicken or chops. Once you get the idea, you can improvise your own pan sauces with whatever you have in your pantry and refrigerator.

WINE AND SHALLOTS

Remove the cooked meat from the pan. Add 1 chopped shallot and cook over medium heat until softened, about 1 minute. Pour in 1 cup dry white wine. Bring to a boil, scraping the bottom of the pan to loosen the browned bits. Boil until the liquid is reduced to about ⅓ cup. Stir in 2 tablespoons chopped fresh parsley.

Remove from the heat and swirl in 1 tablespoon unsalted butter. Season with salt and pepper. Pour over the meat and serve, paired with California Chardonnay.

CAPERS AND MUSTARD

Remove the cooked meat from the pan. Add 1 chopped shallot and cook over medium heat until softened, about 1 minute. Pour in ½ cup chicken stock and ½ cup dry white wine. Bring to a boil, scraping the bottom of the pan to loosen the browned bits. Boil until the liquid is reduced to about ⅓ cup. Stir in 1 tablespoon

(continued)

2. Increase the oven temperature to 500°F. Fill a bowl with ice water and squeeze ½ of the lemon into the water. Working with one artichoke at a time, pull off the tough outer leaves. Trim the bottom and top and snip off any remaining leaf tips with a knife or kitchen shears. Halve the artichoke lengthwise and put both halves in the lemon water. Repeat with the remaining artichokes.

3. Drain the artichokes and pat them dry with paper towels. Toss the artichokes with 2 tablespoons of the olive oil, 1½ teaspoons of the rosemary, and ½ teaspoon of the coarse salt. Place them in a heavy baking dish and squeeze the other ½ of the lemon over them. Sprinkle with 2 tablespoons water. Bake for 20 minutes.

4. While the artichokes are cooking, toss the squid with the remaining 2 tablespoons olive oil, the remaining 1½ teaspoons rosemary, the garlic, the remaining teaspoon salt, and pepper. Spread the squid on a rimmed baking sheet and place in the oven alongside the artichokes when the artichokes have baked for 20 minutes. Bake until the artichokes are tender and the squid is opaque, about 5 minutes. Remove from the oven and combine the squid and artichokes in a bowl. Season with salt if necessary. Arrange the squid and artichokes on a serving plate and sprinkle each portion with bread crumbs. Serve immediately.

SEARED TUNA WITH PRESERVED LEMON

SERVES FOUR • Fennel, coriander, and preserved lemon give this simple seared tuna dish a Moroccan flavor, perfect with Spanish and Italian reds. As always with searing, the seasonings are intensified and bonded to the surface of the fish via the heat of the skillet, making for a very flavorful crust. Sesame seeds pressed into the fish just before cooking provide additional crunch. This is a pretty simple recipe, but the tuna needs time to absorb the spices, so begin the recipe two to four hours before you want to eat. For a compatible starch, serve with couscous or one of the many wonderful Mediterranean flatbreads now available in the deli section of the supermarket.

WINE RECOMMENDATIONS

ITALIAN BARBERA

Pio Cesare Barbera d'Alba,
Clerico Barbera d'Alba,
Contratto Barbera d'Alba

2 teaspoons fennel seeds

½ teaspoon coriander seeds

2 teaspoons kosher salt

1 teaspoon freshly ground black pepper

Four 6-ounce tuna loin pieces, 1 inch thick

¾ cup toasted sesame seeds

½ Preserved Lemon (page 271), cut into ¼-inch-thick slivers

2 tablespoons finely chopped fresh parsley

1 tablespoon black sesame seeds, optional

3 tablespoons olive oil

1. Combine the fennel and coriander seeds in a dry skillet and heat on medium-high, stirring constantly, until browned and fragrant, 3 to 4 minutes. Transfer the seeds to a spice grinder or small coffee grinder and grind. Transfer to a small bowl and stir in 2 teaspoons of the salt and ½ teaspoon of the freshly ground black pepper.

2. Sprinkle each piece of tuna lightly on all sides with the spice mixture. Pat with your fingertips so that the cure adheres. Tightly wrap each piece of tuna separately in plastic wrap. Refrigerate the tuna for at least 2 hours and up to 4 hours to set the seasonings.

3. In a medium skillet, toast the sesame seeds over medium-high heat, shaking the pan frequently, until golden. Transfer to a small bowl and let cool.

4. In another small bowl, combine the preserved lemon and parsley and stir.

5. Stir together the toasted sesame seeds and black sesame seeds, if·using. Place

TRADITIONAL (MAIN-AND-SIDES) DINNERS

WHAT TO COOK	WINE PAIRINGS
MAIN COURSE: Crispy Artichokes and Squid *(page 231)* VEGGIES: sliced summer tomatoes with extra virgin olive oil and fleur de sel, or roasted red peppers STARCHES, ETC.: Toasted Chickpeas with Crispy Sage *(page 191)*	ONCE-A-WEEK ($–$$): Regaleali Rosato (Sicily, Italy) Tormaresca Primitivo (Apulia, Italy) ONCE-A-MONTH ($$$ AND UP): Roda Rioja Reserva (Spain)
MAIN COURSE: Cheese Grits with Shrimp and Chorizo *(page 225)* VEGGIES: Garlic-Braised Collard Greens *(page 189)*	ONCE-A-WEEK ($–$$): Marques de Riscal Rioja Reserva (Spain) Onix Priorat (Spain) ONCE-A-MONTH ($$$ AND UP): Pesquera Ribera del Duero (Spain)
MAIN COURSE: Seared Tuna with Preserved Lemon *(page 233)* VEGGIES: Carrot Slaw with Toasted Pine Nuts and Herbs *(page 39)* STARCHES, ETC.: couscous	ONCE-A-WEEK ($–$$): Contratto Barbera d'Alba (Italy) Pio Cesare Barbera d'Alba (Italy) ONCE-A-MONTH ($$$ AND UP): Clerico Barbera d'Alba (Italy)
MAIN COURSE: Chicken Breasts with Prosciutto and Sage *(page 227)* VEGGIES: spinach and mushroom salad STARCHES, ETC.: Creamy Goat Cheese Polenta *(page 108)*	ONCE-A-WEEK ($–$$): Travaglini Gattinara (Italy) Pio Cesare Nebbiolo d'Alba (Italy) ONCE-A-MONTH ($$$ AND UP): Massolino Barolo (Italy)
MAIN COURSE: Flank Steak Marinated in Spicy Herb Oil *(page 226)* VEGGIES: marinated mushrooms and peppers STARCHES, ETC.: Grilled Corn on the Cob with Pumpkinseed Oil *(page 81)*	ONCE-A-WEEK ($–$$): Faustino Rioja Reserva (Spain) Falesco Vitiano (Italy) ONCE-A-MONTH ($$$ AND UP): Rocca delle Macie Roccato (Italy)
MAIN COURSE: Oloroso Sherry–Glazed Pork Chops with Mushrooms *(page 228)* VEGGIES: Oven-Roasted Fennel *(page 134)* STARCHES, ETC.: soft polenta	ONCE-A-WEEK ($–$$): Finca Allende Rioja Crianza (Spain) Las Rocas Calatayud (Spain) ONCE-A-MONTH ($$$ AND UP): Dominio de Conte Rioja Reserva (Spain)

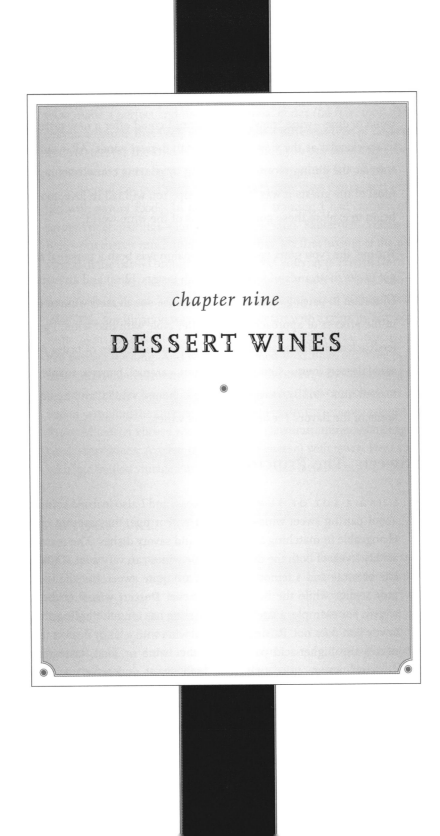

chapter nine

DESSERT WINES

Dessert Wine Categories

DESSERT WINES ARE pretty easy to understand, because there are just five types. Three of them are associated with cool-to-moderate climates, while the other two are associated with warm climates. As with other fruits (think of a Washington-grown apple versus a tropical mango), grapes grown in cool/moderate climates retain more acidity versus those grown in warm climates. Thus the cool-climate wines have prominent acidity (the key component for pairing), while the warm-climate styles are high on sweetness, low on acidity. Here are the five types:

Cool/Moderate Climate

Late Harvest Wines. The grapes are picked later than average, allowing them to become overripe and, thus, very sweet

Botrytis Wines. The grapes picked are infected with botrytis mold, which shrivels and dehydrates them, concentrating their sweetness

Ice Wines. The grapes are picked and pressed while frozen; much of their water content stays frozen as ice, yielding a sweeter, pulpier juice

Warm Climate

Dried-Grape Wines. The grapes are allowed to dry into raisins (either on the vine or after picking); less water content in the grapes yields a sweeter juice

Fortified Wines. The juice is fortified (strengthened) by the addition of alcohol before all the sugar is fermented, yielding a sweet and strong wine

LIQUID GOLD

Dessert wines join French Champagne and red Burgundy on my personal list of splurge-worthy treats. Here are some of the "big guns" to look for when you want to treat yourself to one of the rare classics, or are looking to spend lavishly on a gift for a wine geek (aren't *you* sweet!):

- Vintage Port and Madeira, Portugal (fortified)
- Classified growth Sauternes, France (botrytis)
- Tokaji Essencia, Hungary (botrytis)
- German Beerenauslese and Trockenbeerenauslese (botrytis)
- German Eiswein (ice wine)
- Alsace Selection de Grains Nobles, France (botrytis)

Sugar and Spice, All Things Nice

HERE IS A CHART of the main dessert wine styles and the flavors with which they pair best. It features the most affordable dessert wines—what I consider once-a-week (under $20 per bottle) or once-a-month (under $35) wines.

DESSERT WINE TYPE: **Late Harvest Wines**

SOURCES: California, Washington State, Australia, New Zealand

NAMED FOR: Grape varieties such as Riesling, Gewürztraminer, Semillon, Muscat, Sauvignon Blanc

FLAVOR PARTNERS: Fruit—apples, pears, tropical fruits; custard—crème brûlée, etc.; vanilla, ginger, coconut

---

DESSERT WINE TYPE: **Botrytis and Ice Wines**

SOURCE: France

NAMED FOR: The region—Vouvray, Sauternes

FLAVOR PARTNERS: Tropical fruit, honey, citrus fruit, blue cheese, dried fruits, pears, apples

---

SOURCE: Germany

NAMED FOR: The grape (Riesling) and style (Auslese or Eiswein)

FLAVOR PARTNERS: Tropical fruit, honey, citrus fruit, blue cheese, dried fruits, pears, apples

---

DESSERT WINE TYPE: **Dried-Grape Wines**

SOURCE: Italy

NAMED FOR: The style—Vin Santo, Amarone

FLAVOR PARTNERS: Nuts, caramel, biscotti cookies

SOURCE: Spain

NAMED FOR: The grape (Pedro Ximenez) and region (Jerez/Xèrès/Sherry—the Spanish, French, and English, respectively, for sherry)

FLAVOR PARTNERS: Vanilla, custard, chocolate, figs, dried fruits, maple

---

DESSERT WINE TYPE: **Fortified Wines**

SOURCE: Portugal—Porto

NAMED FOR: The region (Porto) and style (Late bottled vintage [LBV] or tawny)

FLAVOR PARTNERS: LBV—chocolate, vanilla, dark berries; tawny—chocolate, nuts, caramel, honey

SOURCE: Portugal—Madeira

NAMED FOR: The region (Madeira) and either the grape (e.g., Malmsey) or the style (Rainwater)

FLAVOR PARTNERS: Honey, caramel, chocolate, orange peel, dried fruit, maple

---

SOURCE: France

NAMED FOR: The grape (Muscat) and region (Beaumes de Venise)

FLAVOR PARTNERS: Apricot, orange marmalade, chocolate, custard

A Little Goes a Long Way

MANY DESSERT WINES come in half-bottles, yet you still get the same number of servings as with a full bottle of regular wine. That's because, due to their sweetness and, in the case of fortified wines, higher alcohol, the serving size is smaller. A typical serving of dessert wine is three ounces, as compared to six ounces for a glass of regular wine. So before you go into sticker shock at the wine shop, factor this in to figure out the real cost, per serving, of the wine you are buying.

What I Love About Dessert Wines

WHAT'S NOT TO LOVE? Seriously, I think they are God's gift to everyday dinner, because they instantly make it special. And when you do want to turn a meal into an occasion, there is no easier way to make it really memorable and unique. A few years ago I brought different dessert wines to a friend's holiday cookie swap. Gingerbread people with PX sherry, snickerdoodles with Madeira, chocolate-dipped pretzels with tawny Port . . . she says the neighborhood's never been the same!

SIMPLE DESSERTS

So I've talked you into buying a bottle of Port or Madeira, and now you want to enjoy it after dinner with dessert, but don't have time to bake a cake. Not to worry. Dessert wines are an easy way to turn simple desserts based on fresh fruit, or purchased sweets, into something really special. Here are some easy and scrumptious dessert pairing ideas.

FRESH FRUIT DESSERTS

- Strawberries drizzled with best-quality balsamic vinegar, with Banfi Brachetto d'Acqui Italian sparkling rosé
- Fresh figs dusted with cocoa powder, with Fonseca Bin 27 Port, Portugal

- Strawberries, orange zest, and fresh ricotta cheese, with Bonny Doon Muscat Vin de Glaciere, California
- Blueberries, sour cream, and brown sugar, with Rivetti Moscato d'Asti, Italy
- Raspberries and triple crème cheese such as St. Andre, with Moët et Chandon White Star Champagne, France
- Peaches with sweetened whipped cream, with Robert Weil Riesling Auslese, Germany
- Plums with mascarpone and turbinado sugar, with Chambers Museum Muscat, Australia
- Mango and coconut sorbet, with Chateau Ste. Michelle Late Harvest Riesling, Washington State
- Pears with creamy Gorgonzola, with Dr. Parcé Banyuls, France

- Golden pineapple with crushed macaroons, with Huet Vouvray Moelleux, France

CONFECTIONS

- Pecan pie with Blandy's Ten-Year-Old Malmsey Madeira, Portugal
- Biscotti with Castello di Ama Vin Santo, Italy
- Gingerbread and shortbread cookies with Dow's Boardroom Tawny Port, Portugal
- Toasted angel food cake slices with Château Coutet Sauternes, France
- Fruit tarts or turnovers with Selaks Ice Wine, New Zealand
- Chocolate chip cookies with Argueso Pedro Ximenez Sherry, Spain

HONEY- AND LAVENDER-GLAZED FRUIT

SERVES SIX • Infusing honey with lavender is a simple way to add some pretty exotic flavor to complement the smokiness of grilled, glazed fruit. (If you can't find lavender at your market or farmer's market, try using lavender honey. The flavor will be less distinct but still unique.) Choose slightly underripe bananas, the ones that are still a little green, for this recipe. They'll hold their shape on the grill, and the glaze and caramelization from grilling will give them plenty of sweetness. The peaches, too, should be ripe but not soft, or they will fall apart during cooking. This recipe is a snap if you've got a gas grill ready to fire up in the backyard, or if you've already made a charcoal fire to cook dinner, you can later use the cooling coals to caramelize the fruit.

<table>
<tr><td rowspan="3" style="background:black; color:white;">WINE RECOMMENDATIONS</td><td>VOUVRAY FROM THE LOIRE VALLEY

Huet, Champalou, Bourillon-D'Orleans</td><td rowspan="3">½ cup (one stick) unsalted butter, melted

½ cup honey

1 small bunch lavender

1 large ripe pineapple, peeled, quartered, cored, and cut into ½-inch-thick wedges

3 slightly underripe bananas, peeled and sliced in half lengthwise

3 ripe but firm peaches, peeled, halved, pitted, and cut into 1-inch-thick wedges

1 pint vanilla ice cream, optional</td></tr>
<tr><td>SAUTERNES FROM FRANCE

Château LaTour Blanche, Baron Philippe de Rothschild, Château Rieussec</td></tr>
</table>

1. Combine the butter, honey, and lavender in a small saucepan and heat, whisking occasionally, until the butter is melted and the mixture is just coming to a simmer. Remove from the heat and let sit in the pan for 30 minutes. Remove the lavender and discard. Pour the syrup through a fine strainer and into a bowl or measuring cup to remove any stray lavender leaves.

2. Preheat a gas grill to medium and lightly oil the grate. Put all the fruits on a rimmed baking sheet and brush them with the honey glaze. Grill, brushing once or twice with additional glaze, until the fruit is heated through, slightly tender, and caramelized, turning once, about 4 minutes total for the bananas, 6 minutes for the pineapple and peaches. Serve immediately, with a scoop of vanilla ice cream, if desired.

TROPICAL FRUITS "ON THE HALF-SHELL" WITH BANANA CRUNCH TOPPING

SERVES SIX • Miniature golden pineapples make cute containers for tropical fruit. A combination of crushed amaretti cookies and dried banana chips makes this dessert more than just fruit salad. If you haven't tried ice wine, pressed from grapes that have been frozen (either naturally while on the vine, or by putting them in a freezer), here is a good excuse. The wine has tropical fruit flavors and scents, too, making this easy fruit dessert a fabulous match. Dried banana chips are available at most supermarkets, with the dried fruit and nuts, and at natural foods stores.

WINE RECOMMENDATIONS	
ICE WINE Selaks Ice Wine (New Zealand) Bonny Doon Muscat Vin de Glaciere (California) Inniskillin Vidal Ice Wine (Canada)	3 ripe golden baby pineapples 2 cups ripe tropical fruit such as mango, papaya, and/or guava, peeled and cut into ½-inch dice 1 tablespoon fresh lime juice (about ½ a lime) 6 Italian amaretti cookies 2 tablespoons unsalted butter, melted and cooled ½ cup dried banana chips, finely chopped

1. Trim the leafy tops of the pineapples so that the leaves are about 4 inches long. Cut each pineapple in half lengthwise through the leafy tops. Use the tip of a sharp knife to cut out the hard cores, and then cut or scoop out the fruit from each pineapple, leaving the shells intact.

2. Cut the pineapple into ½-inch dice. Place the pineapple, diced tropical fruit, and lime juice in a nonreactive mixing bowl and stir well to combine. (Fruit may be covered with plastic wrap and refrigerated for several hours before serving.) Rub the pineapple shells with half a lime to prevent discoloration, wrap in plastic, and refrigerate until ready to use.

3. Place the amaretti cookies in a heavy zipper-lock plastic bag and crush them with a rolling pin. Place the crushed cookies, melted butter, and banana chips in a bowl and stir well to combine. To serve, spoon the fruit mixture into the half-pineapple shells and sprinkle each with some of the crumb topping.

SOFT CHOCOLATE COOKIE SANDWICHES WITH MASCARPONE AND CHERRY FILLING

MAKES ABOUT EIGHTEEN • Is there an Oreo cookie good enough to break out the dessert wine for? Well, not one you can buy in a package at the supermarket. These meltingly soft chocolate cookies sandwiched with mascarpone and dried cherries, on the other hand, are an excellent way to enjoy the extremely unique Italian sparkling dessert wine called Brachetto d'Acqui. Brachetto is the grape, Acqui the region in Piedmont. The scent of raspberries and rose petals is amazing; the spritz and delicate flavor of berries is gorgeously "poofy" like the cookie filling. Alternatively, Gallo makes a wonderful red spumante right here in California.

Mascarpone is an Italian-style cream cheese with a lighter, more delicate flavor and texture than American cream cheese. It is widely available in the cheese section of supermarkets and in Italian specialty shops. If you can't find dried cherries (look for them in gourmet and natural foods stores), substitute sweetened dried cranberries, which can be found next to the raisins at the supermarket.

<table>
<tr><th>WINE RECOMMENDATIONS</th><th>SPARKLING DESSERT WINE</th><th>FOR THE COOKIES</th><th>FOR THE FILLING</th></tr>
<tr><td></td><td>Banfi Rosa Regale Brachetto d'Acqui or Coppo Brachetto d'Acqui (Italy)

Ballatore Spumante Rosso (California)</td><td>2 cups all-purpose flour
½ teaspoon baking powder
1 teaspoon baking soda
½ cup unsweetened cocoa powder
1 cup sugar
¼ cup vegetable shortening
1 large egg
½ cup buttermilk
½ teaspoon vanilla extract</td><td>1 cup dried cherries or sweetened dried cranberries
½ cup plus 2 tablespoons sugar
1 cup heavy cream, chilled
One 8-ounce container mascarpone cheese, chilled</td></tr>
</table>

1. Make the cookies: Preheat the oven to 425°F. Spray two or three large cookie sheets with nonstick cooking spray. Sift together the flour, baking powder, baking soda, and cocoa powder in a medium bowl and set aside.

2. Combine the sugar and vegetable shortening in the bowl of an electric mixer fitted with a paddle attachment and beat on medium until fluffy, scraping down the

sides of the bowl once or twice as necessary. Add the egg and beat until well-combined. Mix in the buttermilk and vanilla on low. With the mixer running, slowly pour in ½ cup of boiling water and blend until smooth, scraping down the bowl as necessary.

3. Add the flour mixture, one cup at a time, to the wet ingredients, mixing on low and scraping down the sides of the bowl after each addition. The finished batter will be thin.

4. Drop tablespoonfuls of the batter onto the cookie sheets, smoothing each table-spoonful with the back of the spoon into a 2-inch round and leaving 2 inches between each cookie. Bake each sheet for 5 minutes. Let the cookies cool completely on the cookie sheets and then transfer with a spatula to waxed paper.

5. Make the filling: Set aside 2 tablespoons of the cherries in a small bowl. Roughly chop the remaining cherries.

6. Place 2 tablespoons of the sugar in a flat-bottomed bowl and add the 2 table-spoons whole cherries to the bowl. Shake the bowl gently to coat the cherries with sugar, and remove them to a plate. Add the chopped cherries to the bowl and shake them to coat with the remaining sugar.

7. Combine the cream and ½ cup sugar in a large bowl and whip with an electric mixer until the cream just holds stiff peaks. Do not overbeat. Place the mascarpone in another bowl and fold in ⅓ of the whipped cream to lighten it. Fold the lightened mascarpone mixture back into the remaining whipped cream. (Filling may be covered with plastic wrap and refrigerated until ready to use, up to 1 day.)

8. To fill the cookies: Spread a ½-inch layer of filling onto the flat side of a cookie. Use your fingers to sprinkle about ½ teaspoon of the chopped, sugared dried cherries over the filling, and top with another cookie, pressing lightly to make a sandwich with some of the sugared cherries showing at the edge of the filling. Repeat with the remaining cookies. Place the filled cookies on a platter so that they are not touching; cover loosely with plastic wrap and refrigerate until ready to serve, up to 1 day. To serve, unwrap and set alongside a bowl filled with the extra filling, sprinkled with the whole sugared cherries.

GINGERED CRANBERRY-PISTACHIO BISCOTTI

MAKES ABOUT SIXTY • You can substitute whole unblanched almonds for the pistachios, if you like. Biscotti are traditionally served with nutty-raisiny–scented Italian Vin Santo—you drink the Vin Santo, and dip the cookies into it, too. For a change of pace, I developed this version to match the ginger and orange peel scents of French Muscat de Beaumes de Venise.

<table>
<tr><td rowspan="4">WINE RECOMMENDATIONS</td><td>ITALIAN VIN SANTO

Antinori, Castello di Ama

FRENCH MUSCAT DE BEAUMES DE VENISE

Chapoutier, Beaumalric, Jaboulet</td><td>½ cup whole shelled pistachios
Butter or nonstick cooking spray
1½ cups all-purpose flour, plus more for dusting baking sheet
1 teaspoon baking soda
Pinch salt
½ cup packed light brown sugar
⅓ cup dried cranberries
2 tablespoons crystallized ginger, finely chopped, optional
3 large eggs, separated
1 teaspoon vanilla extract
1½ teaspoons finely grated orange zest</td></tr>
</table>

1. Preheat the oven to 350°F. Place the pistachios on a baking sheet and toast until fragrant, about 15 minutes. Cool completely, then coarsely chop.

2. Increase the oven heat to 375°F. Lightly grease or butter a baking sheet and dust with flour, tapping out the excess (or spray with nonstick cooking spray).

3. In a large bowl, sift together the flour, baking soda, and salt. Add the sugar, chopped nuts, cranberries, and crystallized ginger, if using. Stir to combine.

4. In a small bowl, beat together 3 egg yolks and 2 egg whites with an electric mixer, reserving the third white. Stir in the vanilla and orange zest.

5. Pour the egg mixture into the flour mixture and mix together with the electric mixer on low speed until just combined. The dough will be stiff.

6. Turn the dough out onto a lightly floured work surface and divide into thirds. Shape the dough into three 18-inch-long, ½-inch-thick logs. Arrange the logs on the prepared baking sheet several inches apart and brush lightly with the lightly beaten reserved egg white. Bake for 20 minutes.

7. Remove from the oven and let cool slightly on the baking sheet. Reduce the oven heat to 225°F. While still warm, cut the logs into diagonal slices about ½ inch wide. Lay the slices cut side down on the baking sheet and return them to the oven. Bake until crisp and brown, 20 to 30 minutes. The biscotti will keep in an airtight container for 1 to 2 weeks.

GINGER-SPUMANTE CUPCAKES WITH APRICOT-CRANBERRY–CREAM CHEESE CENTERS

MAKES FORTY-EIGHT • The flavors of ginger, apricot, and citrus in these cupcakes are a perfect fit for the festive, spicy fruitiness of the Moscato (Muscat) grape that's used to make spumante (sparkling) and frizzante (lightly sparkling) wines in Italy's Piedmont region. This wine style, which is also made in California, has a touch of sweetness and lower alcohol, which makes this match a great brunch offering, too.

For those who are allergic to dairy, substitute soy cream cheese for regular cream cheese in the filling. If you don't have two large mini-muffin pans you can bake them in batches, one after the other. Cool the pan by placing it in the refrigerator for a few minutes before lining with fresh paper liners and refilling with batter and filling. Another option—make regular-size cupcakes. These may also be baked in regular-size muffin tins. Use paper liners and fill each with a scant ½ cup of batter and 1 heaping teaspoon of filling. Bake until a tester comes out with just a few moist crumbs adhering, 15 to 18 minutes.

WINE RECOMMENDATIONS

SPARKLING MOSCATO

Martini & Rossi Asti Spumante (Italy)

Robert Pecota Moscato d'Andrea (California)

Michele Chiarlo Moscato d'Asti "Nivole" (Clouds), Moscato d'Asti La Spinetta, Rivetti (Italy)

FOR THE FILLING

4 ounces cream cheese, at room temperature

½ cup granulated sugar

Pinch salt

1 large egg

3 ounces dried apricots, finely chopped

½ cup sweetened dried cranberries, finely chopped

1 teaspoon grated lemon zest

FOR THE CAKE BATTER

½ cup Moscato d'Asti wine

½ cup light corn syrup

1½ teaspoons baking soda

1 cup all-purpose flour

½ teaspoon baking powder

1 tablespoon ground ginger

½ teaspoon freshly grated nutmeg

Pinch ground cardamom

2 large eggs

½ cup packed light brown sugar

½ cup granulated sugar

6 tablespoons vegetable oil

2 teaspoons finely grated lemon zest

1. Preheat the oven to 350°F. Line two 24-cup mini-muffin tins with paper liners.

2. Make the filling: Combine the cream cheese, sugar, salt, and egg in the bowl of an electric mixer and beat on medium speed until smooth. Stir in the apricots, cranberries, and 1 teaspoon lemon zest. Set aside.

3. Make the batter: Combine the Moscato wine and corn syrup in a small nonreactive saucepan and bring to a boil. Remove from heat and whisk in ½ teaspoon of the baking soda. Pour into a glass measuring cup or bowl and cool to room temperature.

4. Sift together the flour, remaining teaspoon baking soda, baking powder, ginger, nutmeg, and cardamom in a medium bowl.

5. Whisk together the eggs, brown sugar, and granulated sugar in a large bowl. Whisk in the oil. Whisk in the wine mixture. Whisk in the lemon zest. Add the flour mixture and stir until just combined.

6. Add a scant tablespoon of batter to each muffin cup. Spoon about ½ teaspoon of the filling into the center of each cup, and rap the pan sharply on the counter to eliminate air bubbles. Bake in middle of the oven until golden, and a tester comes out with just a few moist crumbs adhering, 10 to 12 minutes total. (Begin checking at 8 minutes; the cupcakes are small and will overbake quickly once they are done.) If both pans don't fit in the oven at once, or if you have only one pan, bake the cupcakes in batches.

7. Set the cupcakes, still in the pans, on wire racks to cool for 5 minutes, then remove them from the pans and let cool completely on the wire racks. Serve warm or at room temperature. (The cooled cupcakes can be covered and refrigerated for up to 1 day. Let stand at room temperature 1 hour before serving.)

CARAMELIZED BANANA "PIZZA"

SERVES SIX • Placing the sliced bananas back in their peels while you work helps to prevent excessive browning. Oak aging gives tawny Port a nutty-toffee flavor that marries beautifully with the caramel-banana flavors in this fun dish.

WINE RECOMMENDATIONS

PORTUGUESE TAWNY PORT

Fonseca Ten-Year-Old Tawny, Ferreira Dona Antonia, Graham's Tawny

1 cup sugar

1 tablespoon ground cinnamon

Nonstick cooking spray

4 to 6 ripe medium bananas, unpeeled

Three 8-inch flour tortillas

4 tablespoons (½ stick) unsalted butter, softened

1 tablespoon canola oil, plus more if necessary

6 ounces bittersweet chocolate, finely chopped

1. Preheat the oven to 425°F. Combine the sugar and cinnamon in a pie plate or shallow bowl. Spray a baking sheet with nonstick cooking spray.

2. Cut the ends off of each unpeeled banana. With a paring knife, slice just through the peel lengthwise and gently remove the banana, keeping it whole and preserving the peel.

3. Place the banana on a work surface and cut it with the paring knife into ½-inch slices, keeping the banana slices together in a long stack so that they are easy to move and arrange neatly on the pizza. Move the slices back into their peel. Repeat with the remaining bananas.

4. Spread both sides of each tortilla generously with some of the softened butter. In a nonstick sauté pan or skillet, heat ½ tablespoon of the oil on medium-high. When hot, fry the tortillas on both sides, one at a time, until browned and crisp, adding additional oil as needed.

5. As you finish frying each tortilla, place it in the pie plate, coat both sides with the cinnamon sugar, and shake gently over the plate to remove excess sugar. Transfer each coated tortilla to the prepared baking sheet.

6. Carefully lift the sliced banana from its skin and gently fan the slices around on one of the tortillas in a circular pattern. Start on the outside edge and work toward

the center until the tortilla is completely covered with banana slices. Repeat with the remaining bananas and tortillas. Sprinkle the bananas generously with the remaining cinnamon sugar. Bake until the bananas are soft and the sugar starts to bubble and caramelize, 15 to 20 minutes.

7. While the pizzas are baking, make the chocolate sauce: Put 2 inches of water in a medium saucepan and bring the pot to a bare simmer. Combine the chocolate and 3 tablespoons of water in a stainless-steel bowl big enough to rest on top of the saucepan and place the bowl over the simmering water, making sure that the water doesn't touch the bottom of the bowl. Heat the chocolate, whisking occasionally, until it is completely melted.

8. Slice each tortilla into 4 wedges as you would a pizza. Place 2 wedges on each of 6 dessert plates. Serve immediately with chocolate sauce on the side.

SPICED PEAR AND PHYLLO DUMPLINGS

SERVES SIX • Most phyllo dough desserts can be shaped ahead and then chilled, covered, until you are ready to bake them. I like to time the baking so I can serve these warm (but they're good at room temperature, too). To prevent the pears from browning while you prepare the phyllo dough, I suggest that you rub them with a lemon half, but this step can be eliminated if you work quickly and bake the dumplings right away. I have paired this dessert with "discovery" selections—Hungarian Tokaji and Austrian dessert wines that are botrytis, late harvest, or a combination of the two. If you can't find them (though they are worth a search), select any late harvest white wine. I also like to serve this as a breakfast dish with Italian sparkling Moscato d'Asti.

<table>
<tr><td>WINE RECOMMENDATIONS</td><td>DESSERT WINES

Heidi Schrock Ausbruch, Alois Kracher Nouvelle Vague (Austria)

Château Pajzos Tokaji 5 Puttonyos, Royal Tokaji Wine Company Tokaji 5 Puttonyos (Hungary)

Paolo Saracco Moscato d'Asti (Italy)</td><td>6 Bosc or Anjou pears, peeled, with stems intact

1 lemon, cut in half

Nine 17-x-13-inch sheets frozen phyllo dough, thawed

½ cup (1 stick) butter, melted</td><td>6 teaspoons plain dried bread crumbs

3 tablespoons turbinado sugar

½ teaspoon ground cinnamon

½ teaspoon ground allspice

½ teaspoon freshly grated nutmeg</td></tr>
</table>

1. Preheat the oven to 400°F. Line a baking sheet with parchment paper.

2. Core the pears by piercing their blossom (bottom) ends with a paring knife. Cut around the center core to remove it, then use the tip of the paring knife to remove any seeds or tough membranes. Rub the pears all over with a lemon half to prevent browning.

3. To form the dumplings: Place phyllo sheets on work surface. Cut sheets in half crosswise to form eighteen 13-x-8½-inch rectangles. Stack the rectangles on top of each other and cover with plastic wrap, then a damp towel, to prevent drying.

4. Place 1 phyllo rectangle on a work surface; brush with melted butter. Top with second phyllo rectangle, placed perpendicular to the first; brush with melted butter. Top with third rectangle, at the same angle as the first rectangle; brush with melted butter. Sprinkle with 1 teaspoon bread crumbs. Place a pear atop the buttered phyllo sheets. Sprinkle with 1 teaspoon turbinado sugar, and dust with cinnamon and allspice. Grate on some fresh nutmeg.

5. Enclose the filling by lifting the opposite corners of the phyllo and bringing them together at the stem of the pear; pinch gently at the meeting point to close. Lift the remaining 2 corners and pinch together near the stem of the pear. Gently pinch the seams that are formed to seal and neaten the shape. Repeat with the remaining phyllo and pears, to make a total of 6 dumplings.

6. Transfer the dumplings to the prepared baking sheet. Brush dumplings with the remaining melted butter and sprinkle with the remaining sugar. (Dumplings may be prepared to this point and chilled, wrapped in plastic wrap, for 1 day before baking.)

7. Bake phyllo dumplings until golden brown, 12 to 15 minutes, turning the baking sheet halfway through baking to encourage even browning. If the corners or tops of the dumplings begin to brown too quickly, cover the browned edges with bits of foil and continue baking. Serve warm.

PUMPKIN-PEAR MINI SOUFFLÉS

SERVES EIGHT • Everyday soufflés? Yes, because the hard part can be done ahead. I bake these adorable soufflés in ovenproof espresso cups. They are a knockout dish for entertaining because the batter is made and the cups are filled, then popped in the freezer (for up to a week), and bake in just 5 to 7 minutes. Before dinner (even before guests arrive) I have my dessert plates set up with garnishes (toasted almonds, a squiggle of honey, and candied orange peel) so the dessert comes out poofed and beautiful without stress. The spices here connect beautifully with sweet wines based on the Gewürztraminer grape.

You can also serve these for breakfast or brunch when you have weekend guests, baking the soufflés a few at a time as guests wake up. The wafting scent alone will seduce any sleepyhead stragglers to join the living. (And for additional breakfasts, extra pumpkin-pear butter is great spread on toast or with waffles or pancakes.)

WINE RECOMMENDATIONS

LATE HARVEST
GEWÜRZTRAMINER

Hogue Cellars Late
Harvest Gewürztraminer

Columbia Crest Late
Harvest Gewürztraminer

Navarro Late Harvest
Gewürztraminer

1½ cups canned solid-pack pumpkin

1 cup pear nectar

1 large pear, peeled, cored, and grated

½ cup packed light brown sugar

½ teaspoon ground cloves

½ teaspoon ground allspice

1 tablespoon unsalted butter

½ cup granulated sugar

5 egg whites

⅛ teaspoon cream of tartar

Confectioner's sugar for dusting, optional

---

1. Combine the pumpkin, pear nectar, pear, brown sugar, cloves, and allspice in a heavy saucepan and bring to a boil. Reduce heat and simmer, stirring occasionally, until thick and reduced to about 1½ cups, about 1½ hours. Scrape into a bowl and cool completely.

2. Preheat the oven to 450°F. Butter and sugar eight 1-cup soufflé molds or straight-sided coffee cups, knocking out any excess sugar.

3. Measure 1½ cups of the pumpkin-pear butter into a large bowl, reserving any extra for another use. In another large bowl, beat the egg whites with the cream of

tartar until stiff peaks form. Do not overbeat. With a large whisk, incorporate ⅓ of the egg white mixture into the pumpkin-pear butter. With a clean rubber spatula, gently fold the remaining whites into the mixture until smooth.

4. Scoop the soufflé batter into the prepared molds and level the surfaces with a spatula. Run your finger around the top edge of each mold to create a "moat" at the mold's rim. This cleans off excess batter and helps the soufflés rise. (The soufflés can be covered lightly with plastic and frozen for up to a week. Place in the oven straight from the freezer.)

5. Place the molds on a cookie sheet, put the sheet on the lowest rack of the oven, and bake 5 minutes. Then lower the oven temperature to 425°F, and continue baking until the soufflés have risen about 2 inches above the mold, about 2 minutes. Serve immediately, by placing the hot ramekins onto dessert plates (see the headnote for garnish ideas). Sprinkle with confectioner's sugar, if desired. Be sure to let guests know the molds are very hot.

Variation. For Dried Fruit Soufflés, puree ½ cup dried fruits (such as apricots, pears, or prunes) in a blender with ½ cup hot water, ½ cup plus 1 tablespoon sugar, and 2 tablespoons Grand Marnier liqueur until smooth. Cool completely and use in place of the pumpkin-pear butter.

CHOCOLATE-BANANA SORBET

SERVES SIX • I adored banana splits as a little girl. Here is my grown-up version. This is a great way to use overripe bananas that have been sitting on the kitchen counter too long. You can accumulate them over time and just place them in a zipper-lock bag in the freezer until you need them for a simple dessert (or for muffins or banana bread for that matter). The wine—late bottled vintage Port—adds the flavor of the berry topping to this banana split déjà-vu. An ice cream maker is required for this recipe. I use the very low-tech, inexpensive manual type with an insert container that is prefrozen. You put the sorbet mixture in the container, attach the crank and paddle, and crank every few minutes until the sorbet is frozen, about 30 minutes.

WINE RECOMMENDATIONS		
LATE BOTTLED VINTAGE PORT (LBV)	8 ounces bittersweet chocolate, coarsely chopped
	1½ cups sugar
Taylor Fladgate, Noval LB, Fonseca	⅛ teaspoon salt
	4 overripe bananas, frozen in their peels

1. Finely chop the chocolate in the workbowl of a food processor.

2. Combine 3 cups of water, the sugar, and salt together in a heavy saucepan and heat over high until the sugar is dissolved and the syrup comes to a boil.

3. With the processor motor running, gradually add the boiling syrup to the chocolate and process until smooth. Refrigerate the mixture in a bowl until cold.

4. Remove the bananas from the freezer and allow to soften for 10 minutes at room temperature. Cut off the ends of the frozen bananas and remove their peels with a paring knife. (If your hands get too cold, hold the bananas in a towel.) Place the peeled, frozen bananas in the processor with half the chocolate mixture, and process until blended and smooth. Add the banana-chocolate mixture to the bowl with the remaining chocolate and stir to blend well. Scrape the mixture into an ice cream maker and freeze according to manufacturer's instructions. Transfer sorbet to a container and freeze overnight or until ready to serve. Keeps for up to 2 weeks.

PEAR (OR PINEAPPLE) AND PINOT GRIS GRANITA

SERVES SIX • I love the freshness of granita as a light dessert, when I want a late harvest or botrytis dessert wine to star. I've found it's fun to put the granita in a dessert wine glass, then pour the wine over and spoon up the slushy blend. Yum!

WINE RECOMMENDATIONS	DESSERT WINES	One 15-ounce can pear halves (or pineapple chunks) in juice, drained, juices reserved
	Huet Vouvray Moelleux, Baron Philippe de Rothschild Sauternes (France)	½ cup honey
		½ cup Pinot Gris from Oregon, California, or Alsace, France
		1 cup pear nectar (or pineapple juice)
	Chateau Ste. Michelle Late Harvest Riesling (Washington State)	1 tablespoon freshly squeezed lemon juice
		Fresh mint sprigs, optional

1. Combine the pears and honey in a blender and puree until smooth. Pour the reserved pear juice into a 2-cup measuring cup. Add the Pinot Gris and enough pear nectar to measure 2 cups. Pour the juice mixture into the blender, add the lemon juice, and process until well blended.

2. Transfer to a 13 x 9 x 2-inch glass baking dish. Cover with plastic wrap, and place in the freezer until solid, at least 5 hours or overnight.

3. Fifteen minutes before serving, remove the granita from the freezer and allow to sit at room temperature to soften slightly. Using a fork, scrape the surface of the granita to form crystals. Divide the granita among 6 dessert goblets or martini glasses, garnish with fresh mint sprigs, if desired, and serve immediately.

BITTERSWEET CHOCOLATE–CASSIS TRUFFLES

MAKES ABOUT THIRTY • These simple truffles feature a hint of Crème de Cassis liqueur, to pick up the berry flavor in late bottled vintage Port wine. Make sure to finely chop the chocolate before you begin, or it may not completely melt when whisked with the cream. If there are lumps in your truffle mixture, set it over a slightly larger bowl of hot (not boiling) water and stir until melted.

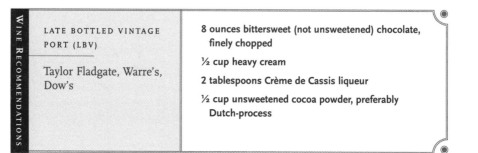

WINE RECOMMENDATIONS

LATE BOTTLED VINTAGE PORT (LBV)

Taylor Fladgate, Warre's, Dow's

8 ounces bittersweet (not unsweetened) chocolate, finely chopped

½ cup heavy cream

2 tablespoons Crème de Cassis liqueur

½ cup unsweetened cocoa powder, preferably Dutch-process

1. Place the chocolate in a medium heatproof bowl. Bring the cream just to a boil in a small saucepan. As soon as it begins to boil, pour it through a fine strainer and into the bowl with the chocolate. Whisk the cream and chocolate together until the chocolate is completely melted. Whisk in the Crème de Cassis. Cover and refrigerate until stiff and cold, at least 3 hours and up to 1 day.

2. Scoop up some of the chilled chocolate mixture with a teaspoon and roll between your palms to make ¾-inch balls (they don't have to be perfectly round). Work quickly so the chocolate doesn't melt in your hands. Transfer the balls to a waxed paper–lined baking sheet, setting them ½ inch apart. Wipe your hands periodically with paper towels to remove any chocolate left behind from rolling. If the truffle mixture becomes too soft to roll, return it to the refrigerator briefly to firm up before continuing.

3. Lightly cover the balls with plastic wrap and return to the refrigerator until cool and firm. Place the cocoa powder in a pie plate or other flat-bottomed dish with sides, and roll the truffles in the cocoa powder a few at a time, until coated. Store the truffles in a waxed paper–lined tin in the refrigerator until ready to serve.

chapter ten

BASIC RECIPES

◉

There are certain basic preparations

that I rely on, almost on an everyday basis, to add wine-friendly flavor to food. Here they are, gathered in one convenient place, to be used as directed in the recipes throughout this book. I hope you will also find creative ways of your own to use these simple recipes to create your own wine-friendly dinners.

BALSAMIC VINEGAR REDUCTION

MAKES ½ CUP • Balsamic vinegar is one of my absolute favorite condiments. Just a drop or two makes so many foods come alive with wine-friendly flavor. Aged balsamic vinegar is a far superior product (and far more expensive) than the balsamic vinegar found on most supermarket shelves. But if you are in a pinch (or just being frugal), you can improve the flavor of the cheaper variety by reducing it as follows.

1 cup balsamic vinegar (not aged)

Place the vinegar in a small saucepan and bring to a boil. Lower the heat to medium and simmer until the vinegar is reduced by half. Pour into a nonreactive container and let cool completely. (Balsamic Vinegar Reduction will keep, covered, in the refrigerator for up to 1 month.)

BALSAMIC VINAIGRETTE

SERVES FOUR TO SIX

1 teaspoon Dijon mustard
2 tablespoons balsamic vinegar
¼ cup extra virgin olive oil
Salt and pepper to taste

Whisk the mustard and the vinegar together in a mixing bowl. Whisking constantly, add 2 to 3 tablespoons of the oil in a thin stream until the mixture thickens. Then in a steady stream, whisk in the remaining oil. Season with salt and pepper to taste. If desired, you can thin the vinaigrette by whisking in a few drops of water.

HERB OIL

MAKES ABOUT ONE CUP • This is a wonderfully versatile, flavor-packed marinade for seared or grilled meat and poultry. Use harissa, a North African chili and vegetable paste, if you want a hot and spicy oil. For other variations, see below. Stir in the chives after the oil comes out of the food processor. If added whole they can gum up the food processor blade.

1 large bunch fresh cilantro, washed, dried, and large stems removed

½ cup firmly packed fresh basil leaves, washed and patted dry

⅓ cup fresh mint leaves, washed and patted dry

2 medium garlic cloves

1 tablespoon harissa, optional

½ cup extra virgin olive oil

2 tablespoons freshly squeezed lemon juice

1½ teaspoons grated lemon zest

1 bunch fresh chives, finely chopped

Kosher salt

Combine the cilantro, basil, mint, garlic, and harissa, if desired, in the workbowl of a food processor. Pulse several times to finely chop. With the motor running, gradually add ½ cup water, the olive oil, lemon juice, and lemon zest. Scrape the mixture into a bowl and stir in the chopped chives and salt to taste.

For Southwestern Herb Oil. Substitute 1 seeded, chopped serrano chili for the harissa, and the grated zest and juice of 1 lime for the lemon juice and zest.

For Asian Herb Oil. Substitute 1 tablespoon Thai chili paste for the harissa. Replace the lemon zest and juice with 2 tablespoons rice vinegar, and add 2 tablespoons toasted pure sesame oil with the olive oil.

INDONESIAN FIVE-SPICE BARBECUE SAUCE

MAKES ABOUT ¾ CUP • I discovered the incredible wine versatility of this sauce while teaching a wine and food pairing class at the Epcot Wine and Food Festival, held every autumn at Walt Disney World. I worked with the chef to choose an array of foods that would allow the students to explore complex spice flavors with wine, and we settled on Jamaican jerk–spiced chicken and grilled shrimp glazed with Indonesian barbecue sauce. Fish lovers will be especially pleased to note that this sauce makes a beautiful bridge between shrimp, scallops, salmon, swordfish, roasted oysters(!), and red wine. My favorite to pair with the grilled shrimp we served at Disney was the Penfolds Kalimna Bin 28 Shiraz, whose clove-and-pepper spiciness echoes the sauce beautifully. For Chardonnay, the tasters noted that a ripe-style one with restrained oak worked best—try Edna Valley Vineyard, Jordan, or my favorite: Chehalem from Oregon.

See Plank-Cooked Salmon (page 45) for another fabulous use for this sauce, and for more wine recommendations.

3 garlic cloves

One 1-inch chunk of peeled fresh ginger, coarsely chopped

½ teaspoon sambal oelek (Indonesian chili paste), or 1 small fresh serrano or jalapeño chili, stemmed and seeded

½ cup packed brown sugar

2 teaspoons Chinese five-spice powder

2 tablespoons tamarind concentrate or paste

1 tablespoon tomato paste

½ cup soy sauce (preferably Tamari)

2 tablespoons fresh lime juice

2 tablespoons peanut or canola oil

Place the garlic and ginger in a blender or the workbowl of a food processor and process to finely chop. Add the chili paste and process again to chop. Add the brown sugar, five-spice powder, tamarind concentrate, tomato paste, soy sauce, lime juice, and oil and process until smooth. The sauce will keep in the refrigerator, covered, up to 1 week.

QUICK MUSHROOM STOCK

MAKES 1½ CUPS • Very often when I am reconstituting dried mushrooms for a recipe, I will also use the strained soaking liquid to add extra flavor to the dish. But even when I don't need the liquid, I always strain it and save it so that I'll have some flavorful stock on hand to stir into plain risotto or to make a quick pasta sauce. There are several types of dried mushrooms to choose from. Dried shiitakes are the least expensive and also the least flavorful; porcinis are the most intense. So, if you have a choice, use the shiitake broth in a recipe with other flavor components and save the porcini broth for times when the broth is the main flavoring ingredient.

1 ounce dried mushrooms such as shiitakes, porcinis, or cèpes

1. Place the dried mushrooms in a heatproof bowl and pour 1½ cups of boiling water over them. Let stand to soften, about 30 minutes.

2. Line a small strainer with a coffee filter, and strain the mushroom liquid through the filter and into a container. Squeeze the mushrooms to extract any excess liquid and strain into the container. (Mushroom stock will keep, covered, in the refrigerator for up to 1 week. Or freeze in an airtight container for up to 1 month.)

3. Rinse the reconstituted dried mushrooms to remove any grit, pat dry with paper towels, and reserve for another use.

ROASTED GARLIC

MAKES ONE HEAD • I use roasted garlic to add flavor to a variety of dishes, including Carrot Slaw with Toasted Pine Nuts and Herbs (page 39) and Chicken Legs Braised in Pinot Grigio Mojo (page 111). It is also a flavorful, rustic spread for grilled bread. Squeeze the skins of the individual cloves to extrude the creamy, surprisingly sweet roasted garlic.

1 head garlic
2 tablespoons olive oil

1. Preheat the oven to 350°F. Remove the loose, dry outer layer of skin from the head of garlic. Slice off the top third of the garlic head to expose the cloves, leaving the stem intact.

2. Place the garlic head on a 12-inch-square piece of aluminum foil and sprinkle with the olive oil. Seal the foil tightly to enclose the garlic. Bake until tender, about 1 hour. Cool to room temperature inside the foil. (Roasted garlic will keep in an airtight container in the refrigerator for up to 1 week.)

Variation. For Roasted Shallots, substitute 4 medium shallots, peeled and quartered, for the head of garlic.

OVEN-CRISPED SAGE LEAVES

As you've probably noticed if you've paged through the previous recipes, I love sage for its wine-loving flavor. These crispy sage leaves achieve the flavor and texture excitement of the fried sage leaves I've enjoyed in restaurants, without the hassle of deep-frying. It is best to use them soon after making them, as they begin to lose their crispness after awhile.

½ cup extra virgin olive oil
1 bunch fresh sage leaves
Kosher salt

1. Preheat the oven to 350°F. Place a wire rack over a rimmed baking sheet.

2. Place the olive oil in a small bowl. Dip each sage leaf in the oil to coat. Let excess oil drip back into the bowl. Place the leaves on the wire rack. Bake until crisp, about 6 minutes. Watch carefully and remove from the oven before they begin to brown.

3. Transfer the leaves to a plate lined with paper towels. Sprinkle with kosher salt. Use immediately or let stand at room temperature for up to 1 hour.

PRESERVED LEMONS

MAKES FIVE • Preserving lemons is a traditional North African technique. I like it because it is a great way to add lemon flavor to a dish without adding too much lemony acidity, which can overwhelm wine. I keep these on hand to garnish starches such as couscous or rice, as well as all kinds of chicken and fish dishes. See Seared Tuna with Preserved Lemon (page 233) to get started.

5 lemons
½ cup kosher salt
1 tablespoon black peppercorns
5 bay leaves
1 cup freshly squeezed lemon juice, plus more if necessary
3 to 4 tablespoons olive oil

1. Rinse a 6-cup glass jar and its lid with boiling water. Pour out the water and allow the jar to air-dry.

2. Scrub the lemons well with a soft brush to clean their skins. Dry thoroughly. Cut each lemon lengthwise into 8 wedges and place in a large, nonreactive bowl. Toss with the salt to coat. Press gently on the lemons with a wooden spoon to extract some of their juice.

3. Pack the lemon pieces into the jar, layering them evenly with the peppercorns and the bay leaves. Add the lemon juice from the bowl and the additional 1 cup lemon juice to the jar so that the juice covers the lemons. Slowly pour the olive oil on top of the lemon juice so that it forms a seal.

4. Put the lid on the jar tightly and let stand at room temperature for 7 days, shaking each day to redistribute the juice and salt.

5. Open the jar and rinse the lemons thoroughly under cold running water before using. Preserved Lemons will keep in their jar in the refrigerator for several months. Reseal with a fresh layer of oil as necessary.

grapes and styles, confident in the fact that enjoying them with a meal will show them at their best. Which brings me to the next point . . .

How should I choose wine to keep around, so that I have it on hand for drinking with dinner? Can you give me a basic shopping list?

I recommend you lay in a supply of the most food-versatile everyday wines, so you can open and experiment with them over the course of many everyday dinners. I still do this all the time, because even after all I've tested and tasted, I constantly come across mind-blowing wine and food combos that my instincts would have vetoed . . . like the time my cousin sheepishly declared the red Rioja (rustic-leathery) as the best match with our takeout Japanese seaweed salad (fishy)—I wasn't even going to go there, but she was right!

My shopping list of keep-around bottles for everyday dinner focuses on moderately priced grapes and styles that are food-versatile and sturdy—meaning they hold up well in the fridge so that if you want to try different wines over the course of several evenings, you don't have to worry about the leftovers going bad quickly (see the next page for how to keep them fresh for as long as possible). These include Italian Pinot Grigio, Washington State Riesling, California Sauvignon Blanc, and Chardonnay for whites; and for reds, French Beaujolais-Villages, California Pinot Noir, Washington State Merlot, Chilean Cabernet Sauvignon, Spanish red Rioja Crianza, Italian Chianti and Dolcetto, and Australian Shiraz. This book includes plenty of under-ten-dollar recommendations for each of these. Whether you're cooking or picking up takeout, start sampling the different styles with everyday dinner. In my house, we usually open up both a white and a red, and I recommend you do the same. You'll see how versatile these styles are, and also how even the simplest of wines can instantly elevate everyday dinner.

I'm always looking for a good deal, but I don't know a lot about buying wine. Is it better to buy my wine at a small shop where I can ask questions, or should I just take this book to the big discount liquor store or warehouse club, where the bottles seem unbelievably cheap? Do you have tips for shopping at a small shop? At a large discount store?

Supermarkets, pharmacies, price clubs, catalogs, boutique stores, websites—you may shop for wine at one or all of these depending on the licensing laws in the state where you live. The laws vary from one state to the next, so for example I can buy wine at the supermarket while visiting my folks in North Carolina, but not back home in Connecticut, where only liquor stores are granted licenses to sell wine. Here are some basic buying tips for different wine shopping environments:

Supermarkets and price clubs. If you know what you want, then price is your main consideration and you'll get your best deals at these venues because, as with their other products from milk to paper towels, they get volume discounts that are passed along to you. So-called "floor stacks" and "end caps" are big showcase displays of wine in a trafficked area or at the end of an aisle, where even bigger price discounts are featured. When you see one of your favorites there, take advantage and stock up or try something new while it's on sale.

Fine wine shops. If you want buying advice, or are buying rare or collectible wines, you're better off in a specialist shop. These stores have trained buyers who taste and know their inventory well; they can help with your decision. The better stores also have temperature-controlled storage for their rare wines, which is critical to ensure you get a product in good condition.

Where should I store my wine? Do I have to worry about the temperature of my cabinet? Does it have to go on a rack or can I store the bottles upright? How long can I keep my inexpensive bottles? A couple of weeks? Months? Longer?

You don't need to get a special wine fridge unless and until you start to acquire wines for long-term storage. Everyday wines will hold up well for up to a year in the typical home environment—kitchen, pantry, or whatever. The ideal area for wine is one with a fairly consistent, moderate temperature (away from the heater, oven, and your refrigerator exhaust) and away from direct light, which speeds the spoilage of wine. If you happen to have a cool basement, that's perfect. If it's for longer than a few weeks, store wines on their sides to keep the cork moist, which will keep the seal tight, thus preventing spoilage due to oxidation of the wine.

Once I open a bottle, how long will it be good? Is it best to store open wine in the refrigerator? What about red wine? Is it worth it to buy one of those vacuum pumps to preserve the freshness of wine, or will re-corking it do if I'm going to drink the rest in a day or two?

At a minimum, close the bottle with its original cork. Most wines will stay fresh a day or two. To extend that freshness window, purchase a vacuum sealer (available in kitchenware shops and wine shops). You simply cork the bottle

I see wine packaged in large boxes or wine in screwtop bottles and automatically think it's of lower quality than conventionally packaged wine. Am I being a snob? How should I shop for wines packaged this way?

> There has been a sea-change in this area. Many producers of high-quality wine are beginning to choose alternative packages such as bag-in-a-box or screwtop bottles to avoid the trouble with corks, and for their convenience for consumers. Neither package requires a corkscrew or other tool to open it, and with a bag in a box, the wine never oxidizes because the bag inside deflates as the package is depleted. If you see brands you've always trusted in a screwcap or bag in a box, buy with confidence and enjoy the convenience.

In the summer, I like my wine chilled. What about red wine? Are there some types of reds that can be served cold?

> I like rosés served cold. French Beaujolais and Gamay wines, Italian Dolcetto and basic Chianti, and lighter-style red Zinfandel are nice with a slight chill. And all red wines are best at around 62°F, which is cooler than the typical "room temperature."

I'm going to dinner at a friend's house and don't know what she's serving, but I'd like to bring wine as a gift. Do you have any everyday favorites that are good for giving?

> I wrote my *Wine Buying Guide for Everyone* for exactly this situation. It includes taste and value-for-money rankings of 600 of the best, most widely available wines on the market. The rankings come from regular consumers all across the country. Please visit andreaimmer.com to contribute your rankings for the next edition.

Where do I get unique, special wines to impress a wine lover and stretch my own horizons without breaking the bank?

> I get this question all the time. There's no reason to spend a fortune in time or money to get hand-crafted wines that are great value. Ask your local fine-wine shop—they will love the challenge. Or check out my wine club at andreaimmer.com. For years, I've been finding small-production wines that I really thought my readers would love—especially for the price. These are the

wines my club members receive in their shipments (along with a perfectly matched recipe, of course!). I also offer a website membership that lets you search my database of thousands of wine-and-food pairings and ask me wine and pairing questions directly.

Burgundy Blowout

An entire dinner devoted to Burgundy is really the best way to experience this region, whose wines are the world benchmarks for Chardonnay and Pinot Noir.

FIRST COURSE

Chablis—Moreau Vaillon or Domaine Laroche St. Martin

Roasted Oysters "Rockefeller Center" *(page 116)*

SECOND COURSE

Côte de Beaune white—Boillot Meursaut or Domaine Leflaive Puligny-Montrachet

Yukon Gold Potato and Cauliflower Soup with Truffle Oil *(page 77)*

THIRD COURSE

Côte de Beaune red—Marquis d'Angerville Volnay or Domaine de Courcel Pommard

Seared Pork Tenderloin with Dried Fig and Mushroom Sauce *(page 146)*, Creamy Goat Cheese Polenta *(page 108)*, Roasted Brussels Sprouts with Garlic and Sage *(page 165)*

FOURTH COURSE

Côte de Nuits red—Roumier Chambolle-Musigny or Domaine Dujac Morey-Saint-Denis

Cheese and garnishes: Saint-Nectaire, Cantal, Manchego, and Bucheron with crusty bread and grapes

An Evening of Bordeaux

This menu showcases Bordeaux's true colors—red, of course, as well as tangy-rich white Bordeaux, and golden Sauternes for dessert.

FIRST COURSE

Barrel-aged white Bordeaux—Château La Louvière or Château Smith-Haut-Lafitte

Tarragon- and Mustard-Crusted Scallops *(page 66)*

SECOND COURSE

Right Bank red Bordeaux—Château Clinet (Pommard) or Château Figeac (St.-Emilion)

Wild Mushroom Phyllo Purses with Pumpkinseed Oil Drizzle *(page 163)*

THIRD COURSE

Left Bank red Bordeaux—Château Lynch-Bages (Pauillac) or Château Lagrange (St.-Julien)

Sirloin Steak with "Beurre-Naise" Sauce *(page 173)*, sautéed spinach

FOURTH COURSE

Sauternes—Château LaTour Blanche or Château Suduiraut

Pumpkin-Pear Mini Soufflés *(page 258)*

Old World–New World Cabernet

This menu explores both Cabernet Sauvignon and Cabernet Franc, comparing the subtler Old World style to the bigger, riper New World style. You'll see the virtues of both, lovingly showcased by carefully paired dishes.

FIRST COURSE

Cabernet Franc—Lang & Reed or Pride Mountain Cabernet Franc (California) and Olga Raffault Chinon (Loire Valley, France)

Salad of Fresh Figs with Manchego, Balsamic Vinegar, and Toasted Pine Nuts *(page 162)*

SECOND COURSE

An elegant "Bordeaux blend"—Estancia Meritage (California) and Château d'Angludet (Bordeaux, France)

Rosemary and Sweet Garlic Roast Chicken *(page 171)*, Wine-Braised Leeks *(page 167)*

Roasted Fingerling Frites *(page 168)*

THIRD COURSE

Cellar-worthy—Viader or Château St. Jean Cinq Cepages (Cabernet blend, California) and Château Gruaud-Larose (Bordeaux, France)

Cheese and garnishes: Peter Vella Bear Flag Dry Jack, Cambazzola, Brin d'Amour, Humboldt Fog, nut bread, grapes

Tour de Rhône

This seriously gourmet menu spotlights the majesty of French Rhône wines, which from white to pink to red to dessert are some of the most exciting to pair. (It's okay to cut out a course or two if you don't want a five-course extravaganza. But remember you can always serve tasting menu portions—four oysters, two lamb chops per guest, etc.—to keep the menu manageable and enjoyable.)

FIRST COURSE

Côtes du Rhône rosé—Domaine Pelaquié or Jean-Luc Colombo

Cool Balsamic and Black Pepper Strawberries with Warm Toasted Mozzarella Flatbread *(page 219)*

SECOND COURSE

White Rhône—Coudoulet de Beaucastel Côtes du Rhône Blanc or Guigal Condrieu

Pan-Crisped Oysters with Sesame Seeds *(page 118)*

THIRD COURSE

Southern Rhône red—Domaine du Cayrou Gigondas or Beaucastel Châteauneuf-du-Pape

Cumin-Crusted Lamb *(page 199)*, Roasted Brussels Sprouts with Garlic and Sage *(page 165)*, Roasted Fingerling Frites *(page 168)*

(continued)

Tour de Rhône *(continued)*

FOURTH COURSE

Northern Rhône red—Chave Hermitage or Jasmin Côte-Rotie

Cheese and garnishes: Brin d'Amour, Reblochon, Brebis, Fourme d'Ambert, flatbread, black olives

FIFTH COURSE

Muscat de Beaumes de Venise—Jaboulet or Beaumalric

Chocolate-Banana Sorbet *(page 260)*

Savor Spain

This lovely menu can be pulled off in a number of ways. For one, you can serve it as a multicourse, seated tasting menu with the wines and foods served in the order listed here—even the rack of lamb main course is easily portioned into a one-chop tasting portion. A more casual approach is to serve all the dishes at once, from platters. Put the different wines on the table and, if possible, have two wineglasses at each place setting. Then just let guests help themselves, sampling the pairings at their own pace. Or, serve the menu as a buffet, with different "stations" for each wine and food combination—Lamb and Ribera del Duero on the sideboard, Crispy Artichokes and Squid on the coffee table, etc. That version is relaxed, and encourages lots of mingling.

FIRST COURSE

Albariño—Burgans, Pazo de Señorans or Morgadío

Shrimp Ceviche with Avocado, Cilantro, and Lime *(page 113)*

SECOND COURSE

Manzanilla sherry—Bodegas Hidalgo La Gitana or Barbadillo

Crispy Artichokes and Squid *(page 231)*

THIRD COURSE

Rioja Reserva—Montecillo or Marques de Arienzo

Salad of Fresh Figs with Manchego, Balsamic Vinegar, and Toasted Pine Nuts *(page 162)*

FOURTH COURSE

Ribera del Duero—Arzuaga or Tinto Pesquera

Cumin-Crusted Lamb *(page 199)* and Oven-Crisped Red Potatoes with Thyme and Pumpkinseed Oil *(page 35)*

FIFTH COURSE

Priorat—Vinicola del Priorat Onix or Mas Igneus Barranc dels Closos

Spanish cheeses—Torta del Casar, Idiazábal, Cabrales, Manchego, Mahón

SIXTH COURSE

PX Sherry—Argueso or Domecq Venerable

Bittersweet Chocolate–Cassis Truffles *(page 262)*

Tour d'Italia

When I first arrived in Italy in 1990, I knew nothing about wine, yet the wine-making families I visited practically adopted me. It seemed my passion and eagerness to learn ignited in them an ardent desire to show me everything wonderful about their Italian wine-country culture. Including the family dinners! For me they were sensory odysseys, with courses coming, corks popping, and conversation flowing on for hours. This menu is modeled on those memories. Gather a group of people you love hanging out with, and make sure they check their "hurry" genes at the door.

FIRST COURSE

Vernaccia di San Gimignano—Teruzzi e Puthod or Falchini

Oven-Charred Asparagus with Cheese and Balsamic Vinegar *(page 190)*

SECOND COURSE

Barbera d'Alba—Vietti, Clerico or Pio Cesare

Fettuccine with Prosciutto, Wild Mushrooms, and Sage *(page 136)*

THIRD COURSE

Barolo—Gigi Rosso or Massolino

Warm Wild Mushroom Salad with Black Truffle Vinaigrette *(page 132)*

FOURTH COURSE

Super Tuscan—Banfi Cum Laude or Ruffino Modus

Flank Steak Marinated in Spicy Herb Oil *(page 226)*, Garlic-Braised Collard Greens *(page 189)*, and Sweet Potato Puree with Garlic, Thyme, and Balsamic Vinegar *(page 166)*

FIFTH COURSE

Vin Santo—Avignonesi or Castello di Ama

Gingered Cranberry-Pistachio Biscotti *(page 248)*

Sources and Resources

The vast majority of ingredients you will need for the recipes in this book are available at your local supermarket. The rest can probably be found at a gourmet shop or specialty grocer. But just in case you have difficulty locating pumpkinseed oil or fenugreek seed, here is a list of mail-order sources that carry some of the harder-to-find items that I like to stock in my pantry.

THE BAKER'S CATALOGUE
P.O. Box 1010
Norwich, VT 05055
800–827–6836
www.kingarthurflour.com
Great variety of sea salts as well as specialty flours, seeds, nuts, dried fruits, and quality chocolate.

THE COOKING SCHOOL OF ASPEN
414 East Hyman Avenue
Aspen, CO 81611
www.cookingschoolofaspen.com

D'ARTAGNAN
280 Wilson Avenue
Newark, NJ 07105
800–327–8246
www.dartagnan.com
For foie gras, demi-glace, duck breasts.

DEAN & DELUCA
Call for store locations or catalog
877–826–9246
www.dean-deluca.com
Truffle oil, olive oils, vinegars, dried mushrooms.

KALUSTYAN'S
123 Lexington Avenue
New York, NY 10016
212–685–3451
www.kalustyans.com
A great source for hard-to-find dried herbs and spices, pappadum, tamarind paste, wasabi peas, and an incredible array of rices, dried beans, mustards, vinegars, oils, nuts, and seeds.

PACIFIC RIM GOURMET

i-Clipse, Inc.

4905 Morena Boulevard, Suite 1313

San Diego, CA 92117

800–910–WOKS

www.pacificrim-gourmet.com

Panko Japanese bread crumbs, wasabi peas, and a variety of Asian spices and ingredients.

PENZEY'S SPICES

P.O. Box 933

Muskego, WI 53150

800–741–7787

www.penzeys.com

For sea salts, black sesame seeds, and difficult-to-find whole and ground spices. The freshness of these spices can't be beat, so if you're placing an order for something exotic, it's worth it to order some everyday spices, too.

SAM'S WINES & SPIRITS

1720 North Marcey Street

Chicago, IL 60614

866–726–7946

www.samswine.com

Source for pumpkinseed oil, olive oils, vinegars, cheeses.

TAYLOR'S MARKET

2900 Freeport Boulevard

Sacramento, CA 95818

916–443–6881

www.taylorsmarket.com

Will send Dufour all-butter puff pastry overnight on ice. Also a good source for oils, vinegars, cheeses, and condiments.

ZINGERMAN'S

422 Detroit Street

Ann Arbor, MI 48104

313–663–3354

888–636–8162

Good selection of oils, vinegars, cheeses, salts.

Index

Abadia Retuerta Sardon de
   Duero, 225
Acacia
   Chardonnay, 92
   Pinot Noir, 140, 153
acidity, wine-food pairing and,
   57, 103, 238
Alban Syrah, 202
Albariño, 15, 284
almonds, 15
   spicy fruited couscous, 193
Aloxe-Corton, 127, 132
Alsatian wines
   Gewürztraminer, 33, 34, 214
   specific recommendations, 36,
      38, 40, 52, 192
   Muscat, 33, 38, 52
   Pinot Gris, 34, 36, 44, 52, 53
   Riesling, 31, 33, 214; specific
      recommendations, 36, 38,
      45, 52, 281
   Selection de Grains Nobles,
      240
Amarone, 241
Anderson (S.) Rosé, 121, 123
angel food cake, dessert wine
   with, 243
angel hair pasta with smoked
   salmon and edamame
   "pesto," 107–8
Antinori
   Vermentino, 113, 123
   Vin Santo, 248
apples
   apple, sage, and onion soup
      with Cheddar-bacon
      croutons, 36–37
   fennel and apple hash, 44
   tarte Tatin with bourbon and
      vanilla, 254–55

apricots
   apricot-cranberry–cream cheese
      centers, ginger-Spumante
      cupcakes with, 250–51
   spicy fruited couscous, 193
Apulian wines, 212, 218, 231, 235,
   236
Archery Summit Pinot Noir, 146
Argentine wines
   Chardonnay, 75, 94, 97
   Malbec, 159
   sparkling wines, 103–4
Argueso Pedro Ximenez Sherry,
   243, 284
Argyle
   Brut, 113, 123
   Pinot Noir, 132, 153
Aria Cava Extra Dry, 113, 123
aromatic whites, 32–34
   See also specific varietals
artichokes and squid, crispy,
   231–32
arugula
   charred tricolore salad, 186
   linguine with walnuts, olives,
      and, 169–70
Arzuaga Ribera del Duero, 284
Asian foods, wines for, 32–33
Asian herb oil, 266
asparagus, 104
   oven-charred, with cheese and
      balsamic vinegar, 190
Asti Spumante, 250
   See also Moscato d'Asti
Au Bon Climat
   Chardonnay, 84, 96
   Pinot Noir, 136, 146
Auslese, 30, 243
Australian wines
   Cabernet-Merlot blends, 162, 178

Cabernet Sauvignon, 161, 175,
   179
Chardonnay, 73, 75; specific
   recommendations, 80, 82,
   92, 96, 97
dessert wines, 241, 243, 281
Merlot, 161
Pinot Noir, 125
Riesling, 31; specific
   recommendations, 42, 45,
   46, 52, 53, 281
Shiraz and blends, 161, 181,
   182, 183, 184; food pairings,
   20, 49, 88; specific
   recommendations, 187, 201,
   202, 206, 207
sparkling wines, 103–4, 114, 123
Austrian wines
   dessert wines, 256
   Grüner-Veltliner, 32–34, 35, 39,
      50, 52, 53
   Riesling, 31, 33, 35, 53
Avignonesi
   Rosso di Montepulciano, 221
   Vin Santo, 285
avocado(s)
   charred corn salad with orzo
      and, 78–79
   mussel salad with seared
      avocado dressing, 68–69
   shrimp ceviche with cilantro,
      lime, and, 113

B&G Merlot, 163, 178
Babcock Sauvignon Blanc, 60
bacon
   butternut squash risotto with
      sage and, 42–43

Cheddar-bacon croutons, apple, sage, and onion soup with, 36–37

in fennel and apple hash, 44

Bailly Sancerre, 65

Ballatore Spumante Rosso, 246

balsamic vinegar, 13–14, 21, 264

balsamic vinaigrette, 265; charred tricolore salad with, 186

balsamic vinegar reduction, 264

cool balsamic and black pepper strawberries with warm toasted mozzarella flatbread, 219–20

and mushroom pan sauce, 230

oven-charred asparagus with cheese and, 190

roasted spaghetti squash with nutmeg and, 38

salad of fresh figs with Manchego, toasted pine nuts, and, 162

strawberries with, 243

sweet potato puree with garlic, thyme, and, 166

banana chips

plantain-crusted chicken, 84–85

tropical fruits "on the half-shell" with banana crunch topping, 245

bananas

caramelized banana "pizza," 252–53

chocolate-banana sorbet, 260

honey- and lavender-glazed fruit, 244

Banfi

Brachetto d'Acqui, 243, 246

Cum Laude, 165, 178, 285

Summus, 222, 235

Banyuls, 243

Barbadillo sherry, 284

Barbaresco, 213, 227

barbecue sauce, Indonesian five-spice, 267

plank-cooked salmon with, 45

Barbera, 14, 170, 212

specific recommendations, 222, 233, 235, 236, 285

barley

pearl barley risotto with mushrooms and carrots, 138–39

Barolo, 213, 227, 236, 285

barrels, oak character and, 74, 128–29, 158

basic recipes, 264–72

balsamic vinegar reduction, 264

herb oil, 266

Indonesian five-spice barbecue sauce, 267

oven-crisped sage leaves, 270

oven-dried plum tomatoes, 272

preserved lemons, 271

quick mushroom stock, 268

roasted garlic or shallots, 269

basic techniques, 17–20, 196

basil, 15

crunchy herb salad, 59

in edamame "pesto," 107–8

herb oil, 266

Basilicata wines, 218, 235

bean and black olive bruschetta with rosemary, 218

Beaucastel Châteauneuf-du-Pape, 283

Beaujolais, 140

Beaulieu Vineyards (BV)

Cabernet Sauvignon, 171

Pinot Noir, 132

Syrah, 201

Beaumalric Muscat Beaumes de Venise, 248, 284

Beaumes de Venise, 241, 248, 284

Beaune, 127

beef

churrasco-style skirt steak, 112

flank steak marinated in spicy herb oil, 226

"red and blue" short rib ragù with pappardelle, 175–76

seared filet mignon with Merlot and mushroom jus, 177

sirloin steak with "beurre-naise" sauce, 173–74

Beerenauslese, 30, 240

Belle (Albert) Crozes-Hermitage, 186

Belle Glos Pinot Noir, 151

Benton Lane Pinot Noir, 16, 138

Benziger

Cabernet Sauvignon, 167

Sauvignon Blanc, 68

Beringer

Chardonnay, 86, 89, 94, 97

Founders' Estate Cabernet Sauvignon, 173, 179

Sauvignon Blanc, 64, 70

"beurre-naise" sauce, sirloin steak with, 173–74

Billecart-Salmon Rosé, 121, 123

biscotti, 243

gingered cranberry-pistachio, 248–49

black bean–hoisin sauce, mushroom-dusted tuna with, 151–52

black olive and bean bruschetta with rosemary, 218

Black Opal Shiraz, 201

black pepper

cool balsamic and black pepper strawberies with warm toasted mozzarella flatbread, 219–20

Shiraz-poached pears with Roquefort and, 187–88

Blackstone Cabernet Sauvignon,
    167, 179
Black Swan Chardonnay, 80, 97
Blanck (Paul)
    Gewürztraminer, 40, 52
    Riesling, 38, 281
Blandy's Ten-Year-Old Malmsey
    Madeira, 243, 254
blueberries, dessert wine with,
    243
blue cheese, 185
    pear, fennel, and blue cheese
        salad with red wine glaze,
        221
    "red and blue" short rib ragù
        with pappardelle, 175–76
    Shiraz-poached pears with
        Roquefort and black pepper,
        187–88
    wine pairings, 56, 214, 239, 243
Bodegas Hidalgo La Gitana
    sherry, 284
Bogle Merlot, 177, 179, 195
Boillot Meursault, 282
Bollinger Champagne, 280
Bonny Doon
    Cardinal Zin, 204, 206
    Muscat Vin de Glaciere, 243,
        245
Bordeaux reds, 156–58
    menus for, 178, 282, 283
    specific recommendations, 163,
        165, 171, 178
Bordeaux-style blends
    Meritage, 158, 166, 169, 179,
        283
Bordeaux whites, 55, 56, 57
    specific recommendations, 62,
        66, 70, 282
    See also Sauternes
Borsao Campo de Borja, 222,
    235
Boscarelli Rosso di
    Montepulciano, 221, 235

botrytis wines, 240, 241
    See also Beerenauslese;
        Sauternes; Tokaji;
        Trockenbeerenauslese
Bottega Vinaia Pinot Grigio, 109,
    122
Bouchard
    Bourgogne La Vignée, 135, 154
    Pouilly-Fuissé, 77, 96
    Savigny-Les-Beaune, 132, 150,
        153
bourbon, tarte Tatin with vanilla
    and, 254–55
Bourgeois (Henri) Pouilly-Fumé,
    65
Bourgogne regional wines, 126,
    135, 154
Bourgueil, 159
Bourillon-d'Orleans Vouvray,
    244
Brachetto d'Acqui, 243, 246
Brancott
    Chardonnay, 82
    Pinot Noir, 142, 154
    Sauvignon Blanc, 58, 70
bread
    bean and black olive bruschetta
        with rosemary, 218
    warm toasted mozzarella
        flatbread, cool balsamic and
        black pepper strawberries
        with, 219–20
"brick-roasted" chicken breasts,
    197–98
brining, 20, 196
    fast-track baby back ribs, 50–51
Broadbent Rainwater Madeira,
    254
broccoli florets, Lucas's sesame-
    ginger, 80
Brundlmayer Riesling, 35
Brunello di Montalcino, 211
bruschetta, bean and black olive,
    with rosemary, 218

Brussels sprouts, roasted, with
    garlic and sage, 165
Brusset
    Côtes du Rhône, 204
    Gigondas, 191
Buena Vista
    Pinot Noir, 142, 154
Burgans Albariño, 284
Burgundy reds, 125, 126–28, 131
    menus for, 153, 154, 282
    specific recommendations, 132,
        135, 138, 140, 144, 146, 148,
        150, 153, 154
    See also specific appellations and
        producers
Burgundy whites, 15, 73–74, 75,
    76
    specific recommendations, 77,
        81, 92, 96, 97, 282, 283
butternut squash risotto with
    bacon and sage, 42–43
buying wine, 273–75, 278–79
    wines to have on hand, 15–16
BV. See Beaulieu Vineyards
Byron Chardonnay, 84

Cabernet Franc, 157, 158, 159,
    165, 283
    See also Chinon
Cabernet Sauvignon, 16, 130,
    155–79
    basics, 155, 156–61
    food pairings, 15, 20, 49, 170,
        230
    menus for, 178–79, 283
    in Priorat, 215
    specific recommendations, 162,
        165, 166, 167, 168, 169, 171,
        173, 175, 178, 179
    in Super Tuscans, 161, 212
    See also Bordeaux reds; specific
        regions and wineries

Cain Musqué Sauvignon Blanc, 60, 71

cake
  angel food, dessert wine with, 243
  ginger-Spumante cupcakes with apricot-cranberry-cream cheese centers, 250–51

Calatayud, 213, 228, 236

Calera
  Chardonnay, 84
  Pinot Noir, 136, 153

California wines
  Cabernet Franc, 159, 165, 283
  Cabernet Sauvignon, 160, 283; specific recommendations, 166, 167, 168, 169, 171, 173, 178, 179
  Chardonnay, 20, 73, 192, 229; specific recommendations, 78, 81, 84, 86, 89, 92, 94, 96, 97, 192, 195
  Chenin Blanc, 50
  dessert wines, 241, 243, 245, 246, 250, 258
  Gewürztraminer, 34, 48; late harvest, 258; specific recommendations, 38, 40, 48, 52, 53, 192, 258
  Meritage, 158, 166, 169, 179, 283
  Merlot, 160, 179; specific recommendations, 162, 177, 178, 195
  Muscat, 34, 38, 243, 250
  Pinot Gris/Pinot Grigio, 34, 111, 122
  Pinot Noir, 16, 125, 131; specific recommendations, 132, 134, 136, 140, 142, 146, 148, 150, 151, 152, 153, 154, 195
  Riesling, 31, 39, 42, 46, 52, 53
  Sauvignon Blanc/Fumé Blanc, 57; specific recommendations, 58, 59, 60, 62, 64, 66, 68, 70, 71, 195
  sparkling wines, 103–4; specific recommendations, 106, 107, 108, 112, 118, 119, 121, 122, 123, 281
  Syrah/Rhône-style wines, 183, 185; specific recommendations, 185, 190, 201, 202, 204, 206, 207
  Viognier, 34
  Zinfandel. See Zinfandel

Cambria
  Julia's Vineyard Chardonnay, 78, 96
  Pinot Noir, 132

Campanas Navarra Rosado, 219, 235

Campos Reales La Mancha, 222

Canadian ice wine, 245

Candido Salice Salentino, 192

Canoe Ridge Merlot, 175

Canyon Road
  Chardonnay, 78, 96
  Sauvignon Blanc, 58, 70

Cape Mentelle Shiraz, 201, 206

caper and mustard pan sauce, 229–30

Caprai Montefalco Sagrantino, 218, 235

caramel
  caramelized banana "pizza," 252–53
  tarte Tatin with bourbon and vanilla, 254–55

Carmenere, 16, 159, 226

carrot(s)
  pearl barley risotto with mushrooms and, 138–39
  roasted root vegetables with oregano, 105
  roasted tomato soup with leeks and, 217

slaw, with toasted pine nuts and herbs, 39

Casa Lapostolle Cuvée Alexandre
  Chardonnay, 78, 96
  Merlot, 162, 178

Cassis
  bittersweet chocolate–Cassis truffles, 262

Castello di Ama
  Chianti Classico, 221, 235
  Vin Santo, 243, 248, 285

Castello di Gabbiano Chianti Classico, 192, 217, 235

Catena Chardonnay, 94, 97

cauliflower
  cauliflower "popcorn," 106
  and okra, spicy roasted, 40–41
  -potato puree, coddled eggs with, 62–63
  and Yukon Gold potato soup with truffle oil, 77

Cava, 98, 102
  specific recommendations, 106, 109, 112, 113, 118, 119, 122, 123, 281

ceviche, 57
  shrimp, with avocado, cilantro, and lime, 113

Chablis, 73, 77, 282

Chalk Hill Chardonnay, 89

Chalone
  Chardonnay, 92, 97
  Pinot Noir, 140

Chambers Museum Muscat, 243

Chambolle-Musigny, 127, 146, 282

Champagne, 14, 98, 99–101
  Champagne-steamed mussels, 119
  menus for, 122, 123, 280, 281
  opening, 102
  rosés, 101, 112, 121, 122, 123, 281

Covey Run Fumé Blanc, 64, 70
cranberries
   apricot-cranberry–cream cheese
      centers, ginger-Spumante
      cupcakes with, 250–51
   gingered cranberry-pistachio
      biscotti, 248–49
   mascarpone and berry filling,
      soft chocolate cookie
      sandwiches with, 246–47
   spicy fruited couscous, 193
Crawford (Kim) "Un-oaked"
   Chardonnay, 82, 96
cream, spinach, and garlic pan
   sauce, 230
cream cheese
   apricot-cranberry–cream cheese
      centers, ginger-Spumante
      cupcakes with, 250–51
Cristom Pinot Noir, 144, 154
croutons, Cheddar-bacon, apple,
   sage, and onion soup with,
   36–37
Crozes-Hermitage, 182
   specific recommendations,
      186, 194, 199, 206, 207
Cuban-style asado pork with vino
   mojo, 94–95
cumin-crusted lamb, 199–200
cupcakes, ginger-Spumante, with
   apricot-cranberry–cream
   cheese centers, 250–51
cured meats, 14
curry
   coconut milk–curry shrimp
      soup, 64
   spicy fruited couscous, 193

Danzante Sangiovese, 231
D'Arenberg Red Ochre Shiraz
   blend, 187, 206
Degrazia, Marco (importer), 210

Dehlinger Pinot Noir, 142
Dei Rosso di Montepulciano, 221
Delas Côte Rôtie, 186
DeLille Cellars Chaleur Estate
   Blanc, 66, 71
   Cabernet Sauvignon, 169, 178
De Loach Gewürztraminer, 40, 53
desserts
   bittersweet chocolate–Cassis
      truffles, 262
   caramelized banana "pizza,"
      252–53
   chocolate-banana sorbet, 260
   gingered cranberry-pistachio
      biscotti, 248–49
   ginger-Spumante cupcakes
      with apricot-
      cranberry–cream cheese
      centers, 250–51
   honey- and lavender-glazed
      fruit, 244
   pear or pineapple and Pinot
      Gris granita, 261
   pumpkin-pear mini soufflés,
      258–59
   simple desserts with wine
      matches, 243
   soft chocolate cookie
      sandwiches with
      mascarpone and berry
      filling, 246–47
   spiced pear and phyllo
      dumplings, 256–57
   tarte Tatin with bourbon and
      vanilla, 254–55
   tropical fruits "on the half-
      shell" with banana crunch
      topping, 245
dessert wines, 238–62
   basics, 238–42
   food pairings, 239, 241; simple
      desserts, 243
   sparkling, 101, 243, 246, 250,
      281

See also specific types and regions
Dolcetto, 212
Domaine Carneros
   Brut, 119, 122
   Pinot Noir, 148
Domaine du Cayrou Gigondas,
   283
Domaine Chandon Brut, 108
Domaine de Courcel Pommard,
   282
Domaine Drouhin Oregon Pinot
   Noir, 146
Domaine Dujac
   Clos Saint Denis, 148
   Morey-Saint-Denis, 146, 282
Domaine Laroche
   Chablis St. Martin, 77, 282
Domaine Leflaive Puligny-
   Montrachet, 282
Domaine Leroy Nuits-St.-
   Georges, 150, 154
Domaine Pelaquié Côtes du
   Rhône rosé, 283
Domaine Santa Duc Gigondas,
   194, 206
Domaine Ste. Michelle sparkling
   wines, 114, 123, 195, 281
Domecq Venerable PX Sherry,
   284
Dominio de Conte Rioja Reserva,
   219, 228, 236
Dom Pérignon Champagne,
   281
Dow's Port, 262
dried fruit soufflés, 259
dried-grape wines, 240, 241
   Vin Santo, 241, 243, 248, 285
Dry Creek Vineyard
   Fumé Blanc, 66, 71
   Zinfandel, 193, 207
Duboeuf (Georges)
   Côtes du Rhône, 192, 194
   Moulin-à-Vent, 140
duck breast, grilled, with red

wine reduction, 142–43
Duck Pond Pinot Noir, 144, 154
dumplings, spiced pear and
    phyllo, 256–57
Dynamite Cabernet Sauvignon,
    168

Ecco Domani
    Chianti, 195
    Pinot Grigio, 109, 122
Echelon Pinot Noir, 146
edamame "pesto," angel hair
    pasta with smoked salmon
    and, 107–8
Edmunds St. John Syrah, 190
Edna Valley Chardonnay, 81, 94,
    97
Edwards (Merry) Pinot Noir, 148
eggplant
    pancetta-wrapped goat cheese on
        roasted ratatouille, 222–23
eggs
    coddled, with cauliflower-
        potato puree, 62–63
    ideas and wine pairings, 195
    poached, with roasted tomatoes
        and crispy sage, 194–95
    scrambled, with corn tortilla
        strips and Monterey Jack,
        82–83
    Spanish-style scrambled, with
        chorizo and Manchego
        fricos, 224
Eiswein, 240
El Coto Rioja Reserva, 225
Empson, Neil (importer), 210
endive
    charred tricolore salad, 186
Engel (René) Nuits-St.-Georges,
    150
Erath Pinot Noir, 138, 153
Eroica Riesling, 39, 45, 52

Escudo Rojo Cabernet
    Sauvignon, 173
Estancia
    Chardonnay, 81, 84, 96
    Meritage, 166, 169, 179, 283
    Pinot Noir, 151, 154
Etude Pinot Noir, 151, 154
Europvin/Christopher Canaan
    Selections, 210

Faiveley
    Corton Clos des Cortons, 148
    Mercurey, 81, 140
Falchini Vernaccia, 105, 285
Falesco Vitiano, 226, 236
Famiglia di Robert Mondavi
    Moscato, 38
FAQs, 273–79
Faustino Rioja Reserva, 226, 236
Felluga (Livio) Pinot Grigio, 111,
    122
fennel
    and apple hash, 44
    oven-roasted, 134
    pear, fennel, and blue cheese
        salad with red wine glaze,
        221
Ferrari-Carano Fumé Blanc, 58,
    70
Ferreira Dona Antonia Port, 252
fettuccine with prosciutto, wild
    mushrooms, and sage,
    136–37
Fetzer
    Gewürztraminer, 38, 40, 52, 192
    Riesling, 31
    Zinfandel, 204, 206
Fiddlehead Cellars Pinot Noir,
    146
figs
    dessert wine with, 243
    dried fig and mushroom sauce,

seared pork tenderloin with,
    146–47
salad of fresh figs with
    Manchego, balsamic
    vinegar, and toasted pine
    nuts, 162
filet mignon, seared, with Merlot
    and mushroom jus, 177
Finca Allende Rioja, 228, 236
fingerling frites, roasted, 168
Firesteed Pinot Noir, 136, 153
fish, 17
    brining, 196
    ceviche, 57
    John's first-date salmon fillets,
        150
    mushroom-dusted tuna with
        black bean–hoisin sauce,
        151–52
    plank-cooked salmon, 45
    seared tuna with preserved
        lemon, 233–34
    spice-painted salmon, 202–3
    trout, 57
    wasabi pea–crusted salmon,
        121
    whole fish baked in a salt crust,
        204–5
five-spice barbecue sauce,
    Indonesian, 267
    plank-cooked salmon with, 45
flatbread
    cool balsamic and black pepper
        strawberries with warm
        toasted mozzarella
        flatbread, 219–20
fleur de sel, 12, 13, 81
foie gras, mushroom-dusted,
    148–49
Fonseca Port, 243, 252, 260
Foris Pinot Noir, 144
fortified wines, 240, 241
    See also Madeira; Port
Franciscan Cuvée Sauvage

Chardonnay, 89, 97
Franco (Nino) Prosecco, 105, 107, 122
Frei Brothers
  Merlot, 177
  Pinot Noir, 150, 154
  Reserve Cabernet Sauvignon, 179
Freie Weingartner Wachau Grüner-Veltliner, 39, 52
Freixenet Cavas, 112, 119, 122, 281
French Culinary Institute, 185
French paradox, 181
French wines
  rosés, 14, 216
  See also specific regions and grape varieties
Frescobaldi Chianti Rufina, 221
fricos, Manchego, Spanish-style scrambled eggs with chorizo and, 224
fruit desserts
  simple, dessert wine with, 243
  See also desserts; specific fruits
fruited couscous, spicy, 193
Fumé Blanc. *See* Sauvignon Blanc

Gallo of Sonoma
  Merlot, 162, 178
  Pinot Noir, 134, 146, 153, 195
  Zinfandel, 193, 207
garlic
  garlic-braised collard greens, 189
  roasted, 269; in carrot slaw with toasted pine nuts and herbs, 39; in chicken legs braised in Pinot Grigio mojo, 111; in Cuban-style asado pork with vino mojo, 94–95; rosemary and sweet

garlic roast chicken, 171–72
  roasted Brussels sprouts with sage and, 165
  spinach, cream, and garlic pan sauce, 230
  sweet potato puree with thyme, balsamic vinegar, and, 166
Garnacha, 213, 215, 216
Gattinara, 227, 236
German wines
  Gewürztraminer, 33, 34
  Riesling, 29–30, 33; specific recommendations, 40, 45, 46, 50, 53, 281; sweet, 30, 240, 241
Gevrey-Chambertin, 127, 140, 153
Gewürztraminer, 16, 32–34, 214
  food pairings, 14, 49, 192, 239
  Gewürztraminer pan sauce, oatmeal-crusted chicken with, 48–49
  specific recommendations, 36, 38, 40, 48, 52, 53, 192
Geyser Peak
  Cabernet Sauvignon, 166, 179
  Chardonnay, 86, 96
  Sauvignon Blanc, 59, 71
Gigi Rosso Barolo, 285
Gigondas, 191, 194, 206, 283
ginger
  gingered cranberry-pistachio biscotti, 248–49
  ginger-Spumante cupcakes with apricot-cranberry–cream cheese centers, 250–51
  Indonesian five-spice barbecue sauce, 267
  sesame-ginger broccoli florets, Lucas's, 80
  gingerbread cookies, dessert wine with, 243
Givry, 126, 138
glasses, 277

Glatzer (Walter) Grüner-Veltliner, 35, 50, 53
Gloria Ferrer Rosé, 112, 122
goat cheese, 185
  creamy goat cheese polenta, 108; lobster with, 89–91
  pancetta-wrapped, on roasted ratatouille, 222–23
  warm crispy goat cheese canapés, 109–10
  wine pairings, 56, 57, 214
Goldwater Dog Point Sauvignon Blanc, 59, 71
Gorgonzola, with pears and Banyuls, 243
Gosset Rosé, 112, 122, 281
Graham's Tawny Port, 252
Graillot (Alain) Crozes-Hermitage, 186, 199, 207
grains. *See* couscous; pasta; polenta; risotto
Gramenon Côtes du Rhône, 189
granita, pear or pineapple and Pinot Gris, 261
greens
  garlic-braised collard greens, 189
Grenache, 182, 183, 184
  blends, specific recommendations, 187, 206
  See also Rhône reds
Grgich Hills Zinfandel, 185
grits, cheese, with shrimp and chorizo, 225
Groffier Bourgogne, 135
Grosset Riesling, 42, 46, 53, 281
Grüner-Veltliner, 32–34
  specific recommendations, 35, 39, 50, 52, 53
Guigal
  Condrieu, 283
  Côte Rôtie, 186, 207
  Côtes du Rhône, 187, 189
  Crozes-Hermitage, 194

ham. *See* prosciutto
hash
　crispy chicken and shallot,
　　140–41
　fennel and apple, 44
health, wine and, 7–8, 181
Heidsieck (Charles) Champagne,
　114, 123, 280
herbes de Provence, 49
herbs, 14–15
　carrot slaw with toasted pine
　　nuts and, 39
　crunchy herb salad, 59
　herbed scallop and potato
　　"Napoleons" with truffle oil,
　　92–93
　herbes de Provence, 49
　herb oil, 266; flank steak
　　marinated in, 226
　lemon-herb-prosciutto shrimp,
　　201
　in rubs for meat, 49
　wine pairings, 14–15
　See also specific herbs
Herencia Remondo Rioja
　Reserva, 228
Hermitage, 182, 199, 207, 284
Hirtzberger Grüner-Veltliner, 39
Hogue Cellars
　Gewürztraminer, 40, 192
　Late Harvest Gewürztraminer,
　　258
　Riesling, 38, 50, 52
　Sauvignon Blanc, 64
hoisin
　black bean-hoisin sauce,
　　mushroom-dusted tuna
　　with, 151–52
honey- and lavender-glazed fruit,
　244
Honig Sauvignon Blanc, 59, 195
Huet Vouvray, 50, 243, 244, 261
Hugel Gewürztraminer, 38, 40
Hungarian Tokaji, 240, 256

ice wines, 240, 241, 243, 245
Indian food, wines for, 32–33
Indian rub, 49
Indonesian five-spice barbecue
　sauce, 267
　plank-cooked salmon with, 45
Inniskillin Vidal Ice Wine, 245
Iron Horse
　Pinot Noir, 134, 153
　sparkling wines, 107, 121, 122,
　　123, 281
Italian dessert wines
　Amarone, 241
　Brachetto d'Acqui, 246
　Moscato d'Asti, 243, 250, 256
　Vin Santo, 241, 243, 248, 285
Italian importers, 210
Italian reds
　Barbaresco, 213, 227
　Barbera, 14, 170, 212; specific
　　recommendations, 222, 233,
　　235, 236, 285
　Barolo, 213, 227, 236, 285
　basics, 208, 209–13, 215
　Chianti, 16, 211; food pairings,
　　14, 88, 170, 192, 195, 214,
　　230; rosatos, 216; specific
　　recommendations, 217, 221,
　　235
　Dolcetto, 212
　emerging regions and grapes,
　　208, 212, 231, 235, 236
　menus for, 235–36, 285
　Nebbiolo, 213, 227, 236
　southern Italy, 218, 231, 235, 236
　Super Tuscans, 161, 212; specific
　　recommendations, 165, 178,
　　222, 226, 235, 236, 285
Italian rosés, 14, 216
Italian whites, 15
　Chardonnay, 74
　Pinot Grigio, 34, 103; specific
　　recommendations, 46, 109,
　　111, 122

Prosecco, 98, 103; specific
　recommendations, 105, 107,
　108, 116, 122, 123
Vermentino, 103; specific
　recommendations, 107, 113,
　122, 123, 192
Vernaccia, 14, 103; specific
　recommendations, 105, 111,
　122, 192
Italian wine menu, 285

Jaboulet
　Beaumes de Venise, 248
　Cornas, 186, 207
　Côtes du Rhône, 187, 206
Jacob's Creek Riesling, 45, 46, 53
Jacquesson Blanc de Blancs, 281
Jade Mountain
　Mourvèdre, 185
　Syrah/Rhône blend, 190, 206
Jadot (Louis)
　Macon, 77, 96
　Puligny-Montrachet, 81
　Santenay Clos de Malte, 140, 150
Jamaican jerk rub, 49
Janodet (Jacky) Morgon, 140
Jasmin Côte Rôtie, 284
Joblot Givry, 138
Joguet (Charles) Chinon, 165
Jolivet (Pascal) Sancerre, 65, 70
Josmeyer Riesling, 36, 45, 52
"J" Pinot Noir, 134, 151
Juge (Marcel) Mercurey, 144
Juillot Mercurey, 138, 153
Jumilla, 213

Kabinett, 30, 33
Kendall-Jackson
　Cabernet Sauvignon, 173
　Riesling, 46, 53

Moscato. *See* Moscato d'Asti; Muscat
Moscato d'Asti, 243, 250, 256
  in ginger-Spumante cupcakes with apricot-cranberry–cream cheese centers, 250–51
Mourvèdre, 182, 183, 184
  specific recommendations, 185, 187, 206
  See also Rhône reds
mozzarella
  flatbread, toasted, cool balsamic and black pepper strawberries with, 219–20
  smoked mozzarella sauce, lobster with confetti vegetables and, 89–91
Mt. Horrocks Cordon Cut Late Harvest Riesling, 281
Mt. Veeder Cabernet Sauvignon, 166
Muga Rioja Reserva, 224, 235
Mumm Champagne, 280
Mumm Cuvée Napa, 118, 123
Murphy-Goode Fumé Blanc, 66, 71
Murray (Andrew) Syrah, 190, 202, 206
Murrieta Rioja Crianza, 231
Muscadelle, 158
Muscat, 32–34, 241
  specific recommendations, 38, 52, 243, 248, 250, 256, 284
mushroom(s)
  and balsamic vinegar pan sauce, 230
  crispy chicken and shallot hash, 140–41
  dried fig and mushroom sauce, seared pork tenderloin with, 146–47
  fettuccine with prosciutto, wild mushrooms, and sage, 136–37

mushroom-dusted foie gras, 148–49
mushroom-dusted tuna with black bean–hoisin sauce, 151–52
Oloroso sherry–glazed pork chops with, 228–29
pearl barley risotto with carrots and, 138–39
quick mushroom stock, 268
seared filet mignon with Merlot and mushroom jus, 177
shallot- and thyme-rubbed roast turkey with, 144–45
warm wild mushroom salad with black truffle vinaigrette, 132–33
wild mushroom phyllo purses with pumpkinseed oil drizzle, 163–64
Musigny, 148
mussel(s)
  Champagne-steamed, 119–20
  salad, with seared avocado dressing, 68–69
mustard
  and caper pan sauce, 229–30
  tarragon and mustard-crusted scallops, 66–67

"Napoleons," herbed scallop and potato, with truffle oil, 92–93
Nautilus Sauvignon Blanc, 58
Navarra wines, 208, 216, 219, 231, 235
Navarro Late Harvest Gewürztraminer, 258
Nebbiolo, 213, 227
  Nebbiolo d'Alba, 213, 227, 236
  See also Barbaresco; Barolo

New York wines
  Chardonnay, 74
  Riesling, 31
New Zealand wines
  Chardonnay, 73, 74, 82, 96
  dessert wines, 241, 243, 245
  Pinot Noir, 16, 125, 131; specific recommendations, 142, 154
  Riesling, 31, 45, 53
  Sauvignon Blanc, 57, 88; specific recommendations, 48, 49, 68, 70, 71
Nigl
  Grüner-Veltliner, 35
  Riesling, 53
Norman (Greg) Shiraz, 207
North African rub, 49
Noval LB Port, 260
Nuits-St.-Georges, 127, 144, 150, 154
nutmeg, roasted spaghetti squash with balsamic vinegar and, 38
nuts, 15
  See also specific nuts

oak character, 158
  Chardonnay, 74
  Pinot Noir, 128–29
oatmeal-crusted chicken with Gewürztraminer pan sauce, 48–49
oil
  herb oil, 266
  olive oil, 12
okra and cauliflower, spicy roasted, 40–41
olive oil, 12
olives
  bean and black olive bruschetta with rosemary, 218

linguine with walnuts, arugula, and, 169–70
with sherry, 56
Oloroso sherry–glazed pork chops with mushrooms, 228–29
Omrah "Un-oaked" Chardonnay, 82
onions
apple, sage, and onion soup with Cheddar-bacon croutons, 36–37
Onix Priorat, 236, 284
opening wine, 276
sparkling wines, 102
Ordoñez, Jorge Tempranillo Imports (importer), 210
oregano, 15
"brick-roasted" chicken breasts, 197–98
charred tricolore salad, 186
roasted root vegetables with, 105
Oregon wines
Chardonnay, 74
Pinot Gris, 34, 44, 53
Pinot Noir, 16, 125, 131; specific recommendations, 132, 135, 136, 138, 144, 146, 153, 154
sparkling wines, 113, 123
Ornellaia Le Volte, 165, 222, 226
orzo, charred corn salad with avocados and, 78–79
Osborne Solaz Tempranillo Penedes, 228
oysters
pan-crisped, with sesame seeds, 118
roasted oysters "Rockefeller Center," 116–17

pancetta-wrapped goat cheese on roasted ratatouille, 222–23

pan sauce(s), 19, 229–30
Gewürztraminer, oatmeal-crusted chicken with, 48–49
Panther Creek Pinot Noir, 146
pantry items
wine pairings, 12–14
wines to have on hand, 15–16, 274
pappardelle, "red and blue" short rib ragù with, 175–76
Parcé (Dr.) Banyuls, 243
Parellada, 102
parsnips
roasted root vegetables with oregano, 105
pasta
angel hair, with smoked salmon and edamame "pesto," 107–8
fettuccine with prosciutto, wild mushrooms, and sage, 136–37
ideas for, 170
linguine with walnuts, arugula, and olives, 169–70
orzo, charred corn salad with avocados and, 78–79
"red and blue" short rib ragù with pappardelle, 175–76
Pauillac, 157, 158
Pazo de Señorans Albariño, 284
peaches
dessert wine with, 243
honey- and lavender-glazed fruit, 244
Peachy Canyon Zinfandel, 204
pear(s)
with Gorgonzola and Banyuls, 243
pear, fennel, and blue cheese salad with red wine glaze, 221
and Pinot Gris granita, 261

pumpkin-pear mini soufflés, 258–59
Shiraz-poached, with Roquefort and black pepper, 187–88
spiced pear and phyllo dumplings, 256–57
pecan pie, dessert wine with, 243
Pecota (Robert) Moscato d'Andrea, 250
Pedro Ximenez, 241
Pedro Ximenez Sherry, 243, 284
Penfolds
Koonunga Hill Cabernet-Merlot, 162, 178
Riesling, 42
Shiraz, 202, 207
Shiraz-Cabernet blends, 187
pepper. See black pepper
peppers
lobster with smoked mozzarella sauce and confetti vegetables, 89
pancetta-wrapped goat cheese on roasted ratatouille, 222–23
Pepperwood Grove Pinot Noir, 132, 153
Perdrix Mercurey, 138, 146, 153
Pernot (Paul) Nuits-St.-Georges, 144
Perrin Reserve Côtes du Rhône, 194, 206
Pesquera Ribera del Duero, 225, 236, 284
Pessac-Léognan, 157, 158
pesto, edamame, angel hair pasta with smoked salmon and, 107–8
Petit Verdot, 157, 158
Phelps (Joseph) Syrah, 185
Phillips (R.H.)
Chardonnay, 86, 96, 192, 195
EXP Syrah, 190, 206

phyllo
    spiced pear and phyllo
        dumplings, 256–57
    wild mushroom phyllo purses
        with pumpkinseed oil
        drizzle, 163–64
Picard (Michel) Sancerre, 65, 70
Pichler Grüner-Veltliner, 50
Piedmont reds, 212–13
    Barbaresco, 213, 227
    Barbera, 14, 170, 212; specific
        recommendations, 222, 233,
        235, 236, 285
    Barolo, 213, 227, 236, 285
    Gattinara, 227, 236
    Nebbiolo d'Alba, 213, 227, 236
    Spanna, 227
Pighin Pinot Grigio, 46
Pikes Riesling, 42, 46, 52, 281
pineapple
    dessert wine with, 243
    honey- and lavender-glazed
        fruit, 244
    and Pinot Gris granita, 261
    tropical fruits "on the half-
        shell" with banana crunch
        topping, 245
pine nuts, 15
    in cauliflower "popcorn," 106
    toasted, carrot slaw with herbs
        and, 39
    toasted, salad of fresh figs with
        Manchego, balsamic
        vinegar, and, 162
Pinot Gris/Pinot Grigio, 32–34,
    103
    food pairings, 14, 170
    pear or pineapple and Pinot
        Gris granita, 261
    Pinot Grigio mojo, chicken legs
        braised in, 111
    specific recommendations, 36,
        44, 46, 52, 53, 109, 111, 122

See also specific regions and
    wineries
Pinot Meunier, 99
Pinot Noir, 16, 124–54
    basics, 124, 125–31
    grilled duck breast with red
        wine reduction, 142–43
    menus for, 153–54
    in sparkling wines, 99
    specific recommendations, 132,
        134, 135, 136, 138, 140, 142,
        144, 146, 148, 150, 151,
        153–54
See also specific regions and
    wineries
Pio Cesare
    Barbera d'Alba, 233, 236, 285
    Nebbiolo d'Alba, 227, 236
Piper-Sonoma Brut NV, 106
pistachios
    gingered cranberry-pistachio
        biscotti, 248–49
    "pizza," caramelized banana,
        252–53
plantain-crusted chicken, 84–85
plums, dessert wine with, 243
Polaner Selections, 210
polenta
    cheese grits with shrimp and
        chorizo, 225
    creamy goat cheese polenta,
        108; lobster with, 89–91
    quick-cooking, 192
Pol Roger Champagne, 116, 123,
    280
Pomerol, 157, 158
Pommard, 127, 135, 282
Poniatowsky (Prince) Vouvray, 50
Ponzi Pinot Noir, 136, 153
pork
    brining, 196
    chops, Oloroso sherry–glazed,
        with mushrooms, 228–29

chops, quick pan sauces for,
    229–30
Cuban-style asado pork with
    vino mojo, 94–95
fast-track baby back ribs, 50–51
tenderloin, seared, with dried
    fig and mushroom sauce,
    146–47
See also bacon; chorizo;
    prosciutto
Port, 240, 241
    with cheese, 56, 239
    specific recommendations, 243,
        252, 260, 262
Portuguese dessert wines. See
    Madeira; Port
potatoes
    cauliflower-potato puree,
        coddled eggs with, 62–63
    herbed scallop and potato
        "Napoleons" with truffle oil,
        92–93
    oven-crisped red potatoes with
        thyme and pumpkinseed
        oil, 35
    roasted fingerling frites, 168
    shrimps in a blanket, 114–15
    Yukon Gold potato and
        cauliflower soup with truffle
        oil, 77
Potel (Nicolas)
    Pommard, 135
    Santenay, 144, 154
Pouilly-Fuissé, 73, 77, 92, 96
Pouilly-Fumé, 55, 57, 65, 70
poultry
    brining, 20
    grilled duck breast with red
        wine reduction, 142–43
    mushroom-dusted foie gras,
        148–49
    shallot- and thyme-rubbed
        roast turkey, 144–45

turkey quesadillas with sesame–sweet potato mole sauce, 86–87
See also chicken
Prager Grüner-Veltliner, 50
Pride Mountain Cabernet Franc, 165, 283
Primitivo, 180, 231, 236
Priorat, 215, 236, 284
prosciutto
  chicken breasts with sage and, 227
  fettuccine with wild mushrooms, sage, and, 136–37
  lemon-herb-prosciutto shrimp, 201
  shrimps in a blanket, 114–15
Prosecco, 98, 103
  specific recommendations, 105, 107, 108, 116, 122, 123
Provençal rosés, 216
Prum (JJ) Wehlener Sonnenuhr, 281
Puligny-Montrachet, 74, 81, 282
pumpkin-pear mini soufflés, 258–59
pumpkinseed oil
  grilled corn on the cob with, 81
  oven-crisped red potatoes with thyme and, 35
  in summer tomato salad, 58
  wild mushroom phyllo purses with pumpkinseed oil drizzle, 163–64
PX Sherry, 243, 284

quesadillas
  ideas and wine pairings, 88
  turkey, with sesame–sweet potato mole sauce, 86–87
Qupé Syrah, 185

radicchio
  charred tricolore salad, 186
Rafanelli Zinfandel, 197, 207
Raffault (Olga) Chinon, 165, 178, 283
ragù, "red and blue" short rib, with pappardelle, 175–76
Rancho Zabaco
  Sauvignon Blanc, 68, 70
  Zinfandel, 197, 207
Rasmussen (Kent) Pinot Noir, 140
raspberries, dessert wine with, 243
ratatouille, roasted, pancetta-wrapped goat cheese on, 222–23
Raymond Napa Cabernet Sauvignon, 169, 178
"red and blue" short rib ragù with pappardelle, 175–76
Redde (Michel) Pouilly-Fumé, 65, 70
red wine(s)
  glaze, pear, fennel, and blue cheese salad with, 221
  growing popularity of, 181
  pantry recommendations, 16
  reduction, grilled duck breast with, 142–43
See also specific wines
Regaleali Rosato, 231, 236
Renwood Zinfandel, 191, 207
Rex Hill Pinot Noir, 138
Rhône Rangers, 183
  See also California wines, Syrah/Rhône–style wines
Rhône reds, 49, 180–207
  basics, 180, 182–84
  food pairings, 12, 15, 214, 230
  menus for, 206–7, 283–84
  specific recommendations, 186, 187, 189, 191, 192, 194, 197, 199, 204, 206, 207
Rhône whites, 34, 192, 283
Ribera del Duero, 214, 225, 236, 284
ribs
  fast-track baby back ribs, 50–51
  "red and blue" short rib ragù with pappardelle, 175–76
Ricasoli 1181 Chianti, 217, 235
rice
  butternut squash risotto with bacon and sage, 42–43
Ridge Geyserville Zinfandel, 185, 204, 206
Riesling, 16, 28–53, 214
  basics, 28, 29–31, 33
  in coq au Riesling with leeks, 46–47
  dry, specific recommendations, 35, 36, 38, 39, 40, 42, 45, 46, 50, 52, 53
  in fennel and apple hash, 44
  food pairings, 14, 15
  late harvest/sweet, 30, 38, 239, 241; specific recommendations, 243, 261, 281
  menus for, 52–53, 281
See also specific regions and wineries
Rioja reds, 16, 213–14
  food pairings, 12, 14, 192, 195, 214, 230
  specific recommendations, 219, 224, 225, 226, 228, 231, 235, 236, 284
Rioja rosés, 219, 235
Rioja whites, 192
risotto
  butternut squash, with bacon and sage, 42–43

pearl barley, with mushrooms and carrots, 138–39
Rivetti Moscato d'Asti, 243, 250
Rocca delle Macie
    Chianti Classico, 221, 235
    Roccato, 226, 236
Rochioli Pinot Noir, 148
"Rockefeller Center" roasted oysters, 116–17
Roda Rioja Reserva, 231, 236
Roederer Estate sparkling wines, 106, 118, 123
root vegetables
    roasted, with oregano, 105
    See also specific vegetables
Roquefort, 239
    Shiraz-poached pears with black pepper and, 187–88
rosemary, 15
    bean and black olive bruschetta with, 218
    crispy artichokes and squid, 231–32
    lemon-herb-prosciutto shrimp, 201
    roasted fingerling frites, 168
    rosemary and sweet garlic roast chicken, 171–72
    shrimps in a blanket, 114–15
    toasted chickpeas with crispy sage, 191
Rosemount
    Chardonnay, 80, 82, 97
    GSM, 187, 206
    Shiraz, 202
Rosenblum Zinfandel, 199
rosés, 14, 216, 278
    dessert wines, 243
    menus for, 235, 236
    sparkling wines, 101, 112, 121, 122, 123, 243, 281
    specific recommendations, 219, 231, 235, 236
Rosso di Montalcino, 211

Rosso di Montepulciano, 211, 221, 235
Rothschild (Baron Philippe de) Sauternes, 244, 261
Roumier
    Chambolle-Musigny, 146, 282
    Le Musigny, 148
Royal Tokaji Wine Company Tokaji 5 Puttonyos, 256
Ruffino Modus, 285
Ruston Sauvignon Blanc, 62, 70

sage, 15
    apple, sage, and onion soup with Cheddar-bacon croutons, 36–37
    butternut squash risotto with bacon and, 42–43
    chicken breasts with prosciutto and, 227
    crispy, poached eggs with roasted tomatoes and, 194–95
    fettuccine with prosciutto, wild mushrooms, and, 136–37
    lemon-herb-prosciutto shrimp, 201
    oven-crisped sage leaves, 270
    roasted Brussels sprouts with garlic and, 165
    toasted chickpeas with crispy sage, 191
Sagelands Merlot, 175, 179
Saint-Aubin, 77
Saintsbury Garnet Pinot Noir, 140, 153
salad dressings, 21
    See also salads; vinaigrette
salads, 20–21
    carrot slaw with toasted pine nuts and herbs, 39

charred corn salad with avocados and orzo, 78–79
charred tricolore salad, 186
crunchy herb salad, 59
mussel salad with seared avocado dressing, 68–69
pear, fennel, and blue cheese salad with red wine glaze, 221
salad of fresh figs with Manchego, balsamic vinegar, and toasted pine nuts, 162
summer tomato salad, 58
warm wild mushroom salad with black truffle vinaigrette, 132–33
salmon, 57
    brining, 196
    first-date salmon fillets, John's, 150
    plank-cooked, 45
    smoked, angel hair pasta with edamame "pesto" and, 107–8
    spice-painted, 202–3
    wasabi pea-crusted, 121
Salomon (Erich)
    Grüner-Veltliner, 50
    Riesling, 35, 53
salsa, charred corn, 79
salt, 12–13
    whole fish baked in a salt crust, 204–5
Sancerre, 55, 56, 57, 65, 70
Sanford Pinot Noir, 146
Sangiovese, 130, 211–12, 216, 231
    food pairings, 170
    See also Chianti; Montalcino; Montepulciano; Super Tuscans
Santenay, 77, 127, 140, 144, 150, 154

Saracco (Paolo) Moscato d'Asti, 256
Sardinian wines, 218
sauce(s)
  "beurre-naise," sirloin steak with, 173–74
  black bean–hoisin, mushroom-dusted tuna with, 151–52
  chocolate, for caramelized banana "pizza," 252–53
  dried fig and mushroom, seared pork tenderloin with, 146–47
  Indonesian five-spice barbecue sauce, 267; plank-cooked salmon with, 45
  Merlot and mushroom jus, seared filet mignon with, 177
  mojo: Cuban-style asado pork with vino mojo, 94–95; Pinot Grigio, chicken legs braised in, 111
  pan sauces, 19; Gewürztraminer, oatmeal-crusted chicken with, 48–49; quick, for chicken or pork chops, 229–30
  sesame–sweet potato mole, turkey quesadillas with, 86–87
  smoked mozzarella, lobster with confetti vegetables and, 89–91
  See also salsa
sausage. See chorizo
Sauternes, 239, 240, 241
  specific recommendations, 243, 244, 261, 282
Sauvignon Blanc, 16, 54–71, 158
  basics, 54, 55–57
  food pairings, 13, 57, 88, 170, 214, 230

menus for, 70–71
  specific recommendations, 58, 59, 60, 62, 64, 65, 66, 68, 70–71, 195
  See also specific regions and wineries
Sauzet Chassagne-Montrachet, 92
Savennières, 34
Savigny-Les-Beaune, 127, 132, 150, 153
scallops
  herbed scallop and potato "Napoleons" with truffle oil, 92–93
  tarragon- and mustard-crusted, 66–67
Schrock (Heidi) Ausbruch, 256
Scott (Allan)
  Pinot Noir, 142, 154
  Riesling, 45, 53
  Sauvignon Blanc, 68, 70
seafood
  basic cooking techniques, 17
  brining, 20
  See also fish; shellfish; specific types
  searing, 17–18, 21
Seaview Brut, 114, 123
Sebastiani
  Chardonnay, 89, 97
  Pinot Noir, 134
Seghesio Zinfandel, 207
Segura Viudas Reserva Heredad Cava, 109, 122
Selaks Ice Wine, 243, 245
Selbach (J&H) "TJ" Riesling, 46, 53
Selene Sauvignon Blanc, 59, 71
Sella & Mosca Vermentino, 107, 122, 192
Semillon, 56, 158
Semillon/Sauvignon Blanc blends, 66
  See also Bordeaux whites

serving wine
  glasses, 277
  opening, 102, 276
  temperature, 278
sesame
  -ginger broccoli florets, Lucas's, 80
  pan-crisped oysters with sesame seeds, 118
  seared tuna with preserved lemon, 233–34
  –sweet potato mole sauce, turkey quesadillas with, 86–87
Shafer
  Cabernet Sauvignon, 171, 178
  Relentless, 185
shallot(s)
  crispy chicken and shallot hash, 140–41
  roasted, 269; in chicken legs braised in Pinot Grigio mojo, 111; in Cuban-style asado pork with vino mojo, 94–95
  shallot- and thyme-rubbed roast turkey, 144–45
  and wine pan sauce, 229
shellfish
  brining, 196
  Champagne-steamed mussels, 119–20
  cheese grits with shrimp and chorizo, 225
  coconut milk–curry shrimp soup, 64
  crispy artichokes and squid, 231–32
  herbed scallop and potato "Napoleons" with truffle oil, 92–93
  lemon-herb-prosciutto shrimp, 201
  lobster with smoked

mozzarella sauce and confetti vegetables, 89–91

mussel salad with seared avocado dressing, 68–69

pan-crisped oysters with sesame seeds, 118

roasted oysters "Rockefeller Center," 116–17

seared shrimp and chorizo bites, 63

shrimp ceviche with avocado, cilantro, and lime, 113

shrimps in a blanket, 114–15

tarragon- and mustard-crusted scallops, 66–67

sherry, 241

in chicken breasts with prosciutto and sage, 227

with olives, 56

Oloroso sherry–glazed pork chops with mushrooms, 228–29

specific recommendations, 243, 284

sherry vinegar, 13, 21

Shiraz. See Syrah/Shiraz

Shiraz-poached pears with Roquefort and black pepper, 187–88

shortbread cookies, dessert wine with, 243

shrimp

brining, 196

ceviche, with avocado, cilantro, and lime, 113

cheese grits with chorizo and, 225

coconut milk–curry shrimp soup, 64

lemon-herb-prosciutto shrimp, 201

seared shrimp and chorizo bites, 65

shrimps in a blanket, 114–15

Sicilian wines, 212, 216, 231, 235, 236

Siduri Pinot Noir, 150

Simi Sauvignon Blanc, 62, 70

slaw, carrot, with toasted pine nuts and herbs, 39

Smith-Madrone Riesling, 42, 52

Sokol-Blosser Pinot Noir, 135, 154

sorbet

chocolate-banana, 260

mango and coconut, dessert wine with, 243

tomato-watermelon, 60–61

See also granita

soufflés, mini pumpkin-pear, 258–59

soup(s)

apple, sage, and onion, with Cheddar-bacon croutons, 36–37

coconut milk–curry shrimp soup, 64

roasted tomato, with leeks and carrots, 217

Yukon Gold potato and cauliflower, with truffle oil, 77

South African wines

Chardonnay, 75

Chenin Blanc, 34

South American wines. See Argentine wines; Chilean wines

Southwestern herb oil, 266

Southwestern rub, 49

soybeans. See edamame

spaghetti squash, roasted, with nutmeg and balsamic vinegar, 38

Spanish dessert wines, 241

Spanish importers, 210

Spanish reds

basics, 208, 209–10, 213–15

emerging regions and grapes,

208, 213, 222, 228, 231, 235, 236

menus for, 235–36, 284

Priorat, 215, 236, 284

Ribera del Duero, 214, 225, 236, 284

Rioja, 16, 213–14; food pairings, 12, 14, 192, 195, 214, 230; specific recommendations, 219, 224, 225, 226, 228, 231, 235, 236, 284

Spanish rosés, 14, 216, 231

Spanish sparkling wines, 98, 102

specific recommendations, 106, 109, 112, 113, 118, 119, 122, 123, 281

Spanish-style scrambled eggs with chorizo and Manchego fricos, 224

Spanish whites, 15, 284

Spanish wine menu, 284

Spanna, 227

sparkling wines, 14, 15, 98–123

basics, 98, 99–104

dessert wines, 101, 243, 246, 250, 281

menus for, 122–23, 280, 281

opening, 102

See also specific regions and wineries

Sparr (Pierre)

Gewürztraminer, 36, 40, 52, 192

Spätlese, 30, 33, 45, 55, 281

spices

Indonesian five-spice barbecue sauce, 267

plank-cooked salmon with, 45

oatmeal-crusted chicken with Gewürztraminer pan sauce, 48–49

plantain-crusted chicken, 84–85

spiced pear and phyllo dumplings, 256–57

spice-painted salmon, 202–3

spice rubs, 49, 50
spicy fruited couscous, 193
spicy roasted cauliflower and
    okra, 40–41
spicy herb oil, 266
    flank steak marinated in, 226
spinach
    lightened-up "creamed,"
        135
    spinach, cream, and garlic pan
        sauce, 230
Spumante, 246
    ginger-Spumante cupcakes
        with apricot-
        cranberry–cream cheese
        centers, 250–51
    See also Moscato d'Asti
squash
    butternut squash risotto with
        bacon and sage, 42–43
    roasted spaghetti squash with
        nutmeg and balsamic
        vinegar, 38
    See also zucchini
squid and artichokes, crispy,
    231–32
steak. See beef
Steen, 34
St.-Emilion, 157, 158, 282
St.-Estèphe, 157, 158
St. Francis
    Chardonnay, 78
    Merlot, 177, 179
    Zinfandel, 185, 197
Stilton, with Port, 56, 239
St.-Joseph, 182
St.-Julien, 157, 158, 282
stock, quick mushroom, 268
Stoneleigh Sauvignon Blanc, 59
Stonestreet Chardonnay, 89
storing wine, 275–76
strawberries
    cool balsamic and black pepper
        strawberries with warm

toasted mozzarella
    flatbread, 219–20
    dessert wine with, 243
Strozzi Vernaccia, 105
Strub Niersteiner Paterberg
    Riesling, 40, 281
St. Véran, 73
Super Tuscans, 161, 212
    specific recommendations,
        165, 178, 222, 226, 235, 236,
        285
Sutter Home
    Chenin Blanc, 50
    Gewürztraminer, 40, 48
sweet potato(es)
    mashed, 192
    puree, with garlic, thyme, and
        balsamic vinegar, 166
    roasted root vegetables with
        oregano, 105
    -sesame mole sauce, turkey
        quesadillas with, 86–87
sweet wines. See dessert wines;
    specific regions and grape
    varietals
Syrah/Shiraz, 130, 161, 180–207,
    226
    basics, 180, 181–84
    food pairings, 14, 15, 49, 88,
        170, 185
    menus for, 206–7
    specific recommendations, 187,
        190, 201, 202, 204, 206,
        207
    See also Rhône reds; specific
    regions and wineries

Taittinger Champagne, 280
Talley Pinot Noir, 146
tannins, wine-food pairing and,
    130
tarragon, 15

"beurre-naise" sauce, sirloin
    steak with, 173–74
herbed scallop and potato
    "Napoleons" with truffle oil,
        92–93
and mustard-crusted scallops,
    66–67
and tomato pan sauce, 230
tarte Tatin with bourbon and
    vanilla, 254–55
Taurino Salice Salentino, 218,
    235
Taylor Fladgate Port, 260, 262
Tempranillo, 130, 213, 214, 215,
    228
    See also Ribera del Duero; Rioja
    reds
Teruzzi e Puthod Vernaccia di
    San Gimignano, 111, 122,
        192, 285
Testarossa Pinot Noir, 146
Thai food, wines for, 32–33
thyme, 14
    lemon-herb-prosciutto shrimp,
        201
    oven-crisped red potatoes with
        thyme and pumpkinseed
        oil, 35
    roasted fingerling frites, 168
    shallot- and thyme-rubbed
        roast turkey, 144–45
    sweet potato puree with garlic,
        balsamic vinegar, and, 166
Tokaji, 240, 256
Tollot-Beaut Aloxe-Corton, 132
tomato(es)
    fried green, pairing, 57
    oven-dried plum tomatoes, 272
    roasted, poached eggs with
        crispy sage and, 194–95
    roasted tomato soup with leeks
        and carrots, 217
    summer tomato salad, 58
    sun-dried, in warm crispy goat

cheese canapes, 109–10
and tarragon pan sauce, 230
-watermelon sorbet, 60–61
Tormaresca Primitivo, 231, 236
Toro, 213
Torres (Marimar) Pinot Noir, 132, 142
tortilla(s)
  caramelized banana "pizza," 252–53
  strips, scrambled eggs with Monterey Jack and, 82–83
  See also quesadillas
Travaglini Gattinara, 227, 236
Trefethen Riesling, 31, 42, 52
tricolore salad, charred, 186
Trimbach
  Muscat, 38, 52
  Pinot Gris, 44
  Riesling, 45
Trockenbeerenauslese, 30, 240
tropical fruits "on the half-shell" with banana crunch topping, 245
trout, 57
truffles, bittersweet chocolate–Cassis, 262
truffles, truffle oil
  black truffle vinaigrette, warm wild mushroom salad with, 132–33
  coddled eggs with cauliflower-potato puree and, 62–63
  herbed scallop and potato "Napoleons" with truffle oil, 92–93
  Yukon Gold potato and cauliflower soup with truffle oil, 77
tuna
  mushroom-dusted, with black bean–hoisin sauce, 151–52
  seared, with preserved lemon, 233–34

turkey
  brining, 196
  quesadillas, with sesame–sweet potato mole sauce, 86–87
  roast, shallot- and thyme-rubbed, 144–45
turnips
  roasted root vegetables with oregano, 105
Tuscan reds, 12, 15, 211–12
  See also Chianti; Montalcino; Montepulciano; Sangiovese; Super Tuscans

Umbrian wines, 212

Vallana Spanna, 227
vanilla, tarte Tatin with bourbon and, 254–55
vegetables, 18–19
  cauliflower "popcorn," 106
  fennel and apple hash, 44
  garlic-braised collard greens, 189
  grilled corn on the cob with pumpkinseed oil, 81
  lightened-up "creamed" spinach, 135
  oven-charred asparagus with cheese and balsamic vinegar, 190
  oven-crisped red potatoes with thyme and pumpkinseed oil, 35
  oven-roasted fennel, 134
  roasted Brussels sprouts with garlic and sage, 165
  roasted fingerling frites, 168
  roasted root vegetables with oregano, 105

  roasted spaghetti squash with nutmeg and balsamic vinegar, 38
  roasting, 18
  sesame-ginger broccoli florets, Lucas's, 80
  spicy roasted cauliflower and okra, 40–41
  sweet potato puree with garlic, thyme, and balsamic vinegar, 166
  toasted chickpeas with crispy sage, 191
  tomato-watermelon sorbet, 60–61
  wild mushroom phyllo purses with pumpkinseed oil drizzle, 163–64
  wine-braised leeks, 167
  See also salads; specific vegetables
Veramonte Cabernet Sauvignon, 166, 179
Vermentino, 103
  specific recommendations, 107, 113, 122, 123, 192
Vernaccia, 14, 103
  specific recommendations, 105, 111, 122, 192
Veuve Clicquot Champagne, 281
Viader Cabernet Blend, 283
Vidal-Fleury Crozes-Hermitage, 194, 206
Vietti Barbera, 222, 285
Viña Santa Carolina Cabernet Sauvignon, 168
vinaigrette, 21
  balsamic, 265; charred tricolore salad with, 186
  black truffle, warm wild mushroom salad with, 132–33
Vincent Pouilly-Fuissé, 92
Vin Divino, 210
vinegar, 13–14, 21

Vineyard Brands, 210
Vino Nobile di Montepulciano, 211
Vin Santo, 241, 243, 248, 285
Viognier, 32–34
Voge (Alain)
  Cornas, 186
  Côtes du Rhône, 204
Volnay, 127, 146, 282
Vongerichten, Jean-Georges, 114, 140
Vosne-Romanee, 127
Voss Sauvignon Blanc, 60, 71
Vouvray, 34, 50
  sweet, 34, 239, 241, 243, 244, 261

walnuts, 15
  linguine with arugula, olives, and, 169–70
Warre's Port, 262
wasabi pea–crusted salmon, 121
Washington State wines
  Cabernet Sauvignon, 160, 169, 178
  Chardonnay, 74
  dessert wines, 241, 243, 258, 261
  Gewürztraminer, 33, 34; specific recommendations, 40, 48, 52, 53, 158, 192, 258
  Merlot, 160, 175, 177, 178, 179
  Riesling, 31, 33; specific recommendations, 38, 39,

45, 50, 52, 261
  Sauvignon Blanc/Fumé Blanc, 57, 64, 66, 70, 71
sparkling wines, 103–4, 114, 123, 195, 281
Syrah, 183, 204
watermelon
  tomato-watermelon sorbet, 60–61
Weil (Robert) Riesling, 45, 46, 53, 243
Weinbach
  Pinot Gris, 44, 53
  Riesling, 281
Wente
  Cabernet Sauvignon, 168
  Riesling, 31, 39, 46, 52
white wine(s)
  pantry recommendations, 16
  and shallot pan sauce, 229
  See also specific wines
Wild Horse Pinot Noir, 142
wild mushrooms. See mushroom(s)
WillaKenzie Pinot Gris, 44
Willamette Valley Vineyard
  Pinot Gris, 44, 53
  Pinot Noir, 135, 146, 154
Williams-Selyem Pinot Noir, 148, 151
wine and health, 7–8, 181
wine-braised leeks, 167
wine FAQs, 273–79
wine glasses, 277
Wright (Ken) Pinot Noir, 135, 146
Wyndham Shiraz, 201, 206

Wynn's Coonawarra Cabernet Sauvignon, 175, 179

Xarel-lo, 102

Yellowtail Chardonnay, 80, 97

Zaca Mesa Syrah, 204
ZAP (Zinfandel Advocates and Producers), 184
Zardetto Prosecco, 116, 123
Zemmer Pinot Grigio, 46
Zenato Prosecco, 108
Zind-Humbrecht Pinot Gris, 36, 52
Zinfandel, 130, 180–207, 226
  basics, 180, 181, 184–85
  food pairings, 14, 15, 49, 88, 170, 185, 214
  menus for, 206–7
  specific recommendations, 185, 191, 193, 197, 199, 204, 206, 207
Zraly, Kevin, 129, 181
zucchini
  pancetta-wrapped goat cheese on roasted ratatouille, 222–23